THE ARCHPRIEST CONTROVERSY,

THE ARCHPRIEST CONTROVERSY.

DOCUMENTS RELATING TO THE DISSENSIONS OF
THE ROMAN CATHOLIC CLERGY, 1597-1602.

Edited from the Petyt MSS. of the Inner Temple

BY

THOMAS GRAVES LAW,
Librarian of the Signet Library, Edinburgh.

VOL. I.

WIPF & STOCK · Eugene, Oregon

Wipf and Stock Publishers
199 W 8th Ave, Suite 3
Eugene, OR 97401

The Archpriest Controversy, Volume 1
Documents Relating to the Dissensions of the Roman Catholic Clergy, 1597-1602:
Edited from the Petyt MSS. of the Inner Temple
By Law, Thomas Graves
Softcover ISBN-13: 978-1-6667-6178-8
Hardcover ISBN-13: 978-1-6667-6179-5
eBook ISBN-13: 978-1-6667-6180-1
Publication date 10/11/2022
Previously published by Camden Society, 1896

This edition is a scanned facsimile of the original edition published in 1896.

COUNCIL OF THE CAMDEN SOCIETY

FOR THE YEAR 1896-7.

President.

THE RIGHT HON. THE EARL OF CRAWFORD, K.T., LL.D., F.R.S., &c., &c.

JAMES J. CARTWRIGHT, ESQ., M.A., F.S.A., *Treasurer.*
REV. J. SILVESTER DAVIES, M.A., F.S.A.
C. H. FIRTH, ESQ., M.A.
JAMES GAIRDNER, ESQ., *Secretary.*
SAMUEL RAWSON GARDINER, ESQ., M.A., LL.D., *Director.*
REV. F. A. GASQUET, D.D.
DAVID HANNAY, ESQ.
REV. W. HUNT, M.A.
ARTHUR W. HUTTON, ESQ., M.A.
REV. CHARLES NEIL, M.A.
J. E. L. PICKERING, ESQ.
H. C. SOTHERAN, ESQ.
HENRY R. TEDDER, ESQ.
CHARLES W. VINCENT, ESQ.
HENRY O. WAKEMAN, ESQ.

The COUNCIL of the CAMDEN SOCIETY desire it to be understood that they are not answerable for any opinions or observations that may appear in the Society's publications; the Editors of the several Works being alone responsible for the same.

TABLE OF CONTENTS.

	PAGE.
INTRODUCTION	ix-xxvii

I.—The Quarrel with the Jesuits, 1597-1598.

1. Letter from John Mush to Dr. Bagshaw	1
2. Responsum Clementis viii. ad orationem sacerdotum, Sept., 1597	4
3. Letter from the Nuncio revoking faculties, Dec. 29	5
4. Abstract of the Memorial against the Jesuits	7
5. Articles for the regulation of the College at Rome	16
6. Circular Letter of Garnet in reply to the Memorial, Mar. 1, 1598	17
7. Letter to Dr. Bagshaw	20
8. Letter from Parsons to Garnet, July, 1598	21
9. Statement of Mush in reply to the preceding	38
10. John Sicklemore to Dr. Bagshaw, Aug. 3	48
11. Mush's Letter to Mr. Wiseman	53

II.—Blackwell's Authority Questioned, 1598-1599.

1. Mush to Bagshaw and Bluet, May 28, 1598	63
2. Mush to Bagshaw and Bluet, July 13	64
3. Three Letters from Charnock to Bagshaw	66
4. Blackwell to Bagshaw and Bluet, Aug. 22	72
5. Draft of Bagshaw's Reply	74
6. Draft of Bluet's Reply	77
7. Letter of Garnet to Clark, Nov. 11, 1598	79
8. Letter from John Maister, Dec. 9	83
9. From "Ed. T." in the Clink to Bagshaw	84
10. Blackwell to Colleton, Mar 1599	85
11. Unsigned Letter [by Mr. Heborne?]	88
12. Letter to Bagshaw, unsigned	89
13. Watson's Thirty Reasons	90
14. The Conditions of Yielding	98

CONTENTS.

III.—THE TWO DEPUTIES AT ROME. DEC., 1598—APRIL, 1599.

PAGE.

1. Dr. Haydock's Letter, Dec. 19, 1598 — 101
2. Cardinal Cajetan to Blackwell, Jan. 12, 1599 — 106
3. A Third Letter of Martin Array, Jan. 18 — 109
4. Fifth Letter from the Proctors, with Account of their Pleadings, Feb. 20 — 115
5. Letter from William Bishop, Feb. 20 — 123
6. Puncta Principalia ; with Letter of Cajetan to Parsons — 126
7. The Libel against the two Priests, Jan. 10 — 129
8. Charnock's Answer to the Libel — 137
9. Draft of Letter to the Deputies by Bagshaw — 148
10. Letter to the Pope in Bagshaw's hand — 149
11. Faculties for the Clergy, Feb. 2, 1599 — 151

IV.—RENEWAL OF THE CONFLICT, JUNE, 1599-JUNE-1601.

1. Letter signed R. B., June 7, 1599 — 154
2. R. B. to Bagshaw — 155
3. Letter from Clark, June 20 — 157
4. Mush to Blackwell, March 2, 1600 — 158
5. Arthur Pitts to Blackwell, April 11 — 160
6. Blackwell to Clark, Feb. 27 — 161
7. Clark's Reply to the foregoing, April 5 — 163
8. Letter by Clark with Narrative of Proceedings to May 3, 1600 — 165
9. Blackwell's Order for Clark's Examination in the Clink, and his Suspension, Mar. 10, 1601 — 173
10. C. R. to John Smith, Low Sunday — 174
11. Letter to a Lady by Father Holtby, June 30, 1601 — 176
12. "Mr. Collington" — 200
13. Letter of Blackwell concerning Robert Benson — 201
14. Letter from R. C. to Mr. B. — 203

V.—DEALINGS WITH THE GOVERNMENT.

1. Memorandum by Bagshaw, Oct. 19, 1598 — 205
2. Fisher's Instructions — 206
3. Statement in the handwriting of Bagshaw — 208
4. Watson to the Attorney-General, April, 1599 — 210
5. Forty-five Articles of Enquiry [by the Bishop of London?], *circ.* Dec. 1600 — 226
6. Answers in Bagshaw's hand to the foregoing — 238
7. Declaration of James Clerk concerning Parsons — 241
8. News from Rome respecting Parsons' Book — 243
9. Swift's Declaration on the state of Douai College, *circ.* Mar. 1600 — 244

INTRODUCTION.

The existence of a mass of Roman Catholic papers of historical interest preserved among the MSS. bequeathed to the Inner Temple by Sir William Petyt (who died 1707) was first made known in the Second Report of the Royal Commission of Historical MSS. by Mr. H. T. Riley, who calendered a portion of them as a specimen. The Rev. W. D. Macray in the Eleventh Report of the Commission (1888) carefully revised and completed Mr. Riley's imperfect catalogue, and again called attention to the value of the documents, of which no public use had been made.

The papers in question do not form a collection apart, and are not arranged in any order, but they occur in groups, mixed up with other documents concerning affairs of State or the Church of England, chiefly in the series numbered 538, vols. 37, 47 and 54. They relate almost exclusively to the dissensions, political and ecclesiastical, which distracted the Roman Catholic clergy during the latter years of the reign of Queen Elizabeth, and which culminated in the famous Appeal to Rome, on the part of a prominent section of the secular clergy, against the government of the Archpriest, Blackwell.

The history of these conflicts has been told, incompletely and with much passion, in the series of books and pamphlets written by the leading partisans on either side in the years 1601 and 1602; but in these books, which have now become exceedingly scarce and little known, are preserved some of the principal documents, papal briefs and official records, upon which the controversy turned. Canon Tierney, in his edition of Dodd's *Church History*, supplemented that historian's rather meagre chapter on "Factions among Catholics," with many valuable annotations and fresh documents derived from the archives of Stonyhurst and other Catholic repositories. But these Petyt papers Tierney had never seen.

By the courtesy of the benchers of the Inner Temple I was enabled to make some use of these materials, and to print *in extenso* a few of the documents for the new edition of Bagshaw's *True Relation*, which I published in 1889 under the title of "A Historical Sketch of the Conflicts between Jesuits and Seculars in the reign of Queen Elizabeth with a reprint of Christopher Bagshaw's 'True Relation of the Faction begun at Wisbich,' and illustrative documents."

The whole of the remaining inedited papers in the collection bearing on this subject, with a few trifling exceptions to be hereafter indicated, will be published in this and a subsequent volume. The present volume takes up the controversy at a point immediately preceding the institution of the Archpriest, and carries it on to the eve of the departure of the four priests sent to Rome to prosecute the Appeal at the end of 1601. The second volume will include the journals and narratives by the Appellants of their proceedings at Rome (Feb.—Oct. 1602) and various documents and memorials in the case laid before the pope and the inquisition. The particulars of these discussions have been comparatively little known ; for the brief of Oct. 5, 1602, by which the pope terminated the controversy, and for a second time, strictly prohibited all publications by either side on the subjects in dispute, was at last obeyed, with the result that the above mentioned journals and memorials remained in manuscript.

To understand rightly the documents here printed, it must be remembered that the institution of the archpriest, upon which the controversy ultimately turned, was in itself the outcome of previous quarrels and disorders, for which that institution was, in some sort, intended by its projectors as a remedy. These disorders had in the course of years passed through many phases and involved various interests; and were, moreover, continually fomented by causes which do not appear on the surface. Their origin must be traced back to the foundation of the English college at Rome in the autumn of 1578.

Dr. Clenock, the first rector, who governed the college with the assistance of certain Jesuit masters, was weak and incompetent. The students almost immediately, *i.e.* early in 1579, rose in open revolt against him, and turbulently demanded a Jesuit superior. They had their way; and Father Agazzari, an Italian, was made rector. A reaction quickly set in, and there were now loud murmurs against the Jesuits, who were accused of using their influence to entice the best scholars into their own order and away from the English mission. Allen hastened to Rome and, to reconcile conflicting interests, proposed that the Jesuits should themselves take part in the mission. Accordingly in the summer of 1580 the Fathers, Parsons and Campion, arrived in England. There were already in the country one hundred missionaries who had been sent from the seminaries in the preceding six years. There is no proof that political designs occupied the minds of these young men;[a] and the older, or Marian priests, were generally credited with sincere loyalty. The northern insurrection of 1569 had been instigated, indeed, by Dr. Morton and other clerical emissaries from abroad, but they had acted independently of Allen and the college of Douai. In 1579 and 1580 Dr. Sanders, as Nuncio, was unfurling the pope's banner in Ireland, and raising rebellion against the Queen with Italian soldiers and secret aid from Spain.

[a] The statement of Froude, Green, Ranke, and others that Cuthbert Mayne, the first Seminarist executed, was caught with the papal bull of deposition about him, is erroneous. It was a harmless bull granting a jubilee which had already expired. For the facts, see the *English Historical Review*, vol. i., p. 141.

But there is no evidence that he was acting in concert with the missionaries secular or Jesuit. Some of the clergy at home, however, showed signs of jealousy or fear of Parsons' masterful energy, and suspected his designs. To disarm all these suspicions of political intrigues on their part the Jesuits exhibited their instructions, which strictly prohibited their intermeddling in any way with affairs of state; and they solemnly made oath of their sincere intention to abstain from all such dealings. Little more than twelve months passed by before Parsons, discerning perhaps the hopelessness of a merely spiritual campaign, was in communication with the Spanish ambassador in London and with Lennox in Scotland, busy with schemes for the liberation of the Queen of Scots: ere long, he had slipped abroad, and along with Allen was restlessly promoting that series of conspiracies which ended in the Armada.

These two chiefs of the missionary body, Jesuit and secular, were not the mere instruments of others. They were the master minds, planning and advocating schemes of invasion, persuading and urging pope and king to the conquest of England, and the transference of the crown to Philip or the Infanta. Yet they still hoped to dissever their dual functions, missionary and militant, so far as to blind the English government to the combination. For there was no open appeal to arms. Their conspiracies were conducted with all possible secrecy, and the priests on the mission were to be kept in ignorance of the projects of their leaders until the moment for action should arrive. The Queen and council, however, were alive to the dangers which thus threatened the crown and country. They saw in every missionary a probable conspirator and in every lay convert a recruit for the army of invasion. Parliament in its indignation made short work of the difficulty of the judges in bringing home treasonable acts to every suspected individual by the barbarous enactment (27th Eliz. 1585) which made it high treason for any English priest, ordained abroad, to enter the country. There was here no attempt to distinguish between loyal and disloyal except by the mere presumption that the Marian priest might be trusted while the Seminarist must be a traitor.

The Armada opened the eyes of many of the priests to what had been going on. Allen now withdrew from active political movements, and partly on this ground and partly owing to the extreme reverence with which he was personally regarded, he escaped the obloquy which was heaped too exclusively upon the heads of the Jesuits, who henceforth became identified with the Spanish party. Parsons, on the other hand, was in Spain, founding seminaries after his own mind, egging on Philip to renewed attacks upon England, and incensing the government by his violent writings. On the death of Allen in 1594 the irritation of the peace party, which had been kept under control by his conciliatory influence, now burst all bounds. The appearance of Parsons' *Conference on the Succession*, which, however, had had the approval and the assistance of Allen, added fuel to the flames. The sorely oppressed clergy might have held speculatively the principles of that book— the principles of the revolution of 1688. But their abstention from rebellion, however justifiable rebellion might have been, was dictated by prudence if not by true patriotism. They thoroughly mistrusted the pretended disinterestness of Spain. If there was to be an appeal to force on their behalf at least it should not come from priests who were pledged to use only spiritual arms; and now by the rash conduct of their false friends they saw their own fidelity compromised, their hopes of toleration dashed, the queen's vindictive measures colourably justified, and innocent men exposed to torture and the gallows, while the true culprits were plotting for the most part in safety abroad. The quarrel spread to every quarter where English Catholics were gathered together. In Flanders the party headed by Charles Paget and Dr. Gifford were denouncing the Jesuits as firebrands of sedition and the worst enemies of their country. Political feeling ran high within the colleges. While at Valladolid, under Parsons' inspiration, the

xiv INTRODUCTION.

scholars were making orations to King Philip and speaking to him of "not our but your England," the students at Rome, to the disgust of their superiors, were glorying over Spanish repulses and mourning at the news of every Spanish success. All scholastic discipline was at an end; and, to add to the disturbance, the Jesuit prefects now brought against the youths criminal charges of a revolting character.

Meanwhile in England there were other causes at work to embitter the older seminarists against their Jesuit brethren. The latter had been invited to take part in the mission as auxiliaries. It had now come about that half-a-dozen Jesuits—for there had been seldom more and often not as many in the country at this time—were apparently taking the lead and directing the policy of some three hundred priests; and in the eyes of the world taking the greater share of such credit as was to be gained from the venture. It indeed could hardly have been otherwise. In such an expedition of volunteers the lead naturally fell to the strongest. The few Jesuits were picked men of capacity and daring, well disciplined, with a definite policy and with a powerful organisation at their back. The public impression of the paramount position held by this handful of men is reflected in the phraseology of the Acts of Parliament and royal proclamations directed against "Jesuits and Seminarists;" and, indeed, the language of some modern historians would lead us to suppose that the country was swarming with Jesuits.[a] The secular priests, on the other hand, although there were among them many men of high character and ability such as Bishop, Colleton, Mush or Blackwell, and many more who, as events showed, were ready or eager to lay down their lives for their cause, were on the whole poorly equipped for their perilous vocation. A number of ill trained youths were too hastily sent from the seminaries, and found

[a] Even Green writes of Jesuits " sent in batches to the Tower " at a time when there was but one Jesuit priest in the Tower and two others (one of whom was unconnected with the mission) at large in the country.

themselves in England without sufficient resources, properly constituted leaders, or unity of purpose; and the better men among them were continually embarrassed by the eccentricities and failings of their weaker brethren. A small but powerful group saw projects of self-aggrandisement or some mischievous plot in every move of the Jesuits, whom they regarded as tyrants bent upon bringing the whole clergy under subjection for their own ambitious ends. Cardinal Allen witnessed with anxiety the growing jealousy, and, it would seem, did not acquit the Jesuits of fault in the matter; but while he lived, as has been said, his commanding influence preserved some show of peace between the rival factions.

In February 1595, began the notorious " Wisbech Stirs."

Father William Weston, who had been confined in Wisbech Castle for many years, declared himself disgusted with the levity and loose behaviour,—" whoring, drunkenness, and dicing " were the terms used—of his clerical fellow prisoners; and with the approval of Garnet, his superior, he accepted the title of " Agent " from eighteen of his companions, and drew up rules for a more regular mode of life, to which it was hoped all would conform. Dr. Bagshaw and Bluet, at the head of a minority of ten or twelve, protested against this assumption of superiority and declared the imputation upon which it was grounded to be a base calumny. Weston withdrew with his friends into separate chambers; and there ensued a violent quarrel, which created a scandal throughout the kingdom. In November Dr. Dudley, and Mush " The Pacificator," effected a temporary reconciliation. But presently after some months of wrangling there was once more a complete rupture, which continued for the next three years.

It is at this point that the papers here printed begin; and as a further guide to them it may be well to give a brief chronological summary of the principal occurrences to which they relate.

1597.

The disturbances in the college at Rome, which had been almost perennial since its foundation, in 1597 reached a grave crisis. In the spring of the year Parsons hastened from Spain, quelled the mutiny among the students, got rid of or sent into England the ringleaders, and, some time afterwards (November, 1598), was himself appointed rector of the college.

There had been, however, active communication between the discontented in Rome, Wisbech and Flanders; and in September by concert between them a passionate memorial against the Jesuits was drawn up in Flanders for presentation to the pope.

Meanwhile a few of the leading clergy, Colleton, Mush, Charnock and others, in despair of obtaining their desire for episcopal government, and anxious for concord with the Jesuits as well as for abstention from politics, proposed a voluntary Association of the secular priests in two divisions, or under two heads, for north and south.

1598.

In order to avert the threatened ruin of the mission, to gain firmer control over the clergy, and, it has been asserted with good ground, to secure unity of political action in accordance with his own views in the event of the Queen's death, Parsons, in consultation with a few priests in Rome early in 1598, suggested and obtained the appointment by Cardinal Cajetan, of Blackwell, a known partisan of the Jesuits, as Archpriest, with jurisdiction over the secular clergy of both England and Scotland. Blackwell was to be provided with twelve assistants and was instructed in all cases of gravity to follow the advice of the superior of the Jesuits in England.

The "Constitutive Letters" of Cajetan were dated March 7, 1598 and reached Blackwell on May 9.

The appointment came as a thunderclap upon the unconsulted and unsuspecting clergy. Submission to the dominant Jesuit influence, self interest, timidity, as well as better motives led some secular priests, perhaps fifty or sixty in number, to sign a letter of thanksgiving to the pope for the appointment.[a] But others, including some of the most respected leaders of the clergy, regarded it is an intolerable evil. The increase of power put thereby into the hands of the obnoxious society the suspected political motive, the provocation given to the government; and the fact that a jurisdiction of so novel a character and so unusually extensive was made not by Bull or Brief, but on the mere word of a Cardinal Protector, and this in the face of the reported promise of the pope that he would give the clergy no superior without ascertaining their wishes, afforded reasonable ground for doubt whether the cardinal had not misunderstood or exceeded his powers, or whether the pope had fully known or intended what was being done in his name.[b] They considered themselves justified, therefore, in using every legitimate plea for disputing the validity of the document, and of "standing off" until the pope's will could be more certainly ascertained.

William Bishop and Robert Charnock were accordingly deputed to go to Rome, to state their grievances, and to do the best they could to get them remedied. They left England sometime after August, arrived at the English college in Rome December 11; and on the 29th, St. Thomas's day, were arrested at their lodgings and brought back to the college as prisoners.

During their absence, in the month of October, Bagshaw, on suspicion of being concerned in the alleged plot of Squiers and Walpole, was summoned by the Privy Council from Wisbech to London and there confined in prison till the following February. In freeing himself and his party from the charge of disloyalty he apparently gave information to the government regarding the differences among Catholics and revealed what he knew, or thought he knew, of the practices of the Jesuits. Weston, possibly on

[a] See p. 88, note.
[b] It is somewhat doubtful if the institution was in fact made by the pope's order. See note to p. 126.

CAMD. SOC.   c

account of Bagshaw's information, was transferred about the same time to the Tower.

1599.

The harsh and injudicious treatment which the two deputies received at the hands of Parsons at the English College, and the unfairness of their trial before the two cardinals, February 17, are evident enough from the reports of their prosecutors printed in the third section of this volume.

On April 6 the papal Brief was issued confirming the appointment of the Archpriest, and declaring it to have been valid *ab initio.*

The deputies were now disgraced, and forbidden to return to the mission (April 21), Bishop being banished to Paris and Charnock to Lorraine.

Meanwhile in England Father Lister, a Jesuit, wrote and disseminated an attack upon the dissentient priests, as ill judged and extravagant in tone as the Memorial itself. He charged them with the sin of schism, and declared that they were *ipso facto* excommunicated. In reply to the remonstrances of the inculpated priests both Blackwell and Garnet made known their approval of the treatise (March 7-26). Mush, Colleton, and Heborne were now suspended by Blackwell.

May 19 the Brief arrived in England, the dissentients without exception at once made their submission, and peace was restored.

Blackwell, however, moved by " a resolution from our mother city,"[a] announced that his former opponents, having undoubtedly incurred the guilt of schism, must make due acknowledgment and reparation for their sin. They refused to admit there had been either schism or disobedience in withholding their recognition of his authority until they heard the result of their deputation to Rome; and they on their side demanded satisfaction for the slander

[a] Said to have come from Warford or Tichbourne, Jesuits residing at Rome.

and the injury done to them. Here was a dead lock. The conduct on both sides was unyielding and exasperating.[a] The resentment of the accused priests was further aggravated by the siding of influential laymen with their Jesuit directors, and the consequent withdrawal of alms and means of support.

The main question in the dispute was now whether the dissentient priests had or had not been guilty of schism or other grave sin.

1600.

January 17. Blackwell, on hearing there was some intention on the part of the accused priests to publish an apology for their conduct, issued a decree forbidding the publication of any such book by a priest under pain of suspension, or by laymen under pain of interdict.

March 14. He further approved the proposition of Father Jones the Jesuit, that anyone who should defend the priests as innocent of schism would himself incur the censures of the Church.

Early in this year, 1600, the priests had referred the question to the decision of the University of Paris.

On May 3 the Faculty of Theology delivered their judgment on the case proposed, that there had been no such schism or sin.

May 29. Blackwell issued a decree condemning the judgment of the University as prejudicial to the dignity of the Apostolic see, and again forbad under penalties of suspension and interdict anyone to defend that judgment by word or writing.

October 17. Blackwell suspended Mush and Colleton.

November 17. A formal Appeal to the Holy See was drawn up at Wisbech and signed by thirty-three priests.[b]

---

[a] The malcontents, however, more than once made offer to submit to the judgment of arbitrators to be chosen from both sides, but all such proposals were scornfully rejected by the Archpriest.
[b] It is printed in English by Tierney, vol. iii. pp. cxxxiii.-cxliv.

About this time the Privy Council appeared to recognise the gravity of these dissensions and the opportunity of turning them to the profit of the State. Searching inquiries were accordingly instituted by Bancroft, Bishop of London, or others.

About Christmas, or early in the following January, thirty-six prisoners at Wisbech were removed to Framlingham gaol.

1601.

The appellants, after the delivery of the appeal, resolved to support it at Rome by a full account of all their grievances against the Jesuits, and against Blackwell whom they regarded as a creature of the Jesuits. They accordingly, in spite of the archpriest's prohibition of all such writings, secretly printed and published, perhaps after some understanding with the Bishop of London : (1) the *Declaratio Motuum* dedicated to the pope by Mush ; (2) *Relatio compendiosa*, dedicated to the Inquisition by Bagshaw ; and (3) for the information of the laity at home, the *Copies of certain Discourses* by Dr. Bishop and others.

March 10. Nine priests were suspended and interdicted by the archpriest.

Bluet, about the same time, with leave of his keepers, visited London to collect alms for the Framlingham prisoners. He was recognised at the Gatehouse and placed *in libera custodia* under the charge of the Bishop of London, who showed him intercepted letters of Jesuits revealing political intrigues, and (so Bluet, at least reports to Cardinals Arrigoni and Borghese) plans for assassinating the Queen. The Bishop maintained to Bluet that the rigorous penal laws were directed against all seminarists in the belief that the seculars as pupils of the Jesuits were conscious of, and accomplices in, their treasons.

At the end of June Bluet was introduced to the Privy Council and had audience of the Queen. Insisting that the secular priests detested the plots and were willing to reveal them and thwart them

INTRODUCTION.   xxi

in every way in their power, he persuaded the Council to consent to " banish " four of the imprisoned priests, and so set them free to go to Rome and prosecute their appeal. The four priests first named were Dr. Bagshaw, Dr. Champney, Bluet and Barneby. They were allowed several weeks to make their preparations and collect funds for their journey.^a Finally Mush was substituted for Bagshaw, who watched proceedings at Paris, and Dr. Cecil took the place of Barneby.

They actually started about the end of September, but, warned by the failures of their previous deputation, they made some stay at Paris in order to secure the protection and goodwill of the French government.

Meanwhile no word apparently had come from Rome in response to the appeal; and a number of books appeared on the side of the appellants, among which was Bagshaw's *True Relation*, and a series of extravagant publications of Watson, ridiculing and insulting Blackwell, and abusing the Jesuits as a body and individually with the utmost license.

1602.

Early in January appeared Parsons' *Briefe Apologie*, in reply to the earlier publications of the appellants.

On January 26, Blackwell published a Brief of the pope, signed August 17, of the preceding year, in reference to the appeal of November 1600. It had been in the archpriest's possession since Michaelmas.

The Brief reproved both Blackwell and the appellants, refused to receive the appeal, condemned Lister's book and other writings,

^a' There is unfortunately little or nothing in the Petyt Papers to throw further light on these transactions, or on any of the affairs of the clergy during the latter half of 1601. Bluet's report to the cardinals of his negotiations with the Council, and of the Queen's speech on the occasion, is printed in *Jesuits and Seculars*, from S. P. Dom. Eliz., cclxxxiii. f. 70, and with this must be compared an extract from his letter to Mush, in Tierney, vol. iii. p. cxlvi.

and strictly prohibited any further publications or controversy on the subject. It was asserted that the Brief was withheld by Parsons' directions until his own book should appear.

The Brief was treated accordingly by both sides as a dead letter. Parsons wrote an *Appendix* to his *Apologie* and then his *Manifestation*. Colleton wrote his *Just Defence*; and the battle of the books continued throughout the greater part of the year.[a]

February 16. The priests, who had left Paris on January 1, arrived in Rome 16 February. The story of their proceedings at Rome, and of the discussion and litigation which continued there for eight months, is told in a series of consecutive narratives embodying some of the main records in the case, to be printed in the second volume, and leaves little to be said here.

The cardinals, commissioned to examine the appeal, separated in the first instance the question of schism from other debatable matter, and on April 4 made known the decision of the pope, which was in accordance with that of the Sorbonne, viz. that the appellants had not been guilty of schism or disobedience and that they had not incurred the loss of their faculties.

In May seven or eight English books were under examination. Parsons' and Blackwell's proctors called for their condemnation as containing a denial of the deposing power, and other propositions scandalous or heretical. The appellants were here placed in considerable difficulty. They declined to be responsible for the later books written after they had left England and in which they had no part, and in particular they repudiated Watson. On the other hand they demanded the examination and condemnation of Parsons' political publications and similar writings calculated to bring odium upon the Church and provoke persecution. They argued that nothing but injury had been done to the English Catholics by the attempts to reduce the country by force of arms; petitioned

---

[a] Twenty-one books are fully described in the section "Biographical Notes" in *Jesuits and Seculars*, cxxxviii.-cl.

for the withdrawal of all Jesuits from the courts and camps of princes, and begged for the strict prohibition of all interference on the part of the Society in affairs of state.[a] The political differences which had fallen into the background during the debates on the question of schism now came again to the front.

In June the appellants were cheered by hearing from the French ambassador that he had received a message from Queen Elizabeth thanking him for his good offices on their behalf. The Spanish ambassador was continually at Parsons' elbow.

On October 5 the Brief, after several revisions, was drawn up in its final shape and signed. The appellants had failed, through the intervention of the Spanish ambassador (so it was believed), in obtaining an explicit prohibition of writings against the state. All publications containing injurious statements against either party were equally condemned without mention of heresy; and silence was imposed upon the disputants in future, under the severest penalties. The same penalties were to be incurred by any one who under whatsoever pretext should communicate with heretics to the prejudice of Catholics. The appellants triumphed, however, in the withdrawal of the offensive clause in the archpriest's instructions bidding him take counsel of the Jesuit superiors.[b] He was now,

[a] The appellants seem to have made little account of the 47th decree of the Fifth Congregation of the Society of Jesus, by which the Society herself in 1593 "gravely and severely" forbad her members to engage in affairs which belong to politics and state government as things repugnant to their profession. This order was issued, it should be observed, before the publication of the *Book on the Succession* (1594), and before the *Memorial for the Reformation* (1596), which was disseminated by Parsons in manuscript. See the decree quoted, with Father Morris' comments, in the *Dublin Review* for April, 1590 (p. 251).

[b] In justice to Blackwell it should be remarked that, whatever the authors of his appointment may have hoped from him, there is no appearance of his ever having entertained disloyal projects. On the contrary, in his examination at Lambeth in June, 1607, he declares his detestation of the treasons in Ireland; and the sincerity of his "Letter to the Priests his brethren for the lawfulness of taking the Oath of Allegiance," on the 7th of July, cannot be questioned. Moreover it must be remembered that the Pope's Brief admonishing clergy and laity not to consent to any Protestant successor to Elizabeth, was committed for publication, in the event of the Queen's death, not to the Archpriest but to Garnet.

on the contrary, "for the sake of peace," forbidden to consult the Jesuits whether in England or Rome; and Blackwell was ordered, as vacancies occurred among his assistants, to select the next three in succession from the ranks of the appellants.

While these affairs were being transacted in Rome, Dr. Bishop and Dr. Bagshaw were in Paris watching the interests of their party there, and in constant correspondence with their new friend the Bishop of London.

On Christmas day the aged Bluet, the author of the "Appeal to Cæsar," as he himself called this secret dealing with Elizabeth, returned once more as a prisoner to the Bishop's palace.

One of the most instructive, or at least the most novel, of the papers in this first volume is that here entitled "Forty-five Articles of Enquiry," (p. 226) written at the end of 1600 and already referred to. It seems to furnish the key to the whole collection of MSS. with which we are dealing, and logically it should be read first. The pulpits of the kingdom are said to have rung with the clamour of the Wisbech Stirs; and particulars of the feud were doubtless brought to the Privy Council by the keeper, Medley, as well as by Bagshaw and perhaps Bagshaw's lay friend and visitor, Dr. Farbeck. They may have provoked ridicule or scandal, but little seems to have come of the disclosures beyond the favour or disfavour occasionally shown by the authorities towards individuals on this side or the other. But Bancroft, who was made Bishop of London in 1597, certainly recognised the grave issues involved, and soon made himself master of the whole controversy.

In May, 1599, we learn from Mush that his letter on the disturbances at Rome, with suggestions for the remedy of existing evils, addressed to Mgr. Morro, was returned from Rome by Parsons, and fell into the hands of the Bishop of London. The *Articles of Enquiry* are almost certainly from the Bishop's pen. The writer, it will be seen, had already in his possession a number of Bagshaw's letters and his paper *Pro instituendo* (p. 149). He had copies of the two important letters of Blackwell's proctors from Rome, a letter of Bishop to Parsons, the Censure of Paris, etc.; and he follows all the phases of the quarrel from the first outbreak at Wisbech with surprising intelligence. He is particularly anxious to see certain other documents of which he knew only the purport as the Memorial (see p. 7), Lister's Treatise on Schism or *Adversus Factiosos*,[a] and Sicklemore's letter (p. 48), the abstracts and copies of which are now in the Petyt Collection; and in almost every paragraph of his methodical survey we meet with such phrases as: 'Some things hereunto may be added;' 'the circumstances are required to be set down more particularly;' as if he were not merely seeking for himself further information but inspiring or dictating the outlines of a book. The replies to these enquiries, set down in the handwriting of Bagshaw (p. 238), are curiously meagre and unsatisfactory. The writer seems reluctant to show his hand too plainly, or is perhaps ashamed of his business. But it is noteworthy that Bagshaw's *True Relation*, published just about twelve months later, runs entirely on the lines sketched by the enquirer and supplies in the amplest manner the particulars wanted. The question of how far these books of the appellants were printed with the aid of Bancroft has often been mooted and never satisfactorily answered. The priests may be believed when they declared that their printing was done under great difficulties, secretly, and at their own cost, but the books can scarcely have been produced without at least the connivance of the bishop, and it is significant that two or three years later (1604) one Jones, an aggrieved stationer, presented a petition to Parliament accusing the bishop of obtaining the release of recusant printers from prison and of otherwise favouring them with the view of criminally aiding and abetting their publication of popish literature. Some of these books bear the imprint of Frankfurt, Rouen, or Rheims, but bibliographers should

---

[a] The text was printed by Bagshaw in his *Relatio Compendiosa*; extracts are given in *Jesuits and Seculars*, pp. 143-5.

have the means of discovering from what London presses they proceeded.

It is not improbable that the bulk of these Roman Catholic papers were collected or copied in the first instance for the use of Bancroft. Many of the endorsements are in a hand closely resembling that of Bluet, who was long in close communication with the bishop. The famous letter of Parsons to Father Holt, dated Genoa, 15 March, 1597, suggesting that the most suitable claimant for the English throne would be "the Infanta with the Prince Cardinal," is marked at the end, "Per famulum magistri Bluet, xvii. Dec., 1601." Certain papers, moreover, would seem to be copied by Bluet. Yet some endorsements in this or a similar handwriting are evidently the work of a Protestant clerk, who uses expressions or makes mistakes which could not have come from a Catholic priest. How these ecclesiastical papers came into the hands of Sir William Petyt, Keeper of the Records in the Tower, is not known; but he was a great collector of MSS., and it is conjectured by Mr. Macray that he acquired the official papers of some one of the law officers of the Court of Arches.

The limits necessarily imposed upon me by the Camden Society in the production of these volumes have made it impossible to include *all* the inedited papers in the Petyt collection which may bear in some degree upon the subject. Certain curious letters of Fisher to Bagshaw, full of personalities and gossip, a letter of U. D. to one of the Wisbech prisoners, "Information from the Keeper of Wisbech Castle," and a long letter of Parsons to Mr. Constable, are not reproduced here, as they are printed either verbatim, or in substance, in Mr. Macray's Appendix to the Eleventh Report (part vii.) of the Historical MSS. Commission. Part of the correspondence of Clark and Blackwell; a badly written draft of a theological reply by Bagshaw to Lister's treatise; and a pious exhortation to obedience, addressed to the dissentients, by some priests who had submitted to Blackwell, have been omitted; also a long document by Watson, entitled " A briefe colleccion of the

INTRODUCTION. xxvii

causes moving me never to yeelde to Jesuites thoughe all other sholde, onely in regard of their Machiavelian practises as heere in parte doe ensue." It adds little to our knowledge of the man or of the controversy. The quarry is, however, not exhausted, and a comparison with other documents of the kind at Stonyhurst or elsewhere may yet throw light on the mysterious relations of the Appellants to the Queen and Council.

The original papers, often hastily written copies, abound in clerical errors of all kinds. Many of these have been corrected or indicated in the text. There remain, however, a few obscurities, verbal or grammatical, which can only be amended by conjecture, and these are left as they stand. Thus for "came in" (p. 193, last line) we should perhaps read "condemned;" for "discents" (p. 213, l. 5 from foot), "descants;" for "ever" (p. 224, l. 5) "never;" for "trice" (p. 218, l. 2), "truce"; and for "oure" (p. 219, l. 6), "their." I have also to ask the reader's indulgence for an unpleasant list of obvious *corrigenda*.

It is more pleasant to record my grateful thanks to the Librarians of the Inner Temple for their unfailing courtesy; to Mr. David Hannay for revising some Spanish transcripts, which are to follow in the second volume; and to the Rev. W. E. Addis, as ever, for constant aid and counsel.

T. G. L.

CORRIGENDA.

Page 27, line 4 from foot, *for* if *read* of.
Page 63, note b, *for* 1801 *read* 1601.
Page 79, line 3, *for* qua *read* quia.
Page 82, line 2, *for* maceria *read* maceriæ.
Page 87, line 18, *for* subjacere *read* subjacete.
Page 96, line 6 from foot, *for* lyft *read* lyst.
Page 128, line 3. *for* dominationum *read* dominationem
Page 128, line 17, *for* gerrere *read* gerere.
Page 153, line 1, *for* Brevium *read* Breviarium.
Page 156, line 5, *for* w^{ch} *read* wth.
Page 164, line 13, *for* qua *read* quæ.
Page 173, line 12, *for* pravibus *read* pravis.
Page 174, line 9, *for* ludificari *read* ludificare.
Page 176, line 6 from foot, *for* as *read* is.
Page 182, line 13, *after* stand out *add* not.
Page 193, last line, *for* disobedience *read* disobedience.
Page 203, line 5, *for* judges *read* judge.
Page 241, line 1 of note, *for* 1680 *read* 1600.

THE ARCHPRIEST CONTROVERSY.

I.

THE QUARREL WITH THE JESUITS.

1. *Letter from M. J. [John Mush] to Dr. Bagshaw.*   38, f. 382.

[1597.]

R. D.,

It is longe synce I hard from you, for M^r. Dud.,[a] and I haue not sene one the other since before Christmas. I heare M^r. D. Nor.[b] is sicke, God comforte him, & that you w^t v. or vj. mo ar at table aparte from the rest in M^r. Blu[ets] chamber. Yf peace wyll be had so you haue done verie well in my opinion, yf yt wyll not, you knowe how to haue patience & make a meritt of yt. Good S^r, as muche as humane frailtie & yor evyll disposed bodies by reason of that infectious place & exasperating companie wyll permitt, giue nor take cause of disquiett to yo^rselfe, and refer the rest to god, who in tyme will send redress as he seethe expedient,

---

[a] Richard Dudley was sent with Mush to Wisbech as arbitrator in the disputes of 1595.
[b] Norden, a priest and doctor of medicine, died suddenly at Wisbech in 1597.

for y{o}{r} name, take no more thought. When I come to the sight of the paper I wyll satisfie y{o}{r} desire to cancell yt, for to what purpose should we kepe yt now, when you ar divided & kepe yt not. Mr. Gwyn[a] tould me that fissher[b] was vngone at his commyng from London. I marvell what the man staieth for all this while? vnless yt be to carrye newes of the foule dealyng of the Jesuits wch bend them selves thus mightely against our association.[c] Your selfe & others haue often warned me to bewarr of them & I was euer to incredulous: but yf I had tyme to lett you vnderstand of their iniurious vsage & slanderous proceeding against me & others aboute this association, & against me about the late tumults at Rome charging me to be the author & beginner of them (whereas before god I was as fre from them as any of you that knewe not of them) & that I am the head of a faction against them, to expell them the realme, &c., &c., you would be more incredulous than I haue bene. for yt is so farr from all not religious & charitable, but honest conceipts also, that no man I thinke can believe them w{t}out his owne experience. for those stirrs of Rome I neuer hard more but what fissher reported, but seing they make me the author of them I intend god wylling to examine and searche them out to the bottom. They make all cleare & tell a faire smothe taile, & ar most innocent I warrant you. for o{r} association yt should haue gone forward by my consent, tho we had bene but 10. to the confusion of all their &

---

[a] Robert Gwyn, Bachelor of Theology, a successful missionary.

[b] Robert Fisher, the reputed compiler of the memorial from materials supplied by the leaders of the anti-Jesuit party abroad, September, 1597.

[c] The association of secular priests for their own better self-government, projected by Colleton, Mush, and other leaders of the clergy, after the dissensions at Wisbech, was partly intended as a means to more effectually resist the aggressive policy of the Jesuits. The unexpected institution of a superior in the character of an archpriest, suggested (it was said) to the Pope by Parsons as a countermove, necessarily put an end to the scheme,

THE QUARREL WITH THE JESUITS.

others slanderous toungs, but yor godsone m^r. mich$^{1\,a}$ & others ar faynt-harted & trepidaverunt timore vbi non erat timor. The Jesuits fearing the creditt of o^r confraternitie to countervaile w^t theirs, wyll neuer endure any vnion of priests yt becometh vs to looke to yt, for vnless we seeke for redress at his handes that can command them, the secular clergy shall haue smale creditt or estimation w^t the people, or concord among themselves. I haue delt most planely in a letter to them. what wylbe the euent god knowethe, but they are men w^t whome I thinke yt is most hard to haue frendship. vnless one flatter & feed their humors in euerye thinge, wch I neuer purpose to do, cheefely (I perceive) they ar bent against me. but god g[rant] me his holy grace & I regard not the worst they can do. co[mend] me to m^r. Bleu. & all w^t you. Jesu kepe you this 8 J. . . . I heare Til^b is come out, but I haue not mett w^t him as yett.

Yo^{rs} vnfeanedly
M. J.

Endorsed by writer : To the right worshp^{ll} m^r. D. Bagshaw these. Wisb.

Endorsement II. : M. J. to Bagshawe of the slanderous dealings of the Jesuits, and how if they prevayle the creditt of secular priests will be overthrowne.

---

^{a} Perhaps John Michell, M.A., Oxford.
^{b} Francis Tillotson escaped from Wisbech and afterwards became a Government spy.

38, f. 371

2. *Responsum S^{mi} Dni nostri Clementis 8 ad orationem Sacerdotum Anglorum quam habuit P. Edwardus Benettus,[a] reliquorum nomine, die 3° Septemb., 1597, cum in Angliam essent decessuri.*

Erant præsentes Il^{mus} Card^{lis} Caietanus, Angliæ Protector, ac P Robertus Personius, quorum nullus, ea de re antea ad Pontificem verbum vllum habuerat, sed admissis Sacerdotibus ad pedum S^æ S^{tis} oscula, et habita oratione, quæ teneros habebat affectus, cum expectaretur, vt Pontifex eadem omnino suauitate (prout solet) responderet, is repræhensionem satis asperam exorsus est, propositis primum beneficijs, quæ istic a sede Apostolica accepissent. Venistis (inquit) ad hanc almam vrbem aliqui vocati, aliqui forsan non vocati, atque hic educati atque instituti fuistis ac multa beneficia accepistis ab hac Sta sede, contra quam aliquorum vestrorum patres blasphemant. Tunc cæpit de Martyrii dignitate ac præstantia agere, ostendens hanc esse supra vires humanas, et proinde sola dei gratia, et humilitate posse acquiri, quam maxime laudauit, ac in spiritum superbiæ, humilitati ac charitati contrarium vehementer est invectus; asserens nihil boni sperari posse ab eo, qui spiritu agitur superbiæ; et tunc dixit magnas fuisse Collegij contentiones ac discordias quæ maxime ei displicebant, et valde (inquit) nos torserunt, et nescio an aliqui hic sint ex illis, sed si fuerint intelligant, non solum se nihil boni in Anglia facturos, nisi hunc spiritum deponant, sed omnino (inquit) timeo ne turpiter labamini. Spiritus enim hic superbiæ in barathrum et abissum vos ducet; hinc iterum cohortatus est omnes vehementer, vt Romæ relinquant

[a] Edward Bennet, the Welshman of whom Dr. Barret wrote to Parsons (Sept., 1596): "This Benet is the greatest dissembler and most perilous fellow in a communitie that ever I knewe" (*Douay Diaries*, p. 386), was a ringleader of "the discontented" at Rome; and subsequently he and his brother John became active leaders of the Appellant clergy. Edward was proposed at one time for the episcopate, and on the death of John Colleton he was made dean of the English Chapter.

spiritum contentionis, et non secum ferant in Angliam. Cum vero finitis omnibus P. Hillus, qui ex præcipuis turbarum erat authoribus, secundo ad eum venisset, post alios multos, vt pro discessu pedes oscularetur, et Pontifex iam desijsset loqui, ac benedictionem indulgentiasque impertivisset, excitatus Pontifex eius aspectu, quem ex seditione præterita recordabatur, redijt iterum in eundem sermonem, dixitque Commendamus vobis omni modo concordiam cum Patribus Societatis in Anglia. Discedentibus vero Sacerdotibus, dixit Pontifex cuidam astanti se P. Hillum ex vultu et prolixa barba[a] agnouisse, et scire illum esse valde seditiosum. Hinc omnes intellexerunt, quam ingrata semper fuerit Pontifici tumultuantium istorum causa, licet vt ipse dicere solet, ne omnino desperatione acti in hæresim laberentur, quod aliqui ei minati fuerunt, motus eorum patientius tulisset.

Endorsed: An answer,[b] . . . papa, 3 Sept., . . . certayne priests tooke their leave for England. The pope noted Mr Hill ye priest to be a factious man.

3. *Copy of a Letter from the Nuncio*[c] *at Brussels to the Clergy in England, revoking the faculties granted to three priests.* 38, f. 370.

Dec. 29, 1597.

Admodum R^di dni Amici in Christo syncere dilecti. Ea est humanæ naturæ deprauatio, seu fragilitas, ut a cæpto syncerioris vitæ instituto et tramite grauibus quibusdam abducti et seducti cupiditatibus facile deflectant: Meruerunt sane præsumpta nedum

---

[a] This long-bearded Thomas Hill, whose faculties were revoked three months later (as will be seen in the following document), is said to have been an Anglican clergyman. He went to Rheims in 1590, and was transferred in 1593 to the College at Rome, where he was ordained priest. He subsequently distinguished himself on the English mission, wrote the *Quatron of Reasons*, was condemned to death in 1612, but was reprieved and banished. He had been admitted while in prison into the Order of St. Benedict. He died at Douai in 1644.

[b] MS. mutilated.

[c] Octavius Mirto, bishop of Tricarico, 1592-1605.

sed et perspecta trium sacerdotum Anglorum, quorum nomina sunt Edwardus Tempestius,[a] Thomas Hillus, ac Robertus Bensonius[b] vitæ innocentia, morum probitas, pietatis et Catholicæ Religionis promovendæ et propagandæ ardens zelus, a sua Beat^{ne} quibusdam facultatibus ad communem Catholicorum in Anglia degentium consolationem, condecorari. Verum enimuero cum cito nimis, proh dolor, perfectioris vitæ studium cupiditatum abrepti blandimentis renunciaverint idque suæ Beat^{ni} notum evaserit, optimo sane consilio, facultates quas vitæ illorum splendore, morum nitore, et pietatis avitæque Religionis ardore allecta et inducta concesserat, audita probæ vitæ exigua perseuerantia, morum depravatione eorundem, reuocandas illas censuit vt quod virtutis intuitu, probitati elargitum fuerat superinducti vitii interuentu improbitati detraheretur. Proinde hisce nostris [literis] patefactum cupimus idipsum R^{dis} D.D. vestris ne a vobis prænominatarum facultatum exercitium ipsis permittatur bullis aut quibuscumque alijs scripturis quantumlibet authenticis, quæ penes eos esse poterunt fidem denegando, quippe cum eæ cassatæ et reuocatæ sint. Præpotens Deus conatus vestros diuino suo favore persequatur, et adiuvet labores in ipsius vineæ decorem cultum et augmentum impensos æterno cælestis vitæ brauio recompensaturus : et valeant. Bruxellis.

Admodum R^{dis} D.D. VV.   xxix Decembris 1597.

           Amantiss^{us} vti frater octauius episcopus
           Tricariensis
           Nuncius Apostolicus

Admodum R^{dis} dnis Amicis in xpo syncere dilectis Presbiteris Catholicis in Angliæ regno residentibus.

---

[a] Edward Tempest had been at the head of an English faction at the college as Bennet was of the Welsh (Foley, *Records*, vi. 36). He was ordained priest March 19, 1594, and was sent into England Sept. 16, 1597.

[b] Robert Benson, *alias* Richardson, was sent from Rheims to Rome in January, 1593.

THE QUARREL WITH THE JESUITS. 7

4. *Abstract of the Memorial and of sundry Letters against the Jesuits. Sept.-Dec.*, 1597.   38, f. 337.

Capita quædam accusationum quibus Doctor Giffordus et Dominus Pagettus, Angli, aliique eorum sequaces societatem Jesu immerito apud summum Pontificem et Ill^{os} Card^{es} aliosque viros præcipuos traduxerunt ; quas iustum est vt vel probent, vel vt societati famu, tam iniquis et manifestis calumnijs inipetita, restituatur.

Omnia proponantur eisdem authorum verbis quantum fieri potuit et breui mittentur scripta ex quibus sunt desumpta.^a

De vniuersa societate patribusque Romanis.

1. Societatis homines adeo esse ambitiosos vt non contenti terminis quos posuerunt patres ipsorum, iam regna et monarchias insatiabili desiderio devorarint. *Giffordus ad Tempestium Romanæ seditionis præcipuum quendam authorem in epistola quadam vt Pontifici Cardinalibusque proponeretur*, 13 *Aprilis* 1596.

---

^a There appears to be no complete copy of the Memorial extant. Certain abstracts of it were drawn up and circulated in MS. by the Jesuits in the hope of putting their adversaries to shame by the extravagance of the charges contained in it. Dr. Bagshaw, however, unashamed, printed in his *True Relation* an English translation of one of these entitled "An Abstract of the Memorial sent by certain Englishmen out of the Low Countries to the Pope's Highness, Clement VIII., against the Jesuits labouring in the English vineyard, Sept., 1597." The present document, also translated by Bagshaw (p. 111), is a more concise "catalogue of slanders," as Parsons term it, extracted partly from the Memorial itself and partly from letters written in support of the Memorial by Dr. Gifford, Dean of Lille and afterwards Archbishop of Rheims, and by others of his party. There are three Latin copies of this paper in the Petyt collection (xxxviii. ff. 333, 337, and 347), one of which is described as *Articuli Patris Personii contra D. Giffordum decanum Insulensem*. Bagshaw gives to his version of the *Capita* the title "Certain chief points of accusations wherewith many Englishmen have justly charged the Jesuits unto the Pope and divers cardinals : taken out of the Memorial and other letters, some of them dated at Rome, 8 of November, 1597." His translation contains some variations from the Latin copies. He, moreover, suppresses the references to the sources of the several charges with the names of their author, which are here supplied by Parsons or the compiler. Paragraphs omitted in Bagshaw's version are here marked with an asterisk.

2. Quod eadem ambitione acti hierarchicam pristinæ ecclesiæ formam præpostero ambitu inuertere conantur. *Idem Giffordus in eadem epistola.*

3. Quod hæc patrum ambitio non tantum in Anglia in carceribus ipsis, in Belgio et in Italia, verum etiam vbique terrarum seditiones excitat. *Ibidem.*

4. Quod hæc ambitio non solum in prouincijs et vrbibus verum etiam in familijs, fratres a se mutuo, coniuges et amantissimos discerpit, et vnum contra alium livore et invidia inflammat. *Ibidem·*

5. Cedendum esse tempori (in controversia Romana) ne dum huic ambitionis impetui obex ponatur disruptis omnis honestatis atque modestiæ repagulis, furenti cursu multos in præcipitium rapiat. *Ibid.*

6. Si hæc ambitio impunita remanserit videbit posteritas illam non solum prælatis sed etiam principibus et monarchis, quibus nascens nunc adulatur, vincula aliquando iniecturam esse. *Ibid.*

7. Rogat Giffordus Pontificem vt hanc longe lateque serpentem societatis ambitionem præscindat securi missa ad radicem arboris, ne suæ sanctitatis authoritate armata, in perniciem aliorum plena vindicta diffundatur, et infinitas animarum ruinas ac strages faciat quod iam in misera Anglia, magna causæ communis iactura, facere cœpit. *Ibid.*

8. Sed neque presbiteris Anglis in exilio locus vllus ab ambitione hac tutus, nisi quis signum eius bestiæ in fronte acceperit. *Ibid.*

9. Quod patres in omnibus Pontificis mandatis querant semper per brachium seculare ea euacuare cum magno multorum scandalo. *Giffordus epistola ad Robertum Marchanium qui ex primis Romæ tumultuantibus erat,* 8 *August,* 1596.

10. Patrum vindictam non terminari nisi cum aduersantium sibi morte et cum infamia mortem consequente. *Ibid.*

11. Quod Jesuitæ (de Romanis loquitur) omnes omnium literas intercipiant itaque ut neque Cardinalium, neque principum quoque, fasciculis parcant. *Ibid.*

12. Deum testatur Giffordus et Angelos eius quod maxima pars

nobilitatis et Cleri Anglicani tam domi quam foris deplorant cum gemitu et lachrimis miserrimum statum suum qui graviora patiuntur sub his novis tyrannis Jesuitis quam ab vllis quotidianis gravibus persecutoribus. *Ibid.*

13. Ideo esse graviorem persecutionem Jesuitarum quam hereticorum Anglorum contra Catholicos quia ab illis ob virtutem, ab his titulo proditionis ac suspectæ fidei Catholicæ patiuntur. *Ibid.*

14. Ita persecuti sunt Jesuitæ sacerdotes aliquot iam martyres, vt eorum mors partim hereticis, partim patribus sit attributa. *Marchianus summus Giffordi amicus in memoriali ad summum Pontificem.*

15. Solemne esse illud apud patres (divide et impera) et ideo Romæ discordias excitant aluntque patres. *Ibid.*

16. Confessarios societatis abuti solere conscientijs scolarium et suorum pœnitentium ad proprium commodum. *Idem, classe* 4^a, *articulo* j^o.

17. Ex 300 sacerdotibus qui Angliam sunt ingressi viz. 6 aut 7 defecisse ex 20, Jesuitis deficisse 8. *Ibid : quæ insignis tamen est calumnia cum ne vnus quidem hactenus ex eis quos societas eo misit defecerit.*[a]

18. Quod patres in Belgio adeo crudeles sunt vt multos viros optimos non solum ad mortem miseram perduxerint sed post mortem infamarint. *fisherus, Pagetti et Giffordi hospes, epistola* 22, *Julii,* 1596.

19. Nihil Cath^{cos} Anglos adeo torquet quam præsentis Pontificis in [ter] Jesuitas contemptus et odium, et Ill^{mis} Card^{bus} Toleto et Alexandrino irrigatæ falso inuriæ, *quas nolentes (inquit Giffordus) audiuimus, et gementes patimur. *Giff. epistola ad Tempes·tium* 19 7^{bris}, 1596.

20. Jesuitas auide expectare mortem sanctissimi domini nostri, et Ill^{mi} Card^{lis} Toleti ;[b] vt quam diu conati sunt cædem et sanguinem

---

[a] This clause, being the Jesuits' denial of the preceding statement, is inadvertently included in Bagshaw's version.
[b] The cardinal died Sept., 1596.

inferant illis omnibus qui illorum tyrannidi se opponere sunt ausi. *Ibid.*

21. Summum (inquit Giffordus) remedium, et in quo cardo totius controversiæ Romanæ vertitur, est, vt collegiorum omnium causæ Ill^{rum} Card^{ium} congregationi regularium cognoscendæ atque decidendæ committantur, nihil enim est (inquit) quod hi tyranni magis verentur quam vt rogentur coram Card^{bus} rationem facti reddere, neque quicquam est quod sic illis laxat insolentiæ habenas sicut ab omni fere tribunali immunitas. *Ibid. et idem multis alijs literis repetit, maxime vero in memoriali, his literis adiuncto, numero vltimo.*

38, f. 334.

22. In festina S^{mi} domini nostri morte sita est eorum spes: quare festinandum est vobis qui Romæ estis, siquidem libertatem nostram potestis. *Ibid.*

*23. Vtimini (inquit) literis meis secreto et efficaciter, quia inimicus si non præveniatur, certam sibi monarchiam persuadet. dum calescit ferrum percutite, dum patroni vestri vivunt peragite. Inimici non aliud quærunt quam ut et tempus lucrentur, et si semel se liberent, et ab angustijs quibus nunc implicantur dominabuntur (mihi credite) tyranicissime. *Giffordus in epistola, 15a Octobris, 1596, et epistola, initio 9^{bris}.*

24. Patres querere regimen quoque collegij Duacensis, neque vllum aliud esse frænum quod timeant et quo infrænari possunt quam vt rectores Jesuitæ subijciantur congregationi regularium. *Ibid., et Marchanus in memoriali.*

25. Quod patres molitionibus machivileanis conantur redigere collegium Duacenum ad dissolutionem. *D. Hugo Griffidius epistola ad Edwardum Bennettum, 26 Aprilis* 1597.

26. Horrendam esse tyrannidem atque insolentiam Jesuitarum maxime eorum qui in Belgio infamant, exauthorisant, deprimunt, vereor etiam (inquit) ne indirecte hostibus prodant quemcunque voluerunt. *Ibid.*

*27. Patres inimicos esse mortales Cardinalis Toleti, optare eius mortem, quotidie loqui de eo turpiter tanquam de Apostata. *Giffordus ad Edw. Bennettum, 15 octobris, 1596.*

*28. Ne detur occasio tyrannidi atque insolentiæ inter Jesuitas S^{mus} dominus noster pro infinita sua prudentia optime statuit in societate (inquit Giffordus) ne quis magistratum apud eos gerat vltra triennium etc. *Epistola ad Tempestium et Bennettum mense* 9^{ris} 1596.

De patribus Societatis Anglicanæ missionis.   38, f. 338.

29. Patres societatis in Anglia inter se dissidere : nominatim vero patrem Henricum superiorem, et patrem Edmundum[a] in carcere Wisbicensi : et esse 16[b] articulos dissentionis. *Pagettus in colloquio ad patrem Bonardum, vt patet ex eius literis* 17 *Sept.*, 1597.

30. Nullam esse Catholicorum domum in qua patres non sint, et pastores et alios habeant deputatos, qui vices suas gerant. *In memoriali quodam per Giffordum et Pagettum Roman transmisso mense Sept.*, 1597. *Eidemque cooperati creduntur ffisherus et D. Hugo Griffin et sigillatim Giffordus in literis.*

31. Si quis sacerdos locum aliquem Residentiæ commodum habuerit in Anglia, patres non cessabunt, quoad eum inde eiecerint, atque hoc modis impijs informando, viz. et suspectum reddendo. *Ibid. Vtrobique tam in memoriali, quam Giffordij epistola ad Marchanum,* 8 *Augusti,* 1596.

*32. Quod neminem permittant Jesuitæ facultatib^{us} sibi etiam a summo pontifice concessis in Anglia vti ; nisi ex speciali licentia patrum. *Memoriale numero* 2, *et Giffordij ad Marchanum.*

*33. Quod patres in Anglia non doctis sacerdotib^{us}, non pijs, non sanctis facultates suas delegant sed indoctis, indevotis, irreligiosis, imo seditiosis. *Numero* 2°.

*34. Quod patres eleemosinas Catholicorum carceribus, aliisque piis vsibus deputatas, omni modo ad se trahunt : easque neque carceribus, neque collegiis, neque presbyteris, neque exulibus distribuunt ; sed seditiosis fabularum fictoribus aliorumque diffamatori-

[a] Edmunds, *i.e.* Weston.   [b] Bagshaw reads 26.

bus, et sanctorum derisoribus in laborum suorum stipendium impendunt. *Numero* 3°.

35. Quod adeo laute et splendide vivunt patres in Anglia, tantumque in personas suas impendunt, vt vnius Jesuitæ expensis possint 20 presbiteri laute splendide et ornate sustentari. *In memoriali, numero* 4°.

36. Quod patres thesauros plurimos trans mare mittunt (vt fertur) vt suo corpori hoc et societati impendant. *Memoriali ibidem, et Giffordij epistola*, 8 *Aug.*, 1596, *ad Marchanum*.

37. Patres extitisse, atque esse modo authores discordiarum et contentionum in carcere Wisbicensi. *Memoriale, numero* 7°. Titiones etiam esse seditionum omnium alibi. *Giffordus in literis.*

38. Patres fæminis blandiri, et suadere vt moniales fiant, modo quæ habent, illis derelinquant: sic de multorum nuptijs: sic de infirmorum testamentis alijsque disponunt, vt semper aliquid cedat in illorum lucrum : ita vt nihil præter pecuniarum quæstum quærere videantur: et ex Angliæ conversione quasi mercaturam conficiunt. *Memor.*, n^{ro} 8.

*39. Quod patres vulgo a plurimis mendacissimi habeantur neque iurantibus illis fides vlla eis adhibeatur: quod a schismaticis vocentur sanguisugæ. *Ibid.*

*40. Patres odio maxime prosequi, contemnere, et omni infamiæ nota lacerare Academicos, et qui studuerunt in Angliæ vniversitatibus, ac laurea aliqua sunt insigniti. *Ibid., numero* 10. Quod Catholici in Anglia magis timent Jesuitas, quam ipsos hereticos. *Memor.*, n^{ro}. 2°.

*41. Quod patres indirecte produnt sacerdotes hereticis persequendo eos. *Ibid., nro.* 7. *Et Giffordus in literis.*

42. Quod patres per fas et nefas simplicem et absolutam monarchiam totius Angliæ quærunt. *Memor., nro.* 7. *Et Giffordus sæpe in literis ad Throgmortonum*, 11 *Julij*, 1596.

43. Patres esse hostes sacerdotum sæcularium vbique fere affirmat *Giffordus, in additione ad literas Hilli*, 21 *Julij*, 1596.

44. Patres esse causam totius discordiæ in gente Anglicana. 38, f. 339. *Giffordus ad Throgmortonum* 11 *Julij*, 1596.

45. A patre Personio, et ab Equite aurato ffrancisco Inglefeldo profectum esse artificium committendi inter se et collidendi Cardinalem Aldobrandinum, Caietanum et Episcopum Cassanensem. *Giffordus ad Throgmortonum*, 11 *Jultj*, 1596.

46. Quod pater Holtus et complices eius loquantur tam in Anglia quam in Belgio dedecorose de summo pontifice, ac de Illmo Card^{le} Toleto. *Giffordus epistola ad Marchanum, 8 Aug.,* 1596.

47. Carolus Pagettus scripsit Card^{li} Alano patrem Holtum reum esse et accusari ab eo posse de rebus turpibus, et infamibus: et de huiusmodi vt eas non audeat literis committere, *vt testatur ipsa Cardinalis epistola ad ipsum Pagettum* 4° *Januarij*, 1591.

48. Quod dicunt pontificem (horrendum inquit dictu de spiritus sancti oraculo) abvsum fuisse clavibus in absolvendo rege Navarrensi. *Ibid.*

49. Patrem Holtum non solum intendere, sed etiam iactitare se velle miseram Angliam sibi et suis in conquistam capere. *Ibid. Giffordus.*

50. Ipse (inquit) suique coegerunt sacerdotes aliquot, qui de hoc ipso apud me cum lachrimis conquesti sunt literis subscribere contra suas ipsorum conscientias. *Ibid.*

51. Massa inquit pecuniarum tanta est, quam pater Holtus, et sui exegerunt à Catholicis in Anglia pro dispensationibus, et sub colore dispensandi eas in bonos vsus, vt multi credibiliter affirment excedere summam quinquaginta millia librarum Anglicanarum, quæ faciunt ducenta millia scuta Italica. *Ibid.*

52. Quod pater Holtus sit fax et titio omnium seditionum et discordiarum. *Ibid.*

53. Quod Jesuitæ viros excellentes ad desperationem impellentes eos vt relicta Anglia religionem aliquam ingrediantur, et etiam [a] viam miserabilem sequantur. *Giffordus. Ibid.*

[a] Bagshaw reads *aut aliam,* " or to take some other miserable course."

54. Quod patres in Anglia artibus quibusdam authoritatem omnem, existimationem, omnemque pecuniam ad se suosque reducunt: domi forisque faciunt quod volunt: emittunt, intromittunt, coeunt, literas intercipiunt atque factiones pro libidine suscitant. *Ibid.*

*55. Loquens Giffordus de literis comendatitijs Card. Toletii quas secum in Belgium ferebant Noricius et Buthonus, ait: Illud præterire non possum Ill^{mi} Card^{lis} Tolleti literas a minimis tirannulis fuisse contemptas, et suorum ludibrio expositas: et R^{mi} patris Generalis literas tanquam sufficientes magis fuisse requisitas. *Epistola ad Tempestium*, 19 *Sept.*, 1596.

*56. Quod pater Holtus in disceptationibus suis asserere non est veritus Anglos exules obligari magis conformare se menti et intentioni ma^{tis} Catholici quam sedis apostolicæ. *Ibid. Giffordus.*

57. Quod pater Holtus in Aula Belgij, et pater Personius in Hispania ad integrum novennium cum infinitis nobilitatis ac Cleri gemitibus fuerunt continuati: et quod ipsi per regios ministros se continuari procuraverunt. *Ibid.*

58. Quod plurima sunt in horum patrum actionibus, qua viros bonos offendunt: nobilitatis contemptus: scholarium omnium a Collegio Duaceno aversio: antiquissimi et quondam florentissimi regni Angliæ in provinciam reducendi conatus: Catholicorum in Anglia sub specie pij vsus per intollerabiles contributiones expilatio: cum hereticis et hominibus suspectæ fidei perpetua tractatio. *Giffordus, ibid.*

59. Curandum est omnino vt æquales facultates, et maiores dentur presbiteris in Anglia quam Jesuitis etc., sic insolentiæ eorum cum authoritate minuatur.[a] *Ibid.*

60. Quod nobiles Angli qui in Belgio sunt mirantur suam sanctitatem permittere Jesuitas in Anglia (qui sunt seditionum titiones) in officio esse dominandi vltra decennium, non obstante

---

[a] Bagshaw reads, "seing their pride by reason of their larger faculties is fenced (as it were) by authority."

clamore miserabili, et lamentis nobilium nostrorum omnium ac generosorum qui oppressi iacent sub gravi iugo insolentiæ ac tirannidis eorum. *Giffordus, epistola ad Tempestium*, 15 *Octobris*, 1596.

61. Patres impedire, ne quis ex Anglia in Belgium veniat, nisi sciant paratum esse, vt scribat, dicat, faciat, quod volent, et vt iuret in eorum verba : et in hoc exercent insignem tirannidem. *Giffordus, scedula quædam ad Tempestium, initio Novemb.*, 1596.

Infinita fere alia huius generis omittuntur, quæ in literis ipis et memorialibus continentur.

---

*Vt obvietur calumniæ vndecimæ, qua falsissime asseritur patres omnium literas intercipere, ferendum est has epistolas ac memorialia quæ hoc catalogo citantur, partim reperta fuisse inter scripta Roberti Marchanii nuper mortui : partim alibi : vel sponte etiam oblata à quibusdam scholaribus post sedatos tumultus.

[At the end of the 3rd copy or abstract of the " Capita"
(38, *f.* 347-8) *follows this note.*]

All this (of the memorial) is written to his holynes in the name of the clergie of England and a letter from the Catholiques put in the end for a confirmacion of the same, though no name be put to in particular, as neyther to the memoryall but yet it is knowne from whome it came in fflaunders and all this ensueth vpon the cominge over of fischer from England.

The same fischer tould to one in secret in fflaunders that his principall busines was wth some matters ther abouts and some partyes there about matters of importaunce, and sayd further he was in greate hope of libertye in conscience in England so that the Jesuitts might be gotten from thence.

Ex literis 2 Decembris 1597.

38, f. 348b.

ffischer hath bene wth m^r D. Thornell [a] a very honest and descreet man and offered him (if he would take against the Jesuitts) that he should be assisted from England and that they priests did oppose themselues to them vniuersallye, and were desirous to send one to Rome to deale for them and in conference had in England vpon the matter, he or Mr. D. Turner,[b] who liveth in Germany, were thought the fittest men, wherefore he sayd if he would be the man, the Catholique Recusants in England would send him yerelye a thousand pounde to mayntayne him in authoritye at Rome.

5. *Articles for the Regulation of the College at Rome.*

A monsieur le provoste de notre dame de Cambraye.

38, f. 340.

1. Quamvis generalis confessarius collegij debeat esse vnus ex patribus societatis nunquam tamen defuerit aliquis Alumnus qui nomen et officium parochi retineat. Cui ad maiorem libertatem, et consolationem Alumnorum confiteri licet, modo non fiat mala fide ad impugnandam dicti confessarij generalis authoritatem.

2. Quoniam in antiquis regulis et consuetudinibus collegij, nihil contra bonos mores, et collegialem disciplinam continetur, sed potius omnia pia admodum et ad institutionem collegij bone proportionata, relinquantur intacta, tam quoad formam verborum, tam quoad sensum, explicationem et praxim.

3. Prohibeatur pater Confessarius sub excommunicatione ne quenquam ex Alumnis ad vllam religionem de proposito alliciat. Hoc tamen non prohibet, quin consilium libere daret in vllam partem sincere provt conscientia illi dictabit, cum pænitens id in secreto confessionis petit.

---

[a] John Thornell, or Thornhill, doctor in both faculties of canon law and divinity. In 1607 he was mentioned, says Dodd, as "candidate for a mitre."

[b] Dr. Robert Turner, of Barnstable, was some time Rector of the University of Ingolstadt and Canon of Breslau. He died at Grätz, Nov. 1599.

4. Quando aliquis ex Alumnis vocationem habuerit ad aliquam religionem approbatam atque resolverit iam ingredi : atque superiores illius religionis admittendum iudicaverint, non permittatur deinceps in collegio vivere.

5. Constituantur de ordinario ex Alumnis tres in Collegio Repetitores quando idonei reperiuntur, quorum electio penes superiores erit. Deficientibus vero Alumnis, substituantur eorum loco patres. Alumnis vicissim idoneis cedant patres.

6. Procuretur quod citissime possit pro summa pecuniæ a pontifice saltem assignata vinea commodior.

7. Vt habere possimus eos superiores qui tradant obliuioni omnia præterita, et qui personas vel partes adversas non agnoscant aut distinguant, sed omnes eadem paterna charitate amplectantur.

8. Vt de examine pro positiva theologia mentio posthac non fiat quod extiterit causa magnæ contentionis iam annis superioribus, nisi forte quod in regulis cautum est post logicas institutiones non convenire iudicetur.

9. Vt fama nostra potissimum per præsidem Duacensem, et alios quamplurimos non sine magno præiudicio status nostri iniuriose dein[te]grata fideliter resarciatur.

These conditions were agreed vpon by ffa. Persons etc. and confirmed by Card. Burghesius. The some of mony mentioned for a vyneyarde was 2000 crownes. Rome, 15 May, 1597.

6. *Copy of circular Letter from Father Henry Garnet in reply to the Memorial against the Jesuits.* 38, f. 360.

March 1, 1598.

Reuerendis Dominis Presbyteris Vniversis per Angliam constitutis ad quos hæ litteræ pervenerint, Henricus G. societatis Jesu Presbyter Salutem optat in Domino sempiternam.

Octodecim iam anni effluxere, ex quo, Illmo patriæ nostræ Patre Gulielmo Alano authore, societas nostra ad hanc domini vineam colendam, vobis præclare antea in ea laborantibus sese adiunxerit. Quo toto tempore (diuina fauente clementia) ita viximus, vt quemadmodum vestrum in nos amorem summum esse sane perspeximus, ita nos vicissim omni ope atque industria conati sumus, vnumquemque vestrum eo quo par erat honore colere, ea qua potuimus sedulitate iuvare, quibus licuit officijs prosequi, amore vero, quantum potest mortalis animus, amplecti. Testis est nobis profecto conscientia nostra, et vero plerique vestrum testimonium perhibebunt, (sine dubio) de nobis neminem vestrum de vlla iniuria vel minima sibi a nobis illata iure conqueri posse. Neque tamen id nobis assumere volumus, nostras actiones omni prorsus culpa vacare, homines enim sumus et in tam lutulento loco nonnihil fortasse pulveris pedibus nostris adheserit. Sed sane quantumvis fragiles atque imperfecti sumus, cupimus profecto fieri meliores, et ab illo facinore nos amor vester facile abduxit, ne quenquam vestrum scienter læderemus. Pervenit nihilominus ad manus nostras summa memorialis cuiusdam S[mo] D.N. exhibiti mense Septembri, superioris anni, in quo ea continentur, quibus nihil magis indignum vestræ authoritati affingi, nihil magis horrendum suæ Sa[tis] auribus obstrepi, nihil immanius ab ipsis hæreticis, de nobis excogitari potuit: Transmissum ante est memoriale illud a duobus e Belgio, sacerdote altero, altero laico, ad suam Sa[tem] nomine cleri Anglicani. Vos igitur appello clerum Anglicanum sementem renascentis Ecc[æ] nostræ, totius Ecc[æ] Catholicæ decus, fortissimorum Christi martyrum illustre seminarium. Dicite obsecro num a vobis hæc prodigia prodierunt. Videte num tunica filiorum vestrorum hæc sit an non? hoc est, an nos amore filios vestros professione fratres invincibili sancti spiritus nexu vestri corporis membra, ac partem etiam tantillam Cleri Anglicani, veris ac iustis coloribus, ac tanquam polymitis vestibus depictos atque indutos memoriale illud exhibeat. Nam si ita est, fera profecto pessima deuoravit nos, monstra sumus teterrima, filii diaboli sumus, indigni hoc sancto consortio vestro, immo et hac luce sumus. Quod si vos viri venerabiles (quod certo scio atque expecto) statim exclamabitis, non nostram hanc esse tunicam, immanissima iniur[ia] nos affici, indignum esse vt huiusmodi calumniatores impune dimittantur, illud consequatur necesse est, vt tunica hæc sit illius pessimæ feræ diaboli, cuius præda detractores omnes deo odibiles futuri sunt, qua nimirum tunica ipse eiusmodi sectatores aliquos suos nuper ornaverit, de quibus scriptum sit induisse eos maledictionem sicut vestimentum. Eripite ergo (pro vestra singulari in deum pietate) eos qui ducuntur ad mortem, eripite pauperem et egenum, de manu peccatoris liberate, vel quod magis est necessarium, vosmetipsos defendite, et famam vestram (sine qua ne vita quidem ipsa vobis iucunda esse debet) tueamini. Parva enim iniuria nostra est si cum vestra conferatur. Nam calumniarum istarum de nobis falsitas, immo etiam vt ita dicam impossibilitas tam manifesta est, vt ipsa per se nullo refellente facile concidat: presertim cum iam Romæ detecta accusatorum nostrorum nequitia sit. At quanta queso iniuria est, vt hec portenta Clero Anglicano affingantur!

Quare vos omnes per Christi viscera hortor et obtestor, vt huic tanto malo remedium opportunum adhibeatis, et vt (si vestris prudentiis expedire videbitur) decem aut viceni aut maiori numero prout provinciæ cuiuslibet numerus ferat, subscriptis nominibus testatum faciatis Illmo protectori, quid in vniversum de hisce Articulis sentiatis.

Nam etsi nonnullis vestrum haud ita familiariter noti sumus, vt omnes falsa esse omnia pronunciare fortasse velint, ex triplici tamen responsione quæ fieri posset, aliqua omnibus conveniet nimirum vt alij scire se omnia falsa esse, alij nihil se habere de quo nos accusent, ac proinde non credere esse vera, alii denique sine vllo scrupulo saltem affirmare possint, se de memoriali illo nunquam somniasse, neque a se vlla ratione illud profectum aut approbatum esse. Quod si mea purgatio vobis suspecta non sit, deum testor atque Angelos eius, nihil eorum de quibus accusamur vel micam habere veritatis. Hæc vero a vobis, vel maxime ita a vobis præstari cupio, vt neque laicis aliquid innotescat nisi vbi prudentiæ vestræ aliter videbitur, neque exemplar vllum harum calumniarum ita servetur, vt in hereticorum manus incidere possit, neque postremo discordia vlla inter presbyteros merito hinc oriri possit: proinde ac summis precibus efflagito, vt nullus ad suum testimonium ferendum moleste vrgeatur, ac sicut polliceor nos nemini infensos fore, eo quod subscribere pro nostra defensione aut neglexerit aut recusauerit. Quoniam autem præter memoriale illud de quo mencionem fecimus (cuius integrum etiam exemplar breui accipiemus) litteræ quædam scriptæ dicuntur ad eundem ss^{mum} D.N. ab omnibus Catholicis quibus de nobis tanquam tyrannulis ac perniciosis conqueruntur, hac etiam in re vestræ charitatis [et] prudentiæ erit, plane ac candide significare, qualem tandem de nobis opinionem pij quilibet Cath^i conceperint. Valete in domino viri verendi, mihi charissimi atque amatissimi. Prima Martij 1598.

R R D^{um} V^{um},
Seruus indignus in Xpo,
HENRICUS.

38, f. 364.   7. *Letter to Dr. Bagshaw.*

[May 10, 1598.]

W^{orll} S^r. according vnto o^r accustomed manner we have sent vnto you for o^r ordinarie marchandise & you shal receave by your ordinarie bearer the summe of xij^l ij^s vj^d. v^s for yo^{r}selfe, v^s for m^r Gar[ret], v^s for Mr Thew[les], & v^s for Mr Arch[er], also ye other ij^s vj^d for Mr Bul[ton], the rest in common. I am hartely sorrie to hear of a certayne memoriall y^t hath bin exhibited vnto ye hygher powers, I know you have harde of it for y^t it doth tooche your particular case, in my opinion it can not be pleasinge nether to god nor man, & I hope you have not anie waye in particular dealte in it; it seems vnto me to require an absolute expulsion of ye Fathers from vs ; & in particular to complayne of f. Ed[monds) we must needes accept of them as patres, fratres & coadiutores, as for absolut superiors they exclame from it. I charge you for god's sake seeke peace vnitie & concord, for this kynd of proceedinge (as you maye better consyder then I) can not but be a scandall vnto the good, a comfort vnto ye enimie, & a disturbanc vnto o^rselfs. yf you think your selfe iniured, have patienc, leave revenge vnto god. & so hopinge to heare from you some more certaynetie & particularitie of ye matter in hast I committ you to god. this 10th of Maye.

Yo^r assured frend to vse,
Parker.

Noted at foot by other hand : This Parker is now assistant.
Endorsed by writer : To the wo^{rth} Mr. S. Bag : D.D.
Second endorsement in same hand as note at foot : Olive Almand To Dr. Bag. He disliketh the memoriall [and wisheth obedience to the ^a]

8. *Copy of Letter from Parsons to Garnet.*[b]

38. f. 416.

[Naples, July 12 and 13, 1598.]

My very loving and deare brother, I was exceeding glad to read yo^{rs} of the 6 and 13 of may, and thereby to vnderstand of yor health wch we greatly desyre & of the good pceeding of yor affayres in gods cause, for wch we pr[a]y dayly and you must have still (as hytherto) greate patience on the one syde and on thother great confidence and courage in hym, for he will not forsake you now

---

[a] These words in brackets erased.
[b] Mr. Macray, following the suggestion of the endorsement, heads this letter: "Parsons to Blackwell." But the marginal note added by Mush to the following draft reply in his own handwriting shows that the letter was written, as the internal evidence also indicates, to Mr. "Walley," *i.e.*, Father Henry Garnet.

the worke he hath begone. Yf we be faithfull humble and perseverant, notw^th standing all the difficulties he permitteth a dextris et a sinistris, wch hymself will overcome, to his owne great glory and o^r more singuler comfort in the end.

I have seene what you write, as also what many other grave priests do write (for it pleased the protecto^rs grace imparte wth me their letters) about the good acceptance of the subordination appointed by his holines order and protecto^rs letter, amonge the clergy there. It was ever presupposed that those servants of god amonge you wold behave themselves in matter of obedience like themselves and Receve most joyfully and comfortably the disposicion of their supreme superiors, in that behalf, seing the only reason that moved his holynes was their owne good and comfort and to prevent such inconveniences as are wont to growe in a body where there is not subordinacion of one member to another: ffor albeit for a tyme and when o^r number was little, et primitiæ spiritus florerent vnusquisque erat sibi lex, nor any externall law or Judge was necessary, yet cold not we expect in this behalf more privilege of perfection in tracte of tyme then had the primitive church: of whom it is written Crescente numero discipulorum factum est murmur grecorum adversus hebreos eo quod despicerentur in ministerio quotidiano viduæ eorum, for wch cause the Apostles were inforced to appoint the order and subordinacion of deacons for the better and quieter governing of that dayly ministry as you knowe. And yf the Apostles successo^r vpon like murmur perhaps of some priests against those of the Society that their autority and faculties were to great and that this tended to the discredit of others (how truly I will not examine), yf I say his holynes followyng the same spirite of the Apostles his predecesso^rs have by this occasion declared that Jesuits neyther had ever nor ever desyred autority or Jurisdiccion over priests in England, and moreouer hath appointed a sweete and a moderate kynd of subordinacion among themselves for the tyme present, it is no lesse to be imbraced and obeyed in every good mans Judgment, then was

the other ordinacion of decons by the apostles themselves. And so
I doubt not but that both you and the rest do and will do, and to
tell you playne the protecto^r was much edified to see the comfort
that you and the rest of yor brethrene of the Society have shewed
by yor letters to have taken by this subordinacion. for it seemeth
to hym a plaine demonstracion of the falshod of the former mur-
muracions against you, and moreouer he was highly pleased to
reade so fervent letters of so many of the principall priests not
only for their good and grateful acceptance of this his hol. ordinacion, but also fo[r] that they shew their great and holy vnion
wth those of the Society, and to disallow wholie and detest that
slaunderous libell written by ffisher (as since hath ben confessed
by himself) at the request of some in ffflaunders at his new arrivall
out of England as by the Authenticall Transscript of his said confession made in Rome and sent vnto you by the protecto^{rs} order
before this I think you have seene wch yet I desyre may be suppressed and burned or kept to yo^{r}selves for charity sake, rather
than to much published so as it come to the hereticks hands, who
wold make his advantage of it. These then were the effects of the
comfort and consolacion that those letters wrought in the protecto^r,
and he said that he doubted not but that they wold worke the very
same in his holynes, wth whom he was presently to imparte them
seing that both their ends and desyrs tended only to o^r love, vnion,
confidence and harty frendship amonge o^{r}selves, whereof they see
evidently and say that all the hope of o^r good successe in the
common cause dependeth, as of the contrary for most certayne
hangeth o^r discredit ruyne confusion and desolacon.

And here now I wold make an end but that wth yo^{rs} you sent me
another letter of a priest to yo^{r}self written (as he pretendeth) in a
frendly manner (and it is good to take it so) thereby to shew you
not so much what hym self beleeveth but what some others discontented do report or complayne of those of the Society. And
for that some of the points wch he obiecteth (thoughe all be not
many) do concerne vs here in these parts and others you there, I

38, f. 416b.

will geve satisfaction for those that touche vs and so do you there, for such as may apperteiyne to matters in England. ffor it is reason that we should yeld satisfaction of o^r doinge to all men that require the same.

The first things (sayeth he) that most troubleth men against those of the Society is their vnquiet governement of the colledge of Rome, where many towardly youthes are cast from their good purposes, much shame spoken of o^r country, and such a fire of dissension kyndled as is to to like to enflame the best parte of England. This is the first obiection.

The second is set downe in these words (yf you Remember) the yonge men may be vnruly, be it so, yet so they were not lightly at their first commyng thither, but the sweet wisdome (me thinketh) of discreet superio^{rs} should in tyme conforme them, and not turne them of so highly discontented.

The thirde foloweth thus, of these tumult^s arise that some (as they say) have their faculties also taken from them by the way, that they may not come to speake what they knowe. Others are sent in wth such large autority, as fewe of the most auncient enioye hiered (as it were before hand) to speke favorably. These are some mens suspicions wch we may chose whether we will beleve or no : but this followyng is certayne that some of yo^{rs} spake so lavishly of certayne priest^s as that these who heare and beleve them take some for little better then spies, who are reputed of them that know them best amonge vs to be right honest men. Some also of yo^{rs} being asked their opinion of that society [a] of priests wch is intended, sayd that they thought it to be a faction against the Society, whereas there is nothing in it, to my seing and many others, towchinge the Society.

These are the points towched in that letter : the latter two certayne (as he sayeth) and the former three suspicions, to those suspicions then I shall answere, and do request you, that both the

---

[a] The Association.

party hym self and all the rest of yor brethren there may knowe 38, f. 417.
the effect therof: and to these latter pointes wch he sayth be
certayne it shall be well that you geve satisfaction, examininge
the particulars, for oftentymes speches are raysed, amplified and
vrged wthout grownde at all or taken in a farre other sense then
they were vttered: whereof ffisher hym self confesseth divers
to have ben fayned against some of the Society and (yf I forgett
not) some of those or the like were also amonge them, and betwene
two bodies that begynne to have emulacion sticklers will never
want notwthstanding the hevy curse that god layeth vpon them for
it. And so much of this.

To the former pointes wch he calleth suspicions, I do greatly
wonder how godly and discrete men can publishe suspicions only
(in so grevous a matter as this to the Reproche of so many their
brethren that desire to be servants of god) wthout examinacion of
of the grounds whether they be like to be true or not, nay rather
when the presumpcions are manifest one the other side, ffor what
indifferent man, hearing of vnquiet people to turmoyle a cyty or
common wealthe, will rather judge the fault to be in the magistrate
then in the subiectes, especially yf the magistrates were knowen to
be godly and well intentioned men, and not ignorant nor voyde of
judgment as the ffathers of the Society do prove themselves in
other governementes daily not to be.

The excessses of the late Tumultuous schollers in Rome have
ben hard of almost throughout the world for these 3 or 4 years
together, and have been condemned by divers great and grave
men that in presence have examined the matters, to witte by their
Cardynall Protecto^r and agayne by another Cardynall visito^r, and
then by two Cardynalls together in commission, and lastly by his
hol., and the fathers proceedings euer iustified, who have for so
longe borne wth patience most manyfold and intollerable iniuryes
and yet have both changed Recto^{rs} to content them and yelded to
all other means of appeasinge and gayning the vnruly party that
wthout offence of god cold be yelded vnto, and all this resteth

vnder Recorde.[a] And yet now as thoughe all the fault were in the fathers and none in the other they are sayd to governe vnquietly and to cast youthes from their good purposes, and for lacke of sweete wisdome to turne them of vndiscreetly.

By this rule and censure, they may condemne the wofull and afflicted father for that his sonne degenerateth and is an vnthrift; the governo^{rs} and superio^{rs} of Religious for all those that lose their vocations and become Apostates as cast by them from their good purposes; the pope and bishops for such as become heretickes or dissolute vnder their charge; Christ and his apostles for the losse of Judas once an apostle, and of Nicholas once an holy deacon; and of Simon Magus once a devout disciple; all wch had once good desyres, and after lost them and became Reprobates. And other many troublesome but yet wthout any fault of their governo^{rs}, and one Apostle excuseth aswell hym self as all the rest in like cases, sayenge, ex nobis prodierunt sed non erant de nobis, nam si fuissent ex nobis vtique permansissent, so that yf some bringe good spirits out of England wth them, persevere not in them, the fault is not to be layed vpon the governo^{rs} but vpon them selves, for from their governo^{rs} they receve nothing but holy instruccion and good example of virtuous life as them selves will confesse I dare say.

38, f. 417b.   And not to examine further [every] particular case of this college of Rome wch seemeth from the begynnyng to have had a certayne infelicity followynge it, above other colleges of the Englisshe nacion, in that some youthes have ben troublesome therein from tyme to tyme, wch seing that in other seminaryes specially those of Spayne vnder the same fathers governement, hath not happened, divers men are of divers opinions why it hath so often and ordinarily fallen out at Rome, and some thinke that it is in good parte the nature of the place that ingendreth highe spirits in them that are not well established in almightie godes

---

[a] The Report upon the English College, Rome, by Cardinal Sega, A.D. 1596, is printed in vol. vi. of Foley's *Records*, pp. 1-66.

grace, ffor commyng thither very yonge and fynding themselves presently placed and provided for abundantly and acquainted dayly wth sights and relacions of popes cardinalls and princes affayres our youthes that were bredd vp at home wth much more simplicity and kept more vnder by their parentes and masters, then the Italian educacion doth comport, forgetteth easily them selves, and breaketh out to liberty. I meane such as have runne astray and lost respect to theire superio^{rs} in Rome, w^{ch} (god be thanked) hath euer ben farre the lesser parte and many have greatly prospered in that place to gods great hono^r and o^r countreyes good.

This opinion of the circumstance of place is greatly encreased by the judgment of straungers both Spaniardes ffrenchmen and fflemynges and other nacions, who affirme that they try by experience their people that live in Rome, yf they be not men of great vertue & prove more heedy afterwarde and lesse tractable then others brought vp at home. But yet to this other men of o^r nacion do adde a second reason, for the English college wch is at Rome, being a place whervnto manye yong men do resort only vpon desire of seing novelties, when any come thither of the English nation, fynding such a commodity of study and mayntenance there and them selves in want and misery, they made suyte for that, wherunto perhaps they had not true vocation from god nor due preparacion in them selves to so holy and highe estate, and so being once admitted, fell afterwards to disorder and to putt out of joint both them selves and others.

A third cause also there was no lesse important perhaps then any of the rest, or more then both together, wch was a certayne disgust geven at the very first foundacion if the colledge vnto a certayne principall man of o^r nacion [a] and his frends then resident in Rome who afterwards, not affecting greatly the governement or governo^{rs} of the sayd college, was ever eyther in Re or in opinion a

---

[a] Dr. Owen Lewis, afterwards a vicar-general of St. Charles Borromeo, and Bishop of Cassano.

backe vnto them that wold be discontented, to wch was adioyned in these latter yeres (as appeareth by their owne writings) an other fountayne of fomentacon from fflaunders that nurished this humo^r and wrought much woe vnto the college wholy.

38, f. 418. And yet all this notwthstandinge this last great broyle, that fell out presently vppon o^r good Cardinall Allen his death, was not begunne wth the multitude of the colledge vppon any dislike agaynst the fathers as appeareth by their owne memorialls, but only by a secreate negotiation of some English abroade in the towne wth others wthin the colledge for the advauncement of the former principall man to the Cardinall his place, wch they attemptinge to do by the generall petition of all the Schollars gott ther hands to hit, neither was the Rector of the Colledge agayst it, but laboured also for it (I meane for the sayd man to have the Cardinalls faculties, for that it seemed over broade to aske the hatt at the first demaunde), but his holynesse, vnderstandinge the drifte, denyed it flattly, and gave the sayd facultyes to the protectors as at both their mouthes I have heard it recompted, wherewith the partyes that did negotiate being offended brought a great parte of the youth to breake wth the sayd protectors & the fathers ther superio^{rs} as causes of this, and to make a common oathe to sticke one to the other, and neuer to leave of. In vertue of wch obligation to iniquitye they wer caryed forth from one discord to an other for almost three parts together wth such headines and obstinacye as neuer was seene or heard of at Rome in youthe of any nation before, as I have heard his holynes often, and diuerse cardinals more often repeate wth exceedinge dishonour to o^r nation, soe as nowe many great and wise men beganne to suspect that the sufferings of o^r blessed martyrs also and Confessors in England was not soe much of vertue and love to gods cause as of a certayne chollere and obstinate will to contradicte the magistrate there, then wch nothing you know can be more opprobrious and iniurious to vs in the world nor to the truthe of godes cause.

Things then standing in this case and much worse in many points then I can expresse, yor frend Robert^a was forced lest all should be lost to take so longe and werysome a jorney from the Spaynish costs to Rome, where he found the colledge as a field wth two hostile campes wthin it, father generall and his assistants wholy aversed, and throughly resolved to leave the governement; the cardinals protecto^r and vice protecto^r throughly weryed, and all the rest of that order extremely scandalised, one namely Baronius, who often told me that o^r youthes bragged muche of martirdome, but they were Refractarij (that was his word) and had no parte of martirs spirite, wch was in humilitie and obedience; His Hol. was greved and vexed as it was a very lamentable thinge to see hym and heare hym speke of the matter; and he told yor sayd frend oftentymes that he neuer was so vexed wth any nacion in the world, ffor one the on syde they pretended zeale and piety and one thother shewed the very spirite of the divell in pryde contumacy and contradiccon, and then he told the meanes he had vsed to appease them, sending to them first his maestro de camera, then the monsignor mora, then cawsing them to be visited by Cardinall Sega, and after to be dealt wth by Cardinall Toledo, and after hym agayne by Cardinall Burghese, and that all wold not serve to bringe them to order, and ever now and then his holynes wold putt his finger to his brayne, signifieng that there stade their sicknes and so wold most of the courte when they talked of Inglesi, and some plainely wold say that Inglesi were *Indiavolati*, and like wordes. His Hol. added also that he knewe not what resolucion to take, for one the one side to punishe them openly wold be a scandall by reason of the hereticks, and yf he should cast them forth of Rome some had told hym that they wold have become hereticks. These and like lamentacions he made to divers.

Now you may imagine how yor frend's hart fared when he harde this and sawe this state of things, having left it in so good case viij yeres before, when he departed from Rome, and had labored so

38, f. 418b.

^{a} Father Parsons.

much in Spayne to sett vp Colledges for the same youthe, of whome he was often demaunded by the Embassado^r and Cardinalls of that nation whether those in Spayne wold not prove also like these in tyme, and namely in hating the kinge and Spaynishe nacion wch these were knowen to do : and the like questions others also did make, wch tended to the disgrace of all the Englishe in Spaine and other places, and to the vtter ouer throwe of those colledges whose case these Romanes did so much neglecte and contemne (I meane o^r discontented scollers of Rome) as they cold not abide to heare of them nor of the benefits there receved at the king's hands. Thoughe diuers of them had there brethren and kinsfolke amonge them, so stronge was their passion against that kinge and nation, and the fathers that had their educacion.

Many other things I passe over, for not to be to tedious, wch yet wold make you wonder, and yor harte rewe to heare, concerning the desperate state wherin matters stoode like to disioint and ouerthrowe o^r whole cause euery where. W^ch yor frend perceyving he first laboured to mitigate mynds abrode intreating them to have patience, and to beare for a while longer, and for what might be brought to passe. And this was as well wth his holynes and cardynalls, as also wth father generall, the Embassado^r and others. And secondly he dealt wth the scollers together (I meane all the discontented parte alone) shewyng them by longe conference of diuers dayes the daungerous state, that they had cast bothe them selves and the common cause of their country into, by their desperate and hedlonge proceedings so farre as they had done, and that they cold not passe one in that course w^thout infinite confusion to fall vpon them before God and man. But fynding them at the first to be most obstynate vpon pretence of reason, and redy to runne into any inconvenience by the invitacion of some amonge them, he to calme and mitigate them resolved to heare wth patience all their reasons, suspicions, clamo^rs and allegacions, demands and peticions, were they neuer so impertynent. And where they might seeme to have any lest reason in the world in any of their accions, there he graunted and rather augmented then dyminished the same; and where they had none at all, he endevored to make them see reason; and where a little reason was ioyned wth much error and passion, there he distinguished the one from the other and so finally brought them to see their evill cause they had in hand, and to geve over their pretences, and namely their seuerall confessions to wch the party hymself that is now in England holpe very muche by yelding ouer his office and persuading them to returne to confesse wth the fathers agayne, and by doing many other good offices. And so all was ended and peace was made, and the fathers of the Societie contente to forgeve all iniuries and slanders wch they had borne and to require no other satisfaction, but only their amendment and good deportement for the tyme to come; wch they promised both in words and protestacions vnto yor frend and by letters to father generall that was then at Naples, who answered them in the like charitable sense as I have sayd, and both their letters are yet extant, and this was all the revenge that the fathers sought of them, or the rigo^r they vsed towards them, thoughe in the tumults past there had ben foure of the busiest expelled by his Hol. order, and by the hand of his vicegerent, wch after vpon entreaty and compassion and promise of amendment being restored to the colledge, they behaved them selves more troublesome than euer before: But now both these and all other were contented (as it semed) and pacified.

This peace was made and ended in the colledge vpon the Ascension day, wch was the vijth of may of this last yere 1597 and so held and contynued in vtter shew vntill the 27th of September next ensuinge, when some being taken at Tavernes vpon a sonday in the morning (as I suppose yo^u have hard) and accused by the Taverners of often repairing thither, and of some worse behavio^r, though not those that then were taken, his hol. commanded a new visitacion to be made by his owne ffiscal; wherevpon ensued after the dismission of some wch you have also hard of and therof some other e[vill] affected have not letted to enforce that the former peace was but dissembled, wch yor frend affirmeth vnto you in al truth and before god to be a false surmise, for that one the fathers syde and specially one his parte there was as full intencion to end and forgeve all by the first peace, as he desireth to be in almightye god for the forgevenes of his synnes, thoughe true it be that a few monthes had passed before some of the former vnquiet beganne agayne secretly to be as troublesome as euer, wch caused yor frend to be more vigilant and to warne them and others their frends of it, and some of them are now there wth yo^u and can testify the same and will not deny it yf they be asked.

But yet the externall peace of the house remained vntill vj or vij (and some of them the principall actors) were quietly dismissed by mission in September and had their ordinary faculties, viaticum and the popes benediction, who made vnto them a very sharpe reprehension at their leave takinge. And soone after their departinge fell out the other disorders that I have signified, wch being examined by his holynes officer, above named, were liked to have receved a severe sentence and punishment had not the good protecto^r and yor foresaid freend entreated hard for mitigacion wch mitigacion came to be so great in the end, that certayne schollers were only sent awaye to live in other colleges, wth viaticum, apparell and very kynde and friendly letters of commendacions, wch they willinglie accepted and have ben so well vsed there (as appereth by their owne letters) and they have also so well behaved them selves as their superio^{rs} give testymonie of them, that euery way exceeding great good hath come thereof: ffor beside the particular good of those sent away the college of Rome hath ben brought vnto so good order thereby, as never it was since the first foundacion, and all occasions of like inconveniences are taken awaye for the tyme to come; and such as remayned there, and had ben deceved have proved since the best and the most contentedest youthes of the house and most beloved of their superio^{rs}.

This then was the mutacion, and thus truly and sincerely proceded the whole matter. And now what good man that is a lover of virtue zealous of the hono^r of god : and of the good of o^r countrey, can mislike the redresse of this so great and daungerous a disease. The cure whereof hath ben the cause of so many great goods together, ffor wch I assure you I have diuers tymes seene his Hol., since it happened lift vp his hands to heaven, and geve god thankes for the same, and so have many other good men done also that knewe the present evill and great daunger hanging ouer vs.

So that heare yor frend fyndeth not why any man there amonge you should call this negotiation of his tyrannicall, Turkish and machiavillian, as some write they have done, thoughe he desire not to know who they be, but he sayeth it is inoughe for him to know that this is spoken in passion, and wthout true knowledge of the matter how it passed, and that it is sufficient for hym to expect his reward from god, and the lesse he hath from man the better : only he addeth this, that he cannot in reason be presumed to have neglected, hated, or hurted these youthes here seing he hath done so muche and doth daylie for them and others of their condicion in other places, in wch respect others have obiected vnto hym the saying of Christ in the gospell, Qui circuitis mare et aridam vt faciatis vnum proselitum, for that not only from England, Ireland, and other countreyes, but even from the straicte prisons gallies and shippes when he passeth he hath gathered euer to this purpose to make schollers, and how many he hath made and procured mayntenance for, these yeres past, wch yet doth endure, is not vnknowen, and the priestes he hath sent towards you since his last departure from Rome may be a sufficient proofe, and therefore much lesse doth he cast any man from his good purposes or wold he have suffered these to have ben sent from Rome, yf it had layen in his power, or that he had thought yt best for them selves or for others or for the common cause to have remayned.

Reason then it seemeth that his worke should rather be beleeved then other men's wordes. And soe, though he might end and answere this sharpe calumniation wth thos sharpe wordes of St.

38, f. 420.

John to Diotrephes, si venero commonebo eius opera, quæ facit verbis malignis garriens in nos, yet will he not but rather wth an other apostle, parco autem ne quis, etc., and wth the same, noli vinci a malo sed vince in bono malum, and soe much of this matter.

There remayneth only that I say a word or two about the facultyes taken away from some in the way towardes England lest they should tell (as is suspected) what they knowe and of others to whom greater were given then the elder sort had as it were hyred thereby to speake frendly, but of this latter poynt I knowe noe grownd at all but rather I knowe it to be most false that any such ample or extraordinarye facultyes have bin given to any since this fact of reformation in Rome happened, for I have bin privy to all and if heretofore at any time difference hath bin mad betweene man and man for givinge them facultyes accordinge to ther talentes in lerninge and other parts it seemeth very vncharitable interp^rtation, that it is done to have them speake or not speake especially in this Romayne action wch speaketh cleare ynoughe of it self and is vnder publique recorde. And thos three from whom the accusation signifyeth that facultyes wer taken from them in the way to the end they should not speake were like to speake the more for that as more displeased, and the lacke of facultyes tyeth noe mans tongue as all the world seeth. The matter then passed thus.

The popes fiscall haveinge made his visitation and taken the depositions of such as could testifye fownd three persons more culpable then the rest, who were departed before towardes England wch haveinge conferred wth his holynes he thought it noe way convenient that thos persons should goe, and live in England in soe [good] a worke vntill they had given better satisfaction, and consequently commaunded the protector to write presently to the nuncio in fflaunders to recall ther facultyes and not so to suffer the sayd persons to passe vnto England vntill he had further order for the same, and to the fiscall his holynes gave commission to draw out soe many articles of his depositions as should be expedient to be shewed vnto the nuncio to examyne them vppon and to require satisfaction.

This is the whole fact [wh]erin yo^u see that the societye hath noe parte at all and consequently noe fault, nor can the procedinge of his holynes or protector herein be rep^rhended or calumniated for that it passed by way of publique iustice and recorde.

Great passion is it then not only to rep^rhend the facte, but also to put soe malignaunt interp^rtation vppon it, as to be done for wicked endes. And when I see such matter come from such mens mouthes as should be temples of the holy ghoast, lovers of veritie, order and discipline, defenders of superiour's doeinges, and charitable interpreters of all mens action that intend to serve god, it maketh me feare greatly that all goeth not well cum homine interiori ; it is St. Paules consequence cum sit inter vos zelus et contentio nonne carnales estis et secundum hominem ambulatis ? 38, f. 420b.

ffor thos of the societye in particular it cannot be denyed but that it is both good and precious to have thes æmulations agaynst them, for wth great love it was spoken sepiam te spinis, and it maketh many to recollect themselves, and to looke more warely vnto ther owne actions humiliatinge ther heartes, and making more frequent recourse vnto almighty god. And yo^u remember what Plutarch sayeth in his booke de utilitate capienda ab inimico that euery vertuous man ought to hyre some body to be his enimye therby to have a watchman ouer him for avoydinge of faultes and that if sometimes this enimye doth calumniate, ther is no more hurt come thereof, sayeth he, then if one for evill will or envye should aduise that you have a spott in yor garment; wch if it be soe then is cause that yo^u take it away, and if it be false it maketh yo^u more carefull that spottes come not there. The like then lett vs doe in this case and pray hartely for them and for o^r selves also.

But to the common cause it must needes be most perilous and pernitious to heare thes contentions and æmulations amongst vs: ne ab invicem consumamur as the holy apostle sayeth dum invicem mordemus ac comedimus and to them that are the particular causes and foundations of thes colers it is wth out all doubt the highe way to the æternall perdition. Yo^u knowe what the same apostle sayeth in the same chapter and matter, portabit iudicium suum quicunque ille est qui conturbat vos, and longe before him the holy ghoast haveinge told vs wth great asseveration that god hated sixe thinges and had the seventh in abomination, nameth this seventh to be in him that soweth sedition amongst brethren.

Therfore my deare S^r let vs all endevour to have o^r handes tongues and hartes free from this heavy curse and neither æmulate nor give any occasion in the world to others of æmulation or hatred against vs, except it be for vertue, of wch arose their æmulation that sayd opprimamus iustum quia est contrarius operibus nostris, for if it come that way it can doe vs no hurt. Yo^u see what o^r fathers suffer vppon this grownde in euery countrye, and it is ther crowne, for in this also must ther imitation be of ther heade, who as he was prophesyed to come not only in resurrectionem, but in ruinam also multorum (though not by his but ther faulte), soe doe I see dayly that this poore society of his is a stumblinge blocke for many to fall and perrishe at, who say, as the others did, gravis est nobis etiam ad videndum quoniam dissimilis est alijs vita illius, et abstinet se a vijs nostris tanquam ab immunditijs, etc.

38, f, 421.

And albeit this do happen often in other places yet I hope in the mercye of o^r Savio^r that it will not happen in England, where euery man ought to be a lanterne the one to the other, and not to envie or emulate but in bonum ; and so I beseche almightie god that it may be, and that they there and we here and in other places labouringe all in one spirite of patience, humility, mansuetude, benignity and charity may prosper in all o^r works, and meete all joyfully one day together eyther in o^r earthly or hevenly country, wch o^r sweete Savio^r graunte and ever preserve you and all that labo^r and serve god wth you. at Naples the 12 of July 1598.

Post script.

Albeit I have ben longe in this letter yet have I written in hast for not to loose the present commodity offred of safe sending the same, and by reason of this hast had I almost forgotten to geve you commission and earnestly intreate you to do my most effectuall harty and humble commendacions to all good frendes there wth you vtriusque ordinis, I meane as well temporall as ecclesiasticall wch are domestice fidei whose holy sent and savo^r is fealt with joy and comfort over all Christendom and their heroicall behavio^r in godes cause doth edifie and sturre vp wonderfully all good people, as also confoundeth faithles negligent, and I hope in Christ Jesus that as he hath geven them so singular courage to resist the externall enemyes furye for so many yeres, so he will geve them light and prudence also to discover this last attempt of the divell, to breke them by domesticall and internall division attempted by a few malcontents either of ignorance or envye. But howsoeuer it be, yf they go forward in that cause, as I hope they will not, they must be eyther corrected by their frendes or contemned, seing they are not only contemptible but odible also to Almighty god in this behalf; and will perish one day wth misery as all those have done lightly that hytherto have had their hands in this worke of iniquity against vnion, peace, order, obedience and vertue, whereof we have here many and most lamentable examples, and many wise men, even strangers, have noted the same wth admiracon and feare; as also one the other syde wth certayne hope of the conversion of England, for that it is evident hereby that god favoureth the cause and fighteth for it and will not have it destroyed by those contradiccions, but only good men exercised and the other punished yf they amend not. And this is so much as sincerely and truly in sight of almighty god occurreth vnto me about this affayre and whether I live or dye this is myne opinion.

My health (I thanke god) is now somewhat better, and I hope these bathes will do me good. My companion is sicke of an ague. M^r. Martin aray is onlie wth me: we have had muche adoe these dayes past aboute the deliuery of xxxiiij english men whom we have found here in the gallies at the ores in extreme misery. But at length god hath geven vs gratiam in conspectu principis and they are deliuered; one was a yonge gentleman of very good parts, whom I have sent to Rome, for god hath geven him great good desyres to follow the life of the semynary. I wrote to you his name and howse before yf I be not deceved, together wth the magistrates patent for their deliuery. And so agayne I byd you hartily farewell this 13th of July, 1598.

Endorsement (in other hand):
Naples 20 (*sic*) July, 1598.
Parsons, as it seemeth to Blackewell, of his ioy y^t the subordination is accepted of by so many: he threateneth such as do oppose themselves: he answereth certayne obiections against ye college at Rome & sheweth why three priests had theire faculties taken from them.

At foot of endorsement (in yet another hand):
John Todde in S^t. Johns Streete ye next house to ye figure of ye Cradle. southwarde.

9. *Statement (in Mush's handwriting) in Reply to the preceding Letter regarding the Dissensions at the English College in Rome.*

54, f. 224.

The continuall discords and contentiones y^t have bene betwene the secular clergie of England, and the Englishe Jesuites, (especially since the deathe of cardinall A. of happie memorie) have muche scandalized as well bothe schismatikes & heretickes as Catholikes: have greatly hindered the increase & progresse of Catholike religion in ye countrie: and have bene verie vngratefull and troublesome to his Holiness. And albeyt there have bene att sundrie times divers meanes attempted for the redressing of these so maine and manifest evills yet hathe there bene no other frute reaped of all those laboures than the increase and multiplication of the same, ffor those that have hitherto laboured in this affayre

THE QUARREL WITH THE JESUITS. 39

attendinge to take a way the imediate cause of the present trobles & discordes, and ether neglectinge, or dispayreinge, or att least faylinge to remove the prime and originall roote frome whence all the rest do springe, have lefte the same intire and vntouched to the new encrease of all the former evilles. Wherefore, least the same effect shoulde folew off all the laboures and travayles that have now bene in redressinge the abvses of the Archprest his authoritie (w^{ch} . . . . . braunches sprange forthe of the same roote whence all the former contentiones have risen) oure desire and intent ys so to bare and lay open the same that by the axe of appostolicall authoritie yt may so be extirpatid as hereafter yt may no more bud forthe.

So yt ys that frome o^r colleges and seminaries, especially this of Rome whence o^r countrie shoulde receave in these times of desolatione the greatest hope, comforthe, and comoditie yt reapethe the increase of miserie and afflictione ffor there hath not bene anie discorde or dissentione (and yet there hathe bene too to muche, wch by all menes confessiones hathe been more hurtefull to o^r countrie then the persecutione of the heretickes) wch hathe not bene hatched and bredd in o^r colledges but cheefly in this of Rome or hathe not risen by the occasione of theyre government, as we shall, wth as muche brevitie as the matter will permitt, demonstrate.

Since the Jesuites entered into the government of this colledge of Rome yt ys well knowne that there have not almost anie two or three yeeres passed wherein there have not bene some so verie great contentiones and iarres betweene the scollers, and thence y^t yf y^t had not beene for the authoritie and moderatione cheefly of Cardi. Alan of happie memorie woulde have brought yt to vtter ruine. W^{ch} contentiones, beinge from time to time rather interrupted or suppressed then ether taken away or ended, have att laste by new occasiones (wch the bande of peace, love, and unione beinge once broken were easely taken) growne into open warres, and have by so much more encreased by how much in process of time bothe

54, f. 224b.

the contendinge parties have multiplied, ffor together wth the number of the persones have increased the diversitie of affectiones whence o[ften] y^t cometh to pass that not only Englande but also all other places where these so diversly affected parties are dispersed are infected wth the same evilles and hereafter will ever so remayne so long as the originall roote frome whence they rise dothe continue.

[Wo]lde god these contentions were so obscurely knowne that they nedd to be p[ro]ved, but alas yt ys farr otherwayes. ffor by the endevoure of oure adv[er]saries (who thaught yt theyre greatest advantage to be the firste trump[et]ers of this newes) a great parte of the Christiane worlde hathe bene so publickely acquaynted therew^th that they can nether be denied nor doubted of. The only thinge that requirethe proofe ys: vpon what roote or occasione these contentiones do rise.

The Jesuites by vniforme consent do attribute them to the evill & perverse dispositione of the scollers. But whether this opinione (wch besides theyre bare assertion hathe no other proofe) be affirmed rather because yt ys true, then to cover the true opinione in dede, we desire others considering these reasons folowinge to iudge.

It ys knowne to all men that knowe anie thinge of the state of o^r affayres, t[h]at these yonge men whoe come to be braught vp in o^r colledges are suche [a]s on the one side have lefte theyre countrie, and manie of them, agaynst [the] willes of theyre owne parentes and frendes, have relinquished large pos[sibi]lities of temporall preferment, and have caste behinde theme the vayne delightes of the worlde: and on the other side have no hope of other temporall benefittes, dignities, or prefermentes, then, after some fewe yeares spent in the studie of vertue and learning vnder collegiall discipline, to returne into theyre countrie wth no other intent then to laboure in convertinge of sowles to god wth manifest danger and iminent perill of no less loss then life yt selfe. Howe therefore ys yt likely that these men who, haveing no other scope then the saveing of other menes sowles do put them selves into suche periil and danger can have so litle care of theyre owne as to caste them away or at least greatly to hazarde theme by obstinate and wilfull contendinge wth theyr superioures.

2. Those prestes who have frome the begininge labored in godes harvest in o^r countrie, haveinge alwayes had a speciall care to send or direct none to the Seminaries but such as do yeelde great good hope of theyre pietie, sinceritie, simplicitie and all other vertu fitt for that vocatione, yt ys not like that they wolde be so farr deceaved as in steede of vine braunches to send thorne bushes or in steede of figg tree plantes to send thistles. Or yf yt be a defect of nature in Englishe men to be contentiouse as some Jesuites have insinuated and therefore harde to be avoyded, why have they alwayes so earnestly laboured to drawe o^r countreemen into theyr religione? or yf they will not heare of that why have they receaved so manie of theme? They cannot be ignorant that one vnquiet spirite ys sufficient to disturbe a whole congregatione, convent or societie; muche more manie that are naturally seditiouse, and contentiouse. Or yf the professinge of religione dothe take away that defect why not the actuall resolutione to vndergoe all iminent perill of deathe for godes sake and the saveinge of sowles? [or why did some of them laboure (pretendinge that defect) to hinder some of o^r countriemen whome gladly they would have had into theyr owne societie to be receaved in a nother religione that was approved 1200 yeares before theyres begann. and some alreadie entred and professed from goinge into Englande? wherin yf they pleade a wronge charge yt will be easely prooved.] ^{a}

3. In all the tumultes of colledge the scollers have alwayes to have [sic] the cause knowne to his holiness and therefore did earnestly desire to be visited by aut[ho]ritie: when of the contrarie part the Jesuites did alwayes laboure [to] hinder all suche authenticall inquisitione of the cause, exceptinge the last

---

^{a} This passage between square brackets is erased in the MS.

visit wch ff[ather] P[arsons] procured by suche meanes as shall hereafter be declared; yt ys therefore [a] signe that the cause of tumultes did not rise vpon the scollers part.

4. The rule of the colledge authoriseing the rectoure to expell anie one that comittethe anie fault whereby the peace of the colledge may be perturbed & gevethe no hope of amendment. Why therefore woulde the Rectoures yf the fault were in the scollers suffer so manie breaches of peace when they mighte so easely have remedied them.

[margin: 54, f. 225b.]

5. Contentiones never risinge but vpon exorbitant or inordinate desires & appetites, yf the scollers ever desired anithinge that was not iust or honest or were ever so obstinate that after the first notice of his holiness his will (the case once knowne) they remayned not fully satizfied or desisted not, they were doubtless faultie therein. But yf the contrarie be true as hereafter yt will appeare most true then the fault wilbe fownde in the Jesuites.

6. Besides that out of Englande are nowe sent but those whoe are of such expectatione as ys before mentioned, yet before the[y] come to Rome ys there another triall made of theme. ffor ordinarily there none comethe to Rome that have not lived some yeares in other seminaries, and by theyre good behavioure there have deserved to be preferred to the missione of Rome, that ys, to be put to live in this colledge wch alwayes hathe bene thaught amongst o^r scollers a preferment.

7. Oure scollers have lived wth so great concorde, peace and tranquilitie in that seminarie that was not vnder the Jesuites government, that never anie like discontentment hapened betweene them and theyre superioures. Besides theyre loyall behavioure in all religiones where they enter ys a signe theyre dispositiones are not so badd but where they have good governoures they may be easely governed.

8. It hathe beene so often tried that now yt needethe no proofe: that those selfe same men whoe liveinge in this colledge of Rome have beene reputed by the Jesuites contentiouse, obstinate, and

seditiouse (both imediately before and after theyre aboade here) have lived in other colledges wth great commendacones of theyre peaceable, yea, and exemplare, behavioure of theyre adversaries. To say nothinge of all those (wch are not few) who bothe by theyre lives in England and deathes have lefte sufficient testimonie to the worlde that they were nether seditiouse nor contentiouse albeyt the Jesuites have labored to make theme so reputed. ffa. p. l're of [the] 12 of July [15]98 to m^r wal:[a]

To conclude: by this and the reasones goinge before besides divers others wch might be alleadged to this purpose yt may be gathered that suche contentiones as have beene betweene these men and the Jesuites have not risen vpon anie evill dispositione in them who vnder other governoures live w^thout anie suche defect. 54, f. 226.

ffather P. being vrged wth these reasones in the behaulfe of the scollers and on the one side beinge as yt seemethe not able to satisfy theme, and on the other obstinatly bent not to admitt them as true, lest thereby he might condeme his owne and his felowes government, ys forced in the fore mentioned letter to forge in theyre excuse certayne reasones why Englishe men in Rome showlde be more contentiouse or troublesome then elsewhere. In this letter he vtterethe manie opprobriouse and contumeliouse speeches of the scollers but vnder the shadow of other menes opiniones ether that they may be of more creditt or to avoyde the answereinge of them yf peradventure he showlde be braught to proofe theme. But his reasons are these:

ffirste, the nature of the place wch by reason of the frequent concurrence of great sightes and relations of popes, cardinalles and princes affayres engenderethe highe spirites in them that are not well established in almightie godes grace. This reasone he confirmethe by the iudgment of other strangeres as Spaniardes ffrenchmen & ffleminges who (as he sayethe) do affirme that experience hathe taught them that this ys true. How true this

---

[a] Father Parsons' letter of the 12th of July, 1598, to Mr. Wal[ley] or Garnet is that printed above, p. 21. The marginal note is in the same hand as the rest of the letter.

reasone ys in father P. him selfe we know not, yett divers circumstances do shewe yt truer in him then peradventure in anie other; but smale truthe yt can have in o^r scollers whoe livinge, as yt were, recluded in the colledge have litle acquayntance wth these great affayres; nether do they hope or expect anie highe places w^{t}hout w^{c}h expectance highe spirites do not often contende.

His 2 reason ys because manie youthes come to Rome only vpon desire to see novelties whither when Englishe men come, falinge into want & finding oportunitie of entertaynment in the colledge: when they are entertayned fall into disorder. But first verie few Englishe men come att all. 2^{ly} there are verie few of those few that are admitted into the colledge. 3^{ly} yf anie of them that are so admitted or anie of the rest do fall into anie disorder the rule of the colledge dothe licence the superioures to expell theme.

His 3 reason (w^{c}h he saythe ys more important then bothe the others) ys the dis[gust] geven at the first fundatione of the colledge to a certayn principall man of ov[r] natione then resident in Rome (he meanethe the Bishope of Cassanae). Who as (he saythe) not affecting the government nor governoures of . . . . . .^{a} was ever in re or in opinione a back vnto them that woulde be discontented. It ys not vnprobable but this good prelate disliked the government as also did Cardinall Alane and others of no small iudgement. And what opinione Gregorie the 13 of happie memorie and Card. Morone then protectoure of o^r colledge had of theyre governmemt yt appearethe by theyre unwillingness to admitt yt into the colledge. But that the fores[ayd Bishope did ever back anie that were w^{t}hout iust cause discontented yt savorethe more of detractione frome him who ys deade ^{b} (w^{c}h ys [no] smale impietie then of anie truthe.

Now what wayght there ys in all these reasones to proove that

^{a} Obliterated. ^{b} He died Oct. 14, 1595.

Englishe scollers in Rome are contentiouse where in other places they a[re] most free frome anie suche note lett the indifferent iudge.

The instance of ffa. m.[a] his government (who to his perpetuall prayes performed that wch none of all his predecessoures nor successoures ever did) ys not so effectuall to proove the defect to be in the scollers as the contrarie, ffor first yt showethe that the scollers are not of so badd a dispositione but that they may be peaceably governed; secondly seeinge that divers who lived under him lived also vnder his predecessoures and successoure, and yett vnder nether w^{t}hout discontentment, yt ys a signe that the defect foloweth the rectoures and not those scollers : ffor else the scollers beinge the same men the woulde have shewed the same affectiones vnder theme all. But yf the reason be asked of vs why that only Rectoure gave such contentment to the scollers we can geve no better reasone then this : that he beinge a Jesuit did not govern like a Jesuit, ffor they amongst vs (what they do else where we know not) desire to be feared more then loved : and he did the contrarie and therefore was he loved of the scollers and also feared where thother Rectoures were nether loved nor feared.

To the other two instances we answere that the peace and tranquillitie of this colledge and also those in Spayne ys suche as ys or woulde have beene betweene the Jesuites in Englande and the prestes notwthstandinge so manie iniuries offered be them to the prestes : ffor yf ffa. P. could as well have hindered the iust complayntes of the prestes from comeinge to the see apostolike (wch he desired and endevored to do) as he dothe of scollers, he would then have sayde there had bene all peace and tranquillitie as now he saythe of these colledges where there ys no less inwarde discontentment then there ys in Englande, albeyt he hath by craftc and violence so braught the matter to pass that it dothe less outwardly appeare.

54, f. 227.

[a] Mutius Vitelleschi, who succeeded Father Joseph Cresswell as rector of the college, April 16, 1592, and was appointed a second time in Oct. 1597. He was afterwards elected sixth general of the society, Nov. 1615.

Now toucheinge the originall causes and occasiones of the contentiones before mentioned this ys our opinione wch how true yt ys we reffere to the particulare proofes.

The Jesuits, by the government of the colledge, ever seeking the private benefit of theyre owne societie w^thout respect of the comone benefitt of o^r countrie; yea further, hopinge by the oportunitie thereof to bringe vnder theyre dominione the whole bodie of the secular clergie of England, have ever directed to this scope all theyre endeavoures, wch manie, as well of the scollers in the colledge as of the prestes, espyinge have alwayes [sou]ght to hinder as [a] thinge uniust and for manie causes inconvenient, vpon wch oppositione have folowed suche endless enmitie and contentiones as now we see. Enmitie we say because those that have not dissembled butt freely shewed their affectiones in these matters agaynst the endevoures of the Jesuites have alwayes beene accompted by theme enemies to theyre societie, contentiouse, seditiouse, factiouse and the like, and when so ever occasione have served have beene entreated by them as suche.

If we here proove the Jesuites endevoures to have beene directed to these endes, to witt to convert the whole benefitt of the colledge to theyre owne societie, and to bringe vnder theme the secular clergie of o^r countrie, yt will remayne manifest and nedless of further proofe, vpone what grownde or roote all the fore mentioned contentiones, discordes, and disagreementes have risen. In this sorte therefore we proove yt. ffirst [they] have ever frome the beginninge wth all arte and cunninge possible lab[o]red to drawe all o^r scollers of anie expectatione ether for talentes of learninge or nobleness of birthe to leave and forsake the end of colledges institutione, and enter into theyre societie.

54, f. 227b. This hathe beene an aunchent complaynt agaynst them prooved by divers particule[r] instances in Cardi. Sega his last visit, confessed by ffa. Holt and not de[nied] by ffa. Per. who in redress thereof promised vpon the worde of a religiouse preste to procure of his Holiness a prohibition vnder excommunicatione for the confessarius of the colledge ever to perswade anie of the scollers ether directly or indirectly to anie religione, wch promise, notwithstandinge his othe, he never performed. Of this practice and of the inconveniences that folow therevpone do springe manie evilles.

1. ffirst, that part of the scollers and prestes that are more zealouse for the conve[r]tione of oure countrie do repute theme selves muche iniured and godes cause much damnified by the alienatinge and divertinge of suc[he] principall partes and members of theyre bodie to another end. This only reasone weyghed so muche wth Card. Boromeo of holy memorie that he for this cause only discharged the Jesuites of the government of his Seminaries att Milane: sayinge yt was more necessarie for godes churche to have learned pastoures then learned religiouse men.

Secundly, by the partiall favoures (an opposite enemie to all peace and vnitie in anie comunitie), wch they shewe to those whome they woulde winn, ys ingendered emulatione in them that ether for want of suche goo[d] partes of nature & birthe, or else for theyre resolutione in theyre owne vocatione, are not partakers thereof. Besides the manifest breache of the colledge rule that forbiddethe all suche singularitie.

3. Thirdly, the Jesuites of purpose deferringe to admitt theme that yelde to they[re] perswationes vntill theyre whole course of studies or a great parte thereof be ended: they remayne still in the colledge and besides that they occu[py] the places of scollers whereas they have forsaken the end of the colledge. They are vsed as instrumentes to draw others into the same mynd and also as spyes to discover other menes affectiones that for feare of disple[asure] do not discover them selves vnless yt be in confidence vnto others. Here[after] folowethe muche ielowsie and suspitione, hurtfull thinges in anie commu[nitie].

4. ffourthely, those scollers that vpon zeale of theyre countries goode ether shewe disliks of this practise or vpon confidence do revayle theyre mynde[s by] mishapp to some secrett Jesuite are

by the Jesuites themeselves reputed [enemies] to theyre socie[tie] and to religiouse perfectione and therefore do they [by] all meanes they [can] cross, vex, and afflict theme : whereby the profitt of theyre studies ys muche hindered and they often times, to redeme theyre uniust vexat[ion]e, [are] compelled to departe the colledge before theyre time : nether are they by this . . . . . ffor before them they sende the infamie of con[tent]iouse, factiouse, and seditiouse spirite, to the great hinderance of theyr laboures in England.

10. *John Sicklemore to Dr. Bagshaw.*

3 Aug., 1598.[a]

38, f. 407. Right Reverend & lerned father and ffrend.

I hope yow doubt not but that (att my being amongst you^u) I faithfullie & trulie deliuered vnto yo^w (soe farre forth as in shorte tyme I could) the effecte & somme of such broyles as latelie hath passed amongst our deerest frendes beyond the seas. Since my departure I haue reflected vpon yor opinion touching the veritie & processe thereof, whereby yo^u seeme to me not to be fullie perswaded that eyther such thinges have happened, or that such lenitie in the persecution hath beene vsed, as was convenyent. ffor the one to weete the truth of my relations I can say no more then I haue vttered, thinking the sworen othe of diverse to be of greater force & credite then the vngrownded surmise of some few (totoo hardlie credilous of verities & totoo easie to suspect vntruthes where noe falshood is thought of). I dare not accuse yo^u as one of this humo^r yet I feare least happilie yor speeches haue seemed to haue some spice thereof, ffor yf yo^u remember, after divers our conferences wch willinglie yo^u harde wthout contradiction, yo^u often asked me what I knew of my proper knowledge, and what I

---

[a] John Sicklemore's name appears in Cardinal Sega's list of the 37 mutineers at the English college at Rome in 1596 (Foley, *Records*, vi. 3)· He is probably the "Humphrey" Sicklemore who left Rheims for Rome in company with Ed. Bennet and six others in May, 1591 (*Douay Diaries*, 239 ; *cf.* Foley, vi. 186).

thought of thes thinges, which question in some maner declared, that yo^u rather were inclined to geue credite rath^r to my censure, then to greater argumentes wch then had bene mentioned. It can not stand, in my iudgement with reason that my worde may be comparable wth the testimony of the right reuerend ff. per[sons] (whose shoues I wish my selfe worthie to kisse), nor my naked thought wth the guiltie conscience of manie, nor my onelie verdicte with the othe of iuridicall confession, wherefore if my sentence might or may prevaile wth yo^w, how much more ought an other mans sinceritie sufficientlie to perswade: whose lerining, wisdome, labours & goodwill to o^r common cause, England hath tried, ffrance ex ore infantium et lactentium testifieth (to confound inimicum et vltorem), Spaine wch erected colledges largelie witnesseth, & Italie, in Rome it self, with established peace most highlie commendeth, finallie credite, yea familiaritie, wth the holiest, most potent, most glorious, most godlie maketh most famous? Yf I say yo^u are content not to misbeleeue me or my opinion, how much more ought yo^w not to discredite that mans dealings & narrations, in whom (as in a verie mirrhour of o^r sinnefull age and afflicted church) god would haue to appeare & abound so manie giftes of his heavenlie grace? Surelie yor wisdome requireth that yor credulitie should be grounded in the fideltie of yor eqvall & superior & not vpon feathers, wauering in each ayre with what wynde soever bloweth. Yo^u know my meaning, verbum sapienti sat est, & you must needes thinke that to touche to nighe the cardinall versions of supreme orbes lacketh not danger of brused bones where too haughtie clyming endeth wth to heavie & perhaps deadlie fall. But lett this suffice for the vertue & dignitie of my auto^r whom to impeach I deeme wilbe as harde, as it is for him easie to defend. Magna veritas et præualet.

To come then to an other pointe, wch is vpon supposition of true crymes, & that yet too great rigour hath bene vsed in the punishment, herein credite me I know not whether it should be called a punishment or noe, or rather a sweete disposition of that wch god in his favourable mercie had ordeyned. True it is, some were dismissed from the Seminarie, and sent elsewhere but thither when I came I found them soe well with there departure contented, as verilie the most of them wth their owne mouth did witnesse & protest vnto me that it was gods verie will that they should remaine whereat they remayned, performing their vsage, & commodious intreatie before that from whence they came, vnwilling to retourne vpon what condition soeuer, in suche trust, loue, favour & likeing wth superior vt nihil supra & farr neerer their retyred & desired home, possiblie they could, yf they had not been dismissed.

The greatest grief in this matter is the publishing of defames, herein what was done in the colledge, was by commaundem^t of the Protecto^r. What was done in England was by the extreame instance of yo^rself & some other w^ch, as it were by force, wrong forth the same, & all this much against the wills of oth^r our superiours & against the minde of such as tould some few thereof. Good Sir, there are onelie some few priestes wch know hereof, noe person as yet is named, it is an easie matter as yet to drowne all before it be imparted eyther to catholike or heretike, ffor gods sake lett vs follow ff : Gar[net] his counsaile in this, which is wholie to conceale thes enormious & beastlie offences. He is wholie bent to yt, that is the mynd of o^r assigned Superio^r Mr Blackwell, of his coadiuto^rs & o^r dearest frendes, Lett vs not one worke an oth^rs shame, otherwise at length I feare maugre our teethe the particular persons wilbe knowen & publickelie punished, & therevpon must of necessitie fall a publicke infamie both of o^r cause, churche & clergie. Whereas now it wilbe & may easilie be forgotten & that privatelie be excused or avoyded, wherevnto ther wilbe noe tergiversation after open proues of particular defamation, wherevnto if this should proceede wch godd forbidd, then whilst we wrest to much one an others iniquities lett vs take heede least to vs pertaine that of the apostle si inuicem mordetis et comeditis videte ne ab inuicem consumamini, let us rather follow the holsome consayle annexed,

Gal.

Dico autem spiritu ambulate et desideria carnis non perficietis. Yf we acknowledg as acknowledge we must that opera carnis be immunditia, impudicitia, luxuria, lett us beware whilst we sifte thes to much eyther against mercie or iustice, (in seeking either to excuse & acquite the guiltie or to checke to cruellie the faultie) that likewise there followe not inimicitiæ, contentiones, æmulationes, iræ, rixæ, dissentiones, sectæ, inuidiæ, ebrietates, comessationes et his similia, quæ, as the same adioyneth, prædico vobis sicut prædixi, quoniam qui talia agunt regnum dei non consequentur. I trust in god that yo^w farre remoue yor actions from thes perills, yet surelie a heauie iudgm^t must needes befall the perturbers of peace in the kingdome of Christ wch is his church. I hope yor spirites are more celestiall & more adioyned to that holie spirite, whose fructes are charitas, pax, patientia, mansuetudo, modestia, fides, continentia, wch as yor profession, or rather sacred confession, requireth & expostulateth of designed, or as it were designed, martyrs, so geue example & testimonie to the worlde & yor poore brethren abroade of semblable lief, si uiuimus spiritu, spiritu et ambulemus, non efficiamur inanis gloriæ cupidi, inuicem prouocantes, inuicem inuidentes. And if often it happeneth that præoccupatus fuerit homo in delicto, uos qui spirituales estis huiusmodi instruite in spiritu lenitatis, considerans teipsum ne et tu tenteris. Alter alterius onera portate et sic adimplebitis legem Christi, then whose behauiour what more meeke? then whose doctrine what more humble? then whose burden what more light? then whose peace what more sweete? then whose example what more patiente? then whose death what more mercifull? And shall we then be most rigorous wth o^r neighbours he being so clement to his offendo^{rs}? or shall those wch are, as it were, in the verie next stepp of reighning wth hym in glorie noe more imitate the pathes wherin he walked, & wherby onelie we can atteine to see his glorious presence? god forbidd. Yo^u are not recluded from the world to disquiett the world, neith^r included for the faith of Christ to perturbe his poore flocke, to offend & scandalize his little ones, but to rest quiett in y[o][r] owne soules & to worke the establishment of peace in others, & to edifie yea the most averted miscreant & infidle whatsoeuer. I pray god the lettre w[ch] yo[u] were in perusing at my departure tend not to some inconvenience, contrarie to that tranquillitie w[ch] his holines conceiveth of our estate. It will be hard to availe much against his determinations, & he wilbe very lothe to impaire the good reformation w[ch] is now in his college there, w[ch] at my comming thence was such as maid him right glad to heare of, & most desirous to continew, & verilie I assure you that verie vnwelcome are they likelie to be, that offer him anie occasion of alteration in a settled quiettnes, & reformed companie, ffor god sake looke what yo[u] doe, & ponder well with whom & what about yo[u] deale. It will be noe little offence in his iudgement anie action enterprised of anie his children, when he vnderstandeth there father therein neglected if not contemned, neith[r] will he suffer it to be vnpunished that we should take anie matter in hand about the common cause, w[th]out his leave, consent and directions whom he hath ordeyned our heade, & substituted as his agent amongst vs in his soe farre absence. I write as having tried how enormious a cryme disobedience is there esteemed, yo[u] may do as it pleaseth god & yo[r]self, for my part by gods grace in pace in idipsum dormiam et requiescam et there shalbe habitatio mea in sæculum sæculi: ffarewell, 3° Aug. 1598.

Y[o][r] faithfull ffrend
Io : SICKLEMORE.

Endorsed (*by writer*) : 1. To his verie good ffrend M[r] docto[r] Baggshaw prison[r] in the castle of Wisbiche be this del[d].

(*by another*) : 2. Sicklemore to D[r]. Bagshaw.

Persons greatly commended.

Certayne lewd actions to be concealed.

He forwarneth: that theire sending to Rome wold haue no good successe.

3 Aug. 1598.

11. *A Copie of a Letter to Mr. Wis:*[a]
[*from John Mush, in vindication of the secular priests*].

Sir, hearinge often by ye relation of diuers good men, yor worthy resolution & industrie to do well, I ioyed much in you, & though we neuer had bin acquainted, nor seene one another, yet did I beare great good affection to you, & thought myself much both benefited & pleasured by o^r vnion in ye family or houshold of god; & by your most fervent labouring, & resolute bestowinge yor self for promotinge of o^r lords worke, ye releif of many, & ye comfort of all his afflicted members, either by yor owne charitable liberality, or by ye good fame of yor vertues spredd alone. We are not acquainted nor like to be: yet surely sir, I neuer can accomnpt myself a straunger to such as you are, we being but as ye diuers members & distant parts of one body, liuinge & receyuinge all o^r good from on[e] & ye same head & spirit. By reason of wch happy coniunction, I doubt not but I may ye rather p^rsume, & be more bold, without giuinge iust offence to admonish you of anythinge y^t may be hurtfull to yo^rself or ye common cause. And again I cannot doubt but hoope for this, at yor charitable & vertuous minde, y^t rather you will take in good part my writing, & amend what is amisse, then be offended with yor freind, or contemne his aduise. Of late certain lines taken out of a book made as they say by you, of 3 fairwelles (if I mistake ye author nihil ad te scriptum putes) were showed to me & others: wherin speakinge of choosing spirituall guides, after y^t you haue exceedingly commended & extolled ye Jesuites aboue other preists within this realme, as more void of passions and affections, more free from errour, more familiar with god, more particularly illuminated in all their meeds & more specially endued with ye spirit of guidinge soules etc: than ye secular preists be in this haruest of god: you adde these words. Onely those I would wish you to take speciall heed of y^t

[a] According to Mr. Macray, "Mr. Wiseman, afterwards Sir William Wiseman, of Broadoaks, Essex."

beinge themselfes not guided by any, are in y^t vnfitt to be guides to others ; such I say I doe not commend you vnto, as are knowne to haue no such relation, wch I speake of, & wch I proued to be so necessarie in all sorts, & much more in them. And as ye times be now without distinction of parishes, or limittes of pastorall chardge, where ye most be at liberty to make choice of theire guides, I would be loth if I were in yor case to choose one y^t were not addicted yt way as I said before. And yet if I had already one that were not so, but were wholy guided by himself : I must tell you y^t as I would not alter him & yt might be inconuenient; so would I very litle relye vpon him a[s] my guide, but further would seeke directi^{on} (as were necessary for me) from some others etc : which words surely, sir, whether they be yo^{rs} without theire knowledge, or theire owne; or yo^{rs} with theire consent & approbation (as yor whole discourse in y^t booke may easyly persuade euery man y^t you would not haue done this or any matter of like importance, without ye priuity & good likinge of them yor spirituall guides) cannot but yeold iust cause of offence & scandall to either all or ye most good secular preists y^t shall heare them, as already they haue moued many, for hereby you & whosoeuer ioyne wth you in this, exceedingly derogate from ye due credit & estimacion of preists, & iniury ye whole order not a litle. for within o^r nation ye greater number without comparison, & ye most sufficient & best labourers euery way, are not guided thus as you speake of [a] . . . . Behold therefore how not onely yo[u] dis[grace] . . . . secular preists, but presume also to checke, controule & reproue o^r superio^{rs} by this position of yours . . . . they be not Jesuits (say you) or not guided by them in theire labours, take speciall heed of them, they [are] vnfitt to be guids to others. Sir, ye spirit & course of o^r superiours, wch happyly beganne this worke . . . . ye Jesuits & haue gone prosperously forward therwith hitherto, with but small

---

[a] Several lines rendered unintelligible from the mutilation of the MS. are here omitted.

assistance or helpe of Jes[uits] in comparison of ye other labourers, theire spiritte, I say, & this of yo^rs differ exceedingly. Theirs hath . . . . all o^r countries good hitherto; yo^rs vnles it be corrected by time will bringe all i[n]to dissention & gar[boyles]. Jesuits cooperate well in ye werke of god, & therefore deserue credit & hono^r amongst good men: other secular preists also labour wth as much pay[n]es & gayne of christian soules as they, and is it reason then there should be speciall heed taken of them, & y^t they be discredited as vnfit pasto^rs for gods people, because the[y] haue noe dependance, relation, direction nor guidinge by Jesuits? Mens vnaduised conc[e]its & inordinate affections may carrie them to inconuenient excesses in valewinge Jesuits or preists & th[eir] deserts; & in m . . . . foolishe blinde & odious comparisons in preferringe religious before others, but this spirit is not of god, nor bese[e]m^th gods people to vse, or his preists, be they religious or secular, to approue or like of. Go[d forb]id y^t [she]epe which [in] all loue, in all humilitye, & in all dutyfull sort, ought to imbrace, to reuerence . . . . . . onourab[ley] . . . . all gods priests, theire pasto^rs, should by inordinate zeale, & disordered affection towards some persons or orders disdain ye rest, or iudge them vnfitt to be theire guides in ye necessities of theire soules, or daungerous & vnworthy labourers in gods vineyarde, wch follow not ye directions or courses of them whom they particularly affect & delight in. It may rightly be thought fowle presumption for ye sheepe to iudge or censure condemne or contemne theire ordinarie pasto^rs in these times of o^rs especially, as vnfitt or insufficient to guide them, & very vnseemly & sinfull it is for you laymen vpon yor owne priuate affections towards either religious or secular, to preiudice ye good estimacion & credit of any yor spirituall fathers: All which I doubt not but they are sufficiently assisted by gods grace when you have to deale with them in yor necessarie occasions touchinge ye saluation of yor soules, so as they can direct you to greater perfection then any of you are arriued vnto as yet, or wilbe ready to follow, & put in

38, f. 331b.

execution. you or whosoeuer bendeth with you y^t way to preferre, or aduaunce either religious or secular preists, with diminishinge ye credit, or derogatinge in any sort from ye other, are badly occupied, & cannot but blowe coales of debate, discord, & emulation amonge brethren, & raise contempt of good men. If you be preferringe & boasting of Paul, an other wilbe of Peter, an other of Apollo; & what is this but vanitie & ye seed of dissention, & a certaine argument of foolish zeale, & indiscrete affection? And must it not also necessarily follow hereupon (you taking this course) y^t you & such other of ye layty wch haue dealinge onely wth Jesuits must not in yor owne conceipts alone, but in ye opinions & estimacion also of all others be iudged of more singular vertue, perfection, & holynesse, then any of ye rest good people can be wch are guided by ye secular preists: yours beinge sufficient to direct you, & theirs vnfitt to guide them? & by these meanes shall wee not haue shortly a foule diuision & emulation amonge ye clergy & people of god? and shall wee not become vaineglorious, factious, & iniurious one towards an other? Sir, for any thinge I haue heard or knowen to ye contrary, all we of ye secular ranke instruct & admonish o^r children to loue, to hono^r, to reuerence, to esteeme most worthyly of, & to accept indifferently in all friendly & dutifull manner, all preistes in respect of him whose messingers they be, & whose person they represent: in regard also of their high order & holy vocation of preisthood, & for ye charitable affayres they haue vndertaken & aduenture theire liues to labour in. we teach them indifferently to carrie their good affections towards all be they Jesuits or secular, & to conceiue & thinke well of all, whom they certainly know not to be evill, & finally to iudge euery one whom god & theire superiours haue approu[ed] and sent to be sufficient & fitt pastors to guide them as theire neede shall require. How you be taught otherwise I know not: But it is a very vndecent & presumptuous rashnes, for ye layty that neither well know themselfes, nor can discerne what true perfection is, and are altogither ignorant of what fitnes preists be to ye dischardge of theire function, to discusse ye matter, & giue theire verdict, as you haue done. myself in mine owne conscience am ye worst & most vnworthy amonge all ye secular preists, yet can I aunswer for my brethren, yt as farre as mans vncertain iudgement can reach & discerne, there be in England ma[ny] secular preists, wch want this dependaunce & relation of yours, as fitt to guide soules in vertuous . . . as many Jesuits be. yea some preists more fitt than some Jesuits, & some Jesuists again more fitt . . . some preists. yet dare I not say or thinke but all on both sides (by ye assistance of gods spirit, and the o[r]dinarie helpes taken in ye felowship of theire brethren) are both fitt & sufficient to dischardge theire dut[i]es in this behalfe. And now especially after they haue passed ye censure, discussion, & approbation of our superiours, & be sent by them into this haruest. Sir, I wish not to diminish in any degree yor good conceipt of ye Jesuits. I also loue & hono{r} them, & thinke them very profitable labourers, & coadiutors in this worke (though I know & heare many of them, & some of you also theire affectionate friends, to be badly conceipted & to report of me, as though aversions, disagreements, & I know not what euill enmities els were on my part against them, but in all these I contemne mens opinions, seinge god must trie ye matter) but I would stay ye excesse of yor affection in magnifyinge them, when it may turne to ye disgrace or discredit of any preist in ye least point yt may be: and would giue you occasion to consider ye worthiness of ye secular preists, yt either you may receiue them also into ye inner parts of yor good affection with them you seeme to loue & like so well of (consideringe they all be fellows & cooperatours in ye principall worke for wch they both are sent & liue here) or els spare hereafter to touch ye one sort with disgrace, for ye great{r} credit of ye other. And therefore I inlarge myself a little more in this case, to giue ye [p]oore men their due. And assure you yt of ye numbers of both sorts, which I haue bin acquainted with in this countrie, I haue knowen & know yett many secular preists (though I be none of them, o{r} lorde graunt me his grace to amende) to be as void of passions & euill affections, as truly mortyfied in theire bodyes & mindes, as free from ambition & vaineglorie, from desire of worldly pompe, credit, riches, hono^{rs}, dignities, & such like vanities, as sincere in all theire dealinges, as discreete, modest & orderly in theire proceedings, as studious of vertuous & pure, as much occupied in meditations & prayers, as temperate in diet, as simple in attyre, as severe towards themselues in fastings, watchings, & other afflictions, as redy by day or night to toyle & trauayle on foote, in heates, in sweats, in colde, in weete, in harde fayre, in stormes & tempests, in darknes, in daungers & solicitude for helpinge & comfortinge christian soules, & finally as desirous & zealous of god^s hono^r, ye saluation of his people & the aduauncement of his holy churches cause, as ye Jesuits be: yea truly, Sir, there be many good & blessed secular preists within this realme, which in all these graces are not behinde ye Jesuits, but may very duly be matched with them, y^t I speake no further. Neither ought, or can this equall comparison of both their virtue[s] displease ye truly religious & humble minds of any, or stirre theire harts or toungues to murmurre, repine, ar mutter one word against it, & to blame me therefore. And for their skill, fittnes, & graces in guiding soules, the effects & fruits of their labours, yeeld manifest proofe & argument, y^t they be no whit inferiours to Jesuits in this point neither: for if wee looke backe to ye beginninge of things, it cannot be denied but y^t they were secular preists wch first breake ye Ise, & entred ye haruest: They trauayled prosperously to the gayninge of many soules, long before any Jesuit came: No, ye Jesuits had not entred ye land, when both the secular preists had watered theire labours with their own blood, by suffringe glorious martirdoms, & their catholike children had learned to contemne all they possessed, & not to shrinke at ye hazard or losse of their liberties, goods, & liues, for defence of god's hono^r, for vpholdinge his catholique religion, & for sauinge their owne soules. Since ye Jesuits entred, indeed ye numbers of gods people zealous and resolute haue increased dayly euery where,

38, f. 332.

the prisons haue bin & are filled with catholiques, many haue bin spoyled of their goods & liuings, many haue constantly sustayned greiuous torments, many haue ioyfully suffred death alredy, & many stand resolutely prepared to endure ye vttermost cruelty of the persecuto^r. But, Sir, yo^{r}self & others must know, y^t ye good industrie of ye secular [preists] (gods holy grace co-operating) hath principally wrought these effects: for y^t to ye most of all these sainets of god onely the secular preists haue bin continually since ye beginninge & are still their pastors & guides, without these relations & guidings of yours. And it cannot be denied (for dayly experience hath euer showed it to be most true) y^t when god permitteth these with whom onely ye secular preists deale, wch you accompt vnfitt guides, to come in question before ye persecutor, but they play ye parts of good & vertuous christians in euery respect, no lesse then ye other doe which haue had their dependance & guidinge wholly by ye Jesuits. In respect of the secular priests [and the p]eople guided by them, the Jesuits & their dependants are but very few. They in all points of christian dutie are not found more faylinge then these, either in good deeds before, or when they come to extreme triall, more faintinge, & all this without yor relation, dependaunce, or guidaunce (I say) for ye most of very good preists & people haue no such dealinge with Jesuits, nor see them scarce once in a whole yeare or twoe. The Jesuits helpe well & doe much good; they also that are wholly guided by them doe well : but in truth ye greatest weight & burthen of ye worke, the chiefe maintenaunce, vpholdinge, & progresse of ye cause, within this realme is principally be ye secular preists, & ye people guided by them. yea Sir (and if you can looke backe on both sides with indifferency, & true comparisons may be without disgrace or offence to any) you may plainly see those catholike houses, which those vnfitt secular[s] guide, not onely to exceede the others guided by Jesuits farre in number, but also fully to matche them (to say the least they deserue) in all good and charitable workes, as in maintaininge ye common cause, as in keepinge most free & liberall hospitalitye, & giuinge comfortable intertainment to all afflicted preists & people of god; as in bestowing almes also & other releife to their abilities where they know necessities to be, & in all su[ch] like deedes of piety. All which they doe to all y^t are knowne to be honest men, in respect onely of god & fulfilling ye duties of good cath : people without all foolish partialitie, or y^t precise or nice acception of persons, or respect whether they be religious or secular preists, or dependinge or guided by either, wch is known & noted to be vsuall in most places where ye Jesuits beare sway, to wch places few or none can be wellcom or be admitted besides themselves & their dependants : for ye most part, the Jesuits haue entred into howses conuerted & guided by the labours of secular preists before theire cominge : If they haue abettered them & brought them to more vertue, let god haue the prayse, they shall not fayle of their merit, & noe gracious soule can repine, but hereupon no man so benefited ought to iudge ye secular preists vnfitt guides. thes vertuous deeds then, wch I have rehearsed & such like beinge ye effects & fruits of the secular preists labours, without yor relation & guidinge show manifestly y^t they be good & profitable guides to gods people, & consequently, it is manifest also, yor position to be very false & pernicious to gods cause & preiudiciall to his preists.

38, f. 532b.   Cease of therefore I pray you, good Sir, this perilous dealinge, proceeding I veryly persuade myself from yor vertuous zeale, & tender affection to ye Jesuits wthout intention (I hoope) to offend or derogate from ye secular, but yet is it not grounded vpon right knowledge, or due consideracion, nor seasoned with discretion as it shoulde be : you cannot offende by honouringe all, by iudginge highly of all, by speakinge the best of all: take the contrary way, and you may both ouershoote yor self to ye offence of god, & also iniurye yor fathers to yor owne & theire harme.   Comparisons of good men are euer odious & disgustfull to vertuous eares : And this extraordinary magnifyinge, extollinge, & preferringe of Jesuits above preists, or this man

aboue that man, specially when they be all good men argueth no
litle vanitie, indiscretion, & fonde affection. Jesuits be good
religious men, & ye better, ye meaner conceipt they carry of themselfes in respect of others as well religious as secular preists.
They labour well, they be fitt spirituall guides. the secular preists
also be all good vertuous men (except myself) they laboure well;
they be sufficient spirituall guides, as appeareth by the effects of
their trauailes in euery corner of the realm. Both sorts spend
their liues, & yeeld their blood with equall courage & constancy
for one & ye same cause. Let not then theire children contend
emulously for ye preferringe or more credit of either, but reuerence
loue, and hono^r all: thanke & prayse o^r lord for them both, y^t
hath giuen such power & graces to younge men, & lefte vs this
seede, for o^r countries further good & hoap. none but he can tell
who be or doe the best: He hath bestowed his giftes & graces
diuersly but all for vnitie, without schisme or partialitie. Of all
sorts some are better and more perfect then others, but yet all
profitable, & worthy of more loue comfort, estimacion, & hono^r
then is giuen them. Of all sorts there wilbe som badde. Apostata
Jesuits, Apostata secular preists: vt omnes timeant dominum: nec
se quisque commendet, sed in domino glorietur. Wee be all frayle
& inconstant creatures. Gratia dei sumus id quod sumus: qui
stat videat ne cadat, et qui se aliquid putat esse, cum nihil sit, ipse
se seducit: Ille solum dum sæuis et periculosis huius vitæ procellis
continue iactatur securius manet, qui in infimo suæ abiectionis
gradu inter sanctos dei reperiri nouerit ac contendit. As for y^e
Jesuits I hoape they are more mindefull of christian perfection, &
more mortified to ye worlde, then either them selves to seeke for
estimacion & credit with gods people aboue ye secular pastors: or
seeme to like & approue, y^t theire affectionate ghostly children
should any way preferre & extoll them before ye ordinary secular
preists: or by these vnseasonable comparisons match them with
the meanest that worke in gods vineyard: consideringe that Paule
would be thought minimus apostolorum, qui tamen plus omnibus

laborabat: and the worst secular in mans deceiptfull conceipt, may euen then in ye true iudgement of god be as good and perhaps more gracious then the best religions preferred before him: dicente ipsa veritate. Nemo scit vtrum odio an amore dignus sit: and qui se exaltat humiliabitur: et qui se humiliat exaltabitur. Iesu keepe you, Sir, and I beseech you make me partaker of youre fervent deuotions.

Yo^rs
M. J.

II.

BLACKWELL'S AUTHORITY QUESTIONED.
May, 1598—May, 1599.

1. *Letter from Mush (alias Ratcliffe) to Bagshaw and Bluet.*   38, f. 380.
May 28, 1598.[a]

R. D.

Mr. Anthony Heb[borne] at his being in thes partes requested me (as he said many also would do the like) to write some particular letter to some in Rome touching thes matters he came to craue o^r consentes in. I haue so done, and giuen what reasons moued & moue me in thes causes, And I thought good to lett them passe by you, that you might censure my writing & amend what you saw amiss, for I am out of vse in writinge latine.[b] Send it to them at London w^t what speede you can, for they ar too to lingring in their businesses & I feare me wylbe preuented. but a good cause wyll euer beare out yt selfe, & preuaile when yt comethe to the

---

[a] At the date of this letter Mush was not aware of the institution of the arch-priest. The official intimation of his appointment had, however, reached Blackwell some weeks earlier (May 9).

[b] The important Latin letter here referred to was addressed to an Italian prelate, Monsignor Morro, and was dated May 27. It was afterwards printed by Mush in his *Declaratio Motuum* (1601). The writer intended to formulate the chief complaints and petitions which the discontented clergy were desirous of laying before the Pope; and it appears that there had been already some project on foot of sending delegates or messengers to Rome to plead their cause before fresh grounds of complaint arose from the appointment of Blackwell. Mush in his letter to Morro had earnestly solicited : (1) the appointment of bishops ; (2) the removal of the Jesuits from the government of the English college at Rome ; (3) the prohibition of all books (such as those written by Father Parsons) treating of the affairs of state ; and (4) liberty for the secular clergy to establish regulations for their own government.

hearing of his Ho. : that is a blessed man, & of timerous conscience. I haue x^{li} to be sent to yor common purse, but this bearer is not fitt to bring yt yt shall come w^t the next I can find conuenient. I hope you be all well and in quietness for I heare nothing to the contrarie. God have mercy on Mr. Stran. soule for we heare nowe he is dead. Commend me to all o^r frendes. Jesu bless you this 28 May.

Yo^{rs} assured,
M. J. Rat.

In another hand, the writer of the second endorsement : A 1597-1598.

Endorsements:

    (1) To the right wor^{fl} & my verie good frendes Mr. D. Bag. & Mr. Blew.

                                 thes

    (2) 28 May, A 1598. Mr. Musshe to D. Bagsh : of his letter to Rome : He wissheth hast, y^t they be not prevented.

In a third hand :

    (3) Musshe the prist.

2. *Mush to Bagshaw and Bluet.*

R. D.   July 13, 1598.

I sent to you aboute the end of May letters concerninge the common business as they had requested me to write, but since we heare of a certaue (as I euer doubted yt would faule out) that the Jesuites haue preuented vs & gotten an Archepres[biter] w^t 12 coadiutores ouer vs, of their owne appointing. Wherevpon perhaps all o^r intendementes wyll surcease & procede no further. yf yt be so, then wishe I my letter backe againe but yf ther be no more than I heare as yett, this they haue done is to smale purpose, & not the greate goodes we were to solicite for the furtherance of Gods cause in the realme, & so no reason why o^r suite should not go forward to the obteyning of better & more needful matters. But you &

they vse yor owne discretions whether to stay, or to procede. My opynion is, that this they haue done should not hinder the prosecution of that we (I hope) all intended for the more honor of God & good of his churche here.

I send you by M^r. Thewless 50^s for the common purse. M^r. Barlow is to pay me aboute 50^s more. caule of him for yt. Other 5^{li} I shall send now by my assured frend Mr. Coope (whom also I commend vnto you as faithfull and sure as my selfe in all things). Yf by any meanes I can borrowe so much in this countrie, for of my owne I haue none here. & when I came owt of Yorkshire I knew nothing of ther commyng, & so brought no monye w^t me, but yf I can not send this other v͂^{li} nowe ye shall haue yt shortely. the whole x͂^{li} is in comon to all. remember me in yor denotions I beseche you. Jesu kepe you this 13 of July

1598 [in another hand]
Yo^{rs} assured
M. J. Rat.

Original endorsement: To the Right Wor^{full} & my Louyng frendes Mr. D. Bag. & Mr Blew. thes
Second endorsement: Musshe the Prist to Dr. Bagshaw .... How he heareth yt there was an Archp. with 12 assistants appointed. But yet thinkes yt insufficient. 13 Jul. 1598.

3. Three letters from Robert Charnock to Bagshaw.

47, f. 298.

1.

Good Mr. B., we labour here as much as lyeth in us to doe, to bring our matters to some good passe, & yf we cannot doe as we would doe, we will attribute it to gods disposition, & think that all thinges are not rype. Absurdytyes are dayly committed hereabout, & so gross as they are to be wondered at. Perchance the prysons are not as yet made ready for vs, wch are threatnd vs, yf we goe to appeale. I hope some good disposed catholickes will doe vs that good, that god doth not permit the hereticks to doe, what will come after thes bitter threatnings, god knoweth, I hope the officer [a] doth speak them but ad terrorem, wch will take little effect in men resolute to suffer in a iust cause. We suspect wth the instructions, wch we have here, & what we shall have els wher we shall goe suffycyently armed to defend o^r selves against such as shall oppose them selves, we make account that all the deuils in hel will doe the vttermost of their power against vs, but we assure our selves that ther is a god, & as I hope some honest men in the world, who hearing the reasonableness of o^r demands, will listen somewhat vnto vs, & give vs so much help as in their owne consciences will stand wth the ho[n]or of god & the good of our contrye, farther then wch we meane not to meddle, we look euery day when we shalbe eased of a litle mony. I wold they wold come for it, that I myght ryde among myne old frends & acquaintance in the meane tyme we liue vppon hope, as many

---

[a] Blackwell first notified the new institution and his own appointment to Colleton and Charnock. They begged him to send to Rome for further information in order to satisfy their doubts as to the validity of Cardinal Cajetan's "Constitutive Letters." On his refusal, the dissentient priests resolved to send messengers with an appeal to the Pope on their own account; and Colleton persuaded Bishop to accompany Charnock on the mission. The three following letters of Charnock refer to their preparations for the journey and their interviews with Blackwell on the subject. They are written in a very slovenly hand, and some words are illegible.

doe that are but neare that thing, they earnestly wish for. I
pray you continew your prayers that we may both begin well, &
end well to all honest mens contentment, no good will shall be
wanting in us. I thanke you for my booke, the copy of the
association let it be kept safly, least our Archip. take the lyke
libertye in denying that, as he hath vsed in some matters of late
This wth most harty . . . . . vnto you, & M^r Bl., Mr Thules,
Mr Coleton [?] and all the rest of our frendes, wth thankes for
your letters you sent. I take, as I hope, a long leave of you &
commend my self most earnestly to y^{or} good devotions.

Agst. 9 [1598 *in another hand*].

Yours most assuredly
R. Ch.

To write under thes^a saveth some laboure in not givinge double
notice of one thinge. No opportunitie etheir heth nor shalbe
hereafter be omitted if the present plott (wch we take most sure)
take not good effect. Ystedaye I was sent for to the archip^rsbiter   47, f. 298b.
where a large discourse in the presence of two laie gentelmen
onlie of they particulers of his authoritie viz. admonere, dirigere,
castigare et providere, he at last charged me to be weetinge to a
parties goynge over, to have written by him for infringing his
archipresbitershippe, and the chief providerre of the charges
towards that iourney, w^{ch} (as he said) must needs be great, and
the necessities of the contrie much needinge and therefore ought
much rather to be imployed that waie. He mistook the partie,
and therebie gave me good scope to answerre what I wold my
selfe, for advantaginge my other designes. Two sheetes ar too
little to abbreviat what passed. He pleaded mightilie that no
appellation culd be made dulie from the authoritie he is invested
in, wch he affirmed was absolute, not dependinge any whit at all
vpon the liking or ganesayinge of priests here. Againe that he

---

^a This postscript is apparently by Wm. Bishop.

had received certaine advertisment that whosoever should be imployed or adventure to goe, and complaine o^r grives, should be fined and imprisoned, order alreadie beinge given to that ende. He affirmed the societie had many thinges to charge me wth, but refused to vtter any in particular, wch must inforce me to write presentlie to Mr. Walley lettinge him to vnderstand so much and intreat notice what they ar. If anye fitt menes fall out right, I meane to see you shortlie and communicate all. Secreat thes I beseeche yo^u, for verilie it is very strange what particular knowledge is given him of all my actions, meetinges, sendinge, iourneyinge, cumpany keepinge, and I know not what as his owne wordes used vnto me bore witnes. In the mene I most heartilie recomend my good will vnto yo^u Mr. Bl. and the residue

Sincerelie and assuredlie yo^{rs} [a]

Endorsed : I. (*by the writer*).
To the right worshipfull his very good frend Mr. Ch. Bag. geue these.
II. Charnock, Bishop.
Charnock. How prisons are threatened if they go to Rome.
Bysshop. How Blackwell sent for hym, and told hym, there laye no appeale from hym ; and y^t they were sure to be imprisoned that should go to Rome in y^t cause etc.

2.

Good M^r. B, althoughe tyme seemeth to have bene ouerslipped in regard that matters haue bene effected contrary to many mens expectation, yet such as ment simply, & sincerely to proceed, & in such sort as they myght very well be awnswerable before god, & the world, are not to thinke any tyme tooe late ether to declare

[a] The signature is an undecipherable monogram.

their owne innocencye, or to discouer the indirect dealing of others, and the iustness of our cause being such, as it is, both before god, & all indifferent parsons, we doubt not but to effect somewhat to some good purpose, yf the world fauour vs not, we know the worst of it, a good conscience is always fauoured of god, who disposeth of all things to his best lyking, how disgustfull soeuer his disposition may seeme to such, as rely not wholy vppon him. wth this confydence therefore in god, good conscience, & iust cause, I hope we shall shortly put our matters in tryall before him, whom we ought not to doubt of, being one most worthy of the worthyest place vnder heaven. wher we intend to declare first what we entend to doe, & vppon what occasion. ; secondly what course was taken [and] what success in that course ; thirdly how we were preuented by wrong imformations, & a gouernour appoynted over vs all wthout any mans knowledge, who not being indifferent is not lykely to make any peace, wch may be shewed many wayes, as we haue set downe, besyde the inconveniences in his authorytye as to send to the cort of Rome (not specyfyed in his letters patents but told vnto such as it pleased him so soone as his authorytye came, to sommon (as it is said) not wthstanding he sent to speake wth them in charytye) also to place & displace, for wch he took occasion although wrongfully to wryght agaynst that, wch we entended to doe, & being perchance afrayd, least many wold not be persuaded by his owne letters (wch to that purpose he writt) to yeld to his authorytye, he hath left this cleane out, & specyfyed only his authorytye to abridg, and annull facultyes, also to suspend from the altar. Our request (after that we have declared as aboue is sayd) wilbe ether to have it drawen backe, and to haue bishops, or our former rules confirmed wth other thinges, wch we sent abroad to haue others consent vnto. also for the superior to haue authorytye to send to the superior of the Jesuits to convent before them both, such as shall iniury any priests by wordes & euil deedes, & to constraine such satisfaction as in conscience ought to be made. also to punish by censure of the Church all such as

70 THE ARCHPRIEST CONTROVERSY.

47, f. 301b.

shall vse any disgracefull speeches agaynst any priests in any contemptible sort to lessen their creditt by comparisons wth others, & what els shall seeme necessarye. at the least to vrdge to haue one in equall authorytye wth the new Archip. wthout whom he shall doe nothing, or els that such as mistrust his euill dealing may be exempted from his authorytye, I pray you yf you think it fit send yor brother B to London with your conceits of thes proceedings & what else you think good, also in what manner your case wilbe best releeued, I pray you send also the book of or rules & the letter, that we may shew the very copye wch was so euell taken, & misconstrued by some; lastly yf you think my Palestina worth the whyle, I pray you send that, and I pray you deale sincerely, as wth one who will not take any thinke otherwise the^n I should at yor hands, if you thinke it not fitt, it shall not be published. fare you well (good M^r B) & I pray you commend me to Mr Blu[et] Mr Cau[erly] Mr Thules, etc., Mr Col[eton] Mr Bis[hop] Mr Heb[borne] etc., haue them com[en]ded most heartyly vnto you, and at this tyme I pray you remember us in your devotions, more particularly from London) wth as m^{ch} hast as we cold, & I pray you be not slack. [a]

Endorsed: Charnocke the Prist to Dr Bagh.
What course he wold use at Rome.
Inconveniences of Mr Blackwelles dealinges.

3.

47, f. 302

Good M^r B, I most hartyly comend me vnto you. our affayres this bearer will relate unto you, to whom you may give creditt (euen in incredible matters but to those who see them) concerning our hast, in long wished courses, hindered by unexpected mischaunces, that, were not the cause iust, & hope great, that god will but try our patience by such accidentes, we shold in some desperat

---

[a] No signature or address, but in the same hand as the preceding

sort lett all goe wch way wind & weather wold carry it. we haue
daylye new comforts, & hope all will torne to the best, god hauing
neuer left the tru meaning to be a pray to others; we haue done,
& doe what lyeth in vs, & although nothing be done, we rest
secure in conscience that no harme can befall vs thorough our
owne default, wch at all tymes wilbe our comfort. It is thought
convenient by vs heare, that a letter be written to his Hol.
that this new order or authorytye was w^thout our pryuytye, & that
many giue their consents vnto it ether for feare of some, who
wth all importunytye persuade them vnto it, or for that they are
made to beleeue that the authorytye is confirmed already by
his Holynes as the Archpriest him self giueth out & spake to
Mr Collint[on] & my self. secondly, that they had rather to haue
the ordynary gouernent of the church by bishops, or at least such
corse as was wholy lyked of by all, before this was devysed to
break of that abruptlye, wch by good, & lawfull order was wished
among vs. also 3^ly that this new devyce is lykely to breed more
disquyet among us then peace, hauing bee[n] hytherto vsed
altogether to disgrace such as were thought forward in the former
course (for soe that case were Mr Col. & Mr Heb[orne] & my self
sommoned so soe [*sic*] as possibly the Archp. cold) & for other
cases, wch the letter may refer to the bearers, we are not vnfor-
nished. & I pray you in what you can, to send yor counsell, &
such a letter wth yor handes vnto it wth the tyme of yor continuance
here for the creditt of ancyent men must ouerpease the multitude
of the yonge, who are caryed away ether wth fayre gyses, or gyftes,
or threatnings, for our Archp. altogether relyeth himself vppon
such as will not spare toung, purse, or any thinge to help him, &
he is altogether ruled by them. It is here repeated that already
one of his assistants doth take uppon him dominari in clero, he
will displace, & place. The Archp. as yet doth not meddle
here about (that I can learne) wth such stuff, but vseth his
authorytye wth very great rigour agaynst some. he vppon
pollycye (as it is to be thought) in his letters (wch he hath

written abroad to the preists to haue them submitt them selves vnto this authoryty) hath concealed his authorytye to place or displace, lest perchance few wold be contented wth any such Archypresbytership. this authoryty cometh only from the Card., who in his letters sayth that he was willed by His Holiness to take some order for acquyeting vs heare (whom Mr Black[well] & Mr Standish did certify the one by his letter, the other by word of moth, to be all at one) especiallye wth the Jesuites (for wch kinde of stryfe Mr Black[well] in his letter to the priests sayth his authorytye was principally given) yet some coming from Rome affirm that they think the pope is certyfyed, what order the Card. had taken, & that yf it shold be here lyked of, that then he wold confirme it of wch you certyfy much as you know, so that (so far forth as we can learne) nothing is confirmed although Mr Black-[well] told vs it was, when we denyed our lyking of it, least by lyking it we shold bring it vppon vs contrary to our wils, Mr Dol seemed very loth to haue his hand goe out of the land, when we [desired] to have it heretofore, I pray you procure him to sett his hand vnto yor letter, & as many as you can, we must s[u]pply by report thereof, whose mindes we know. yf so the hast be not as wold be wished, we must comend our matters vnto god, ass[u]re yor self that nether ther hath bee[n] nor shalbe any neclignece. thes wth my good wishes I comitt you & yor good company to almightye god, not forgetting most harty comendations to Mr Blu., Mr Powel [?], Mr Thul., etc. all me[n] here sal[u]te you.

4. *Copy of Letter from Blackwell to Bagshaw and Bluet.*

Aug. 22 [1598]

Reverendi viri patres et fratres,

Qui plurimos ætate, eruditione, et dignitate anteceditis, miror quod vos quidquam contra authoritatem et institutionem vestri Superioris inconsideratius effunderetis. Ea est vestra conditio, vt quales effingitis vosmetipsos ad nutum et voluntatem superioris vestri, tales inferiores vestros erga vos, qui cæteris præitis invenietis. Exemplar enim estis quod multi ad imitandum sibi proponunt. Collocati estis in altissimo loco. Plurimorum oculi in vos coniecti sunt. Itaque vos debetis curare diligentius, vt verba vestra, moresque sic temperetis, vt superioris vestri authoritas nihil inde detrimenti capiat. Nostis quod omnis offensio tanto conspectius in se crimen habet, quanto maior, qui peccat, habetur. Hinc ego non minimum hausi dolorem, quod pristinus splendor omnis in moribus vestris obsolevit: imo, quod multa peccastis, et in bonorum offensionem incurristis. Non enim dubito, quin peccatum hæreat in eis, qui nostri illustrissimi D. Protectoris institutiones sua petulanti lingua liberius exagitant: qui permittunt ad se fieri crebros excursus hominum, qui disciplinam ecclesiasticam repellentes, multa contra publicam pacem et suo proprio cerebro excudunt : qui scriptum exemplar literarum nuncii Apostolici discerpunt : qui pænas ex mandato supremæ authoritatis inflictas accusant : qui in me, propter impositum mihi officium, nonnulla parum modeste iaciunt, non dicam iniuriosius immittunt. Quæ si vos admiseritis, ego obsecro vos et admoneo, vt studia vestra vocesque ad quandam moderationem inflecteretis. Quamvis enim gaudeam in contemptu, quem mihi privatim impingitis ; illud tamen prætermittere non possum, quia subditus ; nec debeo permittere quia præpositus sum vobis, vt vel ineptis verbis nostri superioris authoritatem violetis ; vel aliquid turbæ et negotij importetis ordini præstituto vobis ; in quo non vmbris et falsis rerum imaginibus vtimur, sed veri iuris germanæque iustitiæ solidam, et expressam effigiem habemus et circumferimus.

Vt igitur vobis non asciscatis tantum malum nolite committere vt vestram industriam in nescio quam sodalitatem illigetis : vnde suscipiatis defensionem quorundam non bene sentientium á quibus recens orta est et nimis imminens nostræ quieti tempestas. Spem omnem malis negotij facessendi præcidi cupimus. Scimus quam libenter illi vellent in nominis et authoritatis vestræ præsidio conquiescere. Sed quoniam prospicitis, quo fluat illorum audacia, et quid turbæ ex fervidioribus ingenijs struatur rerum illi dispositioni, quæ profecta à sede Apostolica iam ad nos deducta est: ego à vobis immensum in modum contendo, vt fæcem istam dissentientium humorum eijciatis : vt ab aculeis verborum contra superiores nescio quo elisu iam excussis, abstineatis : vt accessu authoritatis vestræ ad officij nostri propugnationem, qui litigiosi sunt, illi exterminari spem suam videant, et penitus evanescere. Arripite ergo patrocinium æquitatis, et nolite pati quidquam residere apud vos, quod impediat cursum authoritatis mihi delatæ, quo minus libera et soluta progrediatur ad pacis et pietatis studia promovenda: quibus neglectis, nos certe, ab excitata status nostri conditione ad inclinatum, et prope iacentem devolveremur. Sitis denique sic animis affecti, et comparati, vt æquum bonumque plus apud vos omni in re ponderis habeat, quam vlla vllius perversitas, aut immodesta contentio. Ita fiet vt mihi adiumentum, pijs solatium, impijs terrorem, et communi nostræ causæ subsidium non vulgare, sed præcipuum adferatis. Valete et orate pro me.

Augusti 22

Vester humillimus
Servus
Georgius Blackwellus Archip^rsbiter.

Spectatissimis viris Dr Doctori Bagshawo, et D. Bluetto.

38, f. 400. 5. *Draft (in Bagshaw's hand) of Letter to Blackwell in reply to the preceding.*

Sept. 2.

Litteræ tuæ, Reverende frater, ad nos datæ quatuor contra nos accusationes continent : 1 Illustrissimi Protectoris institutiones exagitatas : 2 Permissos ad nos excursus hominum indisciplinatorum : 3 Discerptum exemplar litterarum nuncij Apostolici : 4 Pœnas ex mandato supremæ authoritatis inflictas, (verbis tuis vtendum quo sensu tu videris) accusatas. Quæ præterea objicis, inconsiderationem, conspectius crimen, obsoletum omnium[?] in moribus splendorem, multa peccata et inhærentia, bonorum offensionem, linguæ petulantiam, parum modestiæ, contemptum, fæcem dissentientium humorum, aculeos verborum, et alia nescimus quo elisu excussa, maturius vtinam tecum considerasses, ne forte ex eis sint, quæ conviciantis potius vanitatis, quam convincentis veritatis, sanctus appellat Augustinus. Ad accusationes autem singulas quod spectat, cum veritas sit, non paucis conscijs, tempore non multum elapso, et loco tam vicino, exploratu facillima, nec tibi tamen explorata, miramur quomodo tibi nolenti imponi possit, mirari desistimus si in plurimis Anglicanæ Ecclesiæ negotijs Pontifici aut Cardinali, ab aliquo forte terræ filio surreptum fuerit.

1 Equidem pro fide Catholica, et quem diligimus decore domus dei, vincula, tormenta, et plurimorum annorum incarcerationem perpessi, nihil tamen magis dolenter huevsque pertulimus, quam quæ maxime hæreticis placuit et profuit, perpetuam apud nos, etiam annosam, repagulis omnibus solutis, grassantem detractionem. Quæ iam tandem Deo permittente ita in peius profecit, vt hoc ipso tempore non solum fratres nostros eorumque multos fortes confessores et inclytos martyres invaserit, sed vt collegijs nostris transmarinis labem nefandam, et ordini sacerdotali non ferendam ignominiam invsserit, immo nec Cardinalibus adeoque nec ipsis summis Pontificibus pepercerit. Quo tandem erumpet deus novit. Cum superiores nostri bene informati non possunt non ægerrime ferre, authoritatis suæ prætextu armari aut [non] vetari nec eorum nomina molitionibus illis quæ ad destructionem non ad ædificationem tendunt, populariter prætendi debent. Quicquid sit de institutionibus Cardinalis aut præpositura tua quam nescientibus et refutantibus obtrudis, nobis compertum non est, illud vero compertissimum, si vineam plantant superiores nostri, expectant vt uvas faciat non autem labruscas.

2 Quo minus visitaremur in carcere et sustentaremur, et eorum qui foris sunt leges malitiosæ et aliquorum qui intus esse videntur linguæ maledicæ diu multumque vel lites et calumnias etiam

creando amicorum nonnullis viris integerrimis et omni exceptione maioribus contenderunt. Sed deus non deficit sperantibus in eum. Si qui huc excurrunt disciplinam ecclesiasticam repellentes, multa contra publicam pacem ex suo proprio cerebro excudentes, non bene sentientes, tempestatem cientes, muti[?], audaces, turbas ex fervidioribus ingenijs struentes, litigiosi, perversi, immodeste contentiosi, tibi quippe qui sic describis et accusas non possunt non esse valde noti: nobis certe si innotescerent, essent ingratissimi. Quod si frates nostros huc accedentes designes, quales soli nobis placent a quibus servata et patienter et leniter charitas animi, collegij honor, vinculum fidei, concordia sacerdotii : id quod apparet quia sodalitati cuidam quam nescire te dicis, præiudicare tamen non metuis, vereor, vt horum verborum quæ in dei sacerdotes quorum confessionem gloriosis initijs dominus illustravit, effundis in tremendo dei iudicio [aut] coram legitimo in terris magistratu rationem reddere valeas.

3 Discerptæ litteræ Apostolicæ non minus contra nos pro crimine conspectissimo vrgeantur quam dirempta manus Arsenij contra Athanasium.

4 Pænæ quas accusatas nominas, inauditis absentibus, inscijs infliguntur, et vt sperare debemus innocentibus. Pænarum infamia omnes indiscriminatim sive nocentes sive innocentes, immo et collegia ipsa, addimus etiam et religionem nostram involvit. Id quod Topclefo et similibus cordi erit si innotesceret nobis tristitiam affere debet immensam. Unde sic animis affecti et comparati sumus, vt cum apud nos plus valeat æquum et bonum quam ulla quocunque modo palliata factio, nihil ardentius cupimus quam summum pontificem ad quem iam diu provocavimus et iam denuo appellamus, syncere et incorrupte de Ecclesiæ Anglicanæ statu informari. Nec est quod stomacho concaleas si innocentiam nostram fratrumque nostrorum tueri, et qualemlibet pro iusticia persecutionem sustinere, non formidemus.

Datum 2 Sept.

In another hand:
   Mʳ. Dʳ. Bagshawe & Mʳ. Bluetts appellation to yᵉ Pope from Blackwelles accusations.

6. *Draft of Letter from Bluet to Blackwell in answer to his Letter of Aug. 22.*   38, f. 401.

Legi literas tuas fra: charissime, quas per duos fratres misisti nec dilectione fraterna nec ecclesiastica disciplina nec sacerdotali censura dignas, sed animositatis contumeliarum ac detractionum satis plenas. Equidem iam vigessimum secundum in vinculis agens annum a te propter antiquam consuetudinem vuas et non labruscas meliora quæque et viciniora saluti expectabam. Credideram te tandem iam ad meliorem et pacatiorem mentem converti, quod in præteritum tam nefanda tam turpia tam etiam hereticis execranda, aut audisses de nobis temerè aut credidisses: sed in literis tuis etiam nunc animadverto eundem te adhuc esse qui prius fueras, eadem te de nobis credere, et in eo quod credideris perseverare, et in mores nostros diligenter inquirere vt qui multa te iudice peccavimus et a prisco decore excidimus quia dolenter sacerdotum infamiam et facultatum revocationem tulimus. multum nobis displicet fateor quod hæreticis placet, sed utrum ex merito presbiterorum aut insidijs aliorum hoc malum evenerit, non est meum curiose perquirere: lamentari vero ac dolere didici quia homo sum, et humani nihil porto à me alienum et qui hoc prohibet ac vitio vertit inhumanus est. dicente Paulo quis infirmatur et ego non infirmor, quis scandalizatur et ego non vror: si in hoc peccavi cum Paulo peccavi: non est igitur cur mihi irascatur reverentia tua. Quod autem exageras et ad sydera extollis literarum dilacerationem agnosco peccatum esse gravissimum Diabolo instigante commissum idque excommunicatione dignum, sed alienum, non nostrum: tu autem nulla inquisitione facta reum absolvis vt innocentem condemnes, cum dicit dominus descendam et videbo, vtrum clamorem qui venit ad me opere compleverint, an non est ita vt sciam. Quod quia non fecisti, ideo turpiter lapsus es. Insilis insuper in nos quod fratres et compresbiteri pro sua dilectione cupidi sunt ad conveniendum et visitandum fratres, confessores bonos quos illustravit iam gloriosis initijs divina dignatio ; sic et persecutores et plebs, sic turgidus Toplevus indignum esse facinus clamitant, ac nocte dieque student quo modo huic negotio sese opponant, molestias et tribulationes nobis exhibentes et ita gravati supra modum aliquando et supra virtutem sumus vt tæderet vivere: sed de tantis malis et periculis nos deus noster eripiet in quem speramus quod et adhuc eripiet. Alienum igitur a fraterna charitate iudicatur si homo dei cum illis adiungatur. Quod si aliquis forte terræ filius nobis inconsultis imo renitentibus fraudulenter irrepsit summæ potestati : scias tamen frater charissime sententiam Romanæ sedis posse in melius commutari, cum aut surreptum aliquid fuerit, aut ipsa pro consideratione ætatum vel temporum seu gravium necessitatum dispensatione quædam ordinare decreverit quoniam et egregium Paulum Apostolum dispensatione quadam fecisse legimus, quæ postea reprobasse legitur. Nullus invitis debet Episcopus dari, sed cleri plebis et ordinis consensus et desiderium requiratur. Si aliter fit, clericis facultas renitendi, si viderint prægravari : et quos sibi ingeri ex transverso agnoverint, non timeant refutare : et quidem iustus mediator non est, qui vno litigante et altero absente amborum emergentes lites decidere non formidat. Necesse quippe est secundum sacrum scripturarum documentum ac secundum iustitiæ tramitem et accusatum et accusatorem simul adesse, et vnam partem quantacunque et qualicunque prædita sit authoritate sic prorsus audiri, vt alteri parti nullum præiudicium irrogetur. Quod vero suspecti et inimici iudices esse non debeant, et ipsa ratio dictat, et plurimis probatur exemplis. Nam quid gratius et amabilius dare quis inimico potest, quam si ei ad impetendum commiserit, quem lædere forte voluerit. Quamobrem Re : ffr : et pace salva et reverentia illæsa, quia gravamina sunt multa et gravia, et afflictiones multiplicantur afflictis, cum præter iustitiæ tramitem et Canonum regulam non iudicis sed accusatoris personam induis aliena nobis impinges crimina, et (qua ipse laboras linguæ petulantia) non sine summo dolore et tristitia magna cogimur sanctiss: dominum nostrum C[lementem] 8 appellare, cuius sententiam et iudicium expectabimus: cuius sermones sani et recti sunt firmantes et dantes intellectum.

Tho:[a] Bluet.

7. *Copy of a Letter from Henry Garnet, S. J., to William Clark.* 47, f. 292.
11 Nov., 1598.

My verye reuerend sir

If you be sinisterlie talked of for wronginge o^r societie: blame not him I beseech yo^u, who for all yor straungenes, ceaseth not to love you, and whome, for yor hurtfull proceedings, love inforceth to pittie you.

It hath beene alwaies my desyre since that we purged o^r selves (I hope sufficientlye) from the malitious slaunders of some impudent lybellers, that all things should (as much as is possible) be utterlye forgotten: and if all could not be induced to love and affect vs to beare their aversion wth patience and sylence, wthout followinge any course or pursuite against them, so that if you heare either yor selfe or by any others, any sinister reports against yo^u, you may examine them best, whether they be true; and the reporters are to give account on what grounde they vtter them.

True it is, that as it hath pleased god to give o^r societie parte in many glorious [*sic*] wch his holly church are continuallie atcheiuers; so also very often tymes yea ordinarilye doth he make vs partakers of the afflictions & difficulties wch doe thence aryse; and if any worthie thinge be accounted worthie of blame, we are lightlie the first wch are blamed.

It hath pleased his hollines of late to ordaine a certeine government among vs. It hath been received wth singuler likinge of the

[a] In the manuscript it looks more like Ro than Tho.

moste and best. God forbid but that I and all my brethren should have been most readye to runne whither charitie and obedience did call us, least by disobedience we should contemne o^r superior, or by schisme and division be cut of from the heade.

Some have refused to acknowledge this heade, much more to obaye him. Their pretences are in every ones mouth that have heard of this authoritie. It is a thinge devysed by the Jesuits. The superior is one of their owne choosinge. Why should the Jesuits appoint us a superior more than we a generall vnto them. It is the fyne heade of father Persons that hath invented this. He hath given wronge information to the Cardinall & his hollines. The Cardinall was alwaies partiall on Jesuits syde. Some of necessitie must be sent to informe better. The messengers must procure that some assistants be chosen who may not be thought to be partiallie affected to the Jesuits. They must propound to have the Government of the Colledge inlarged, as being over straite or indiscreete for o^r nation. Yea they must make suite that the Jesuits be removed from the government of all seminaries of o^r nation. And touchinge the mission of England in particuler all the Jesuits must needs be called awaye. These and the like speaches havinge been vttered by such as either gathered voyces for another government, or are knowen not to favour this. What can yt argue els, but that such oppose themselves against the societie, as if no authoritie weare to be liked, but wch maye beate down the Jesuits, or set them and other reverend preists together by the eares. And verilye the successe of matters since the authoritie of o^r reverend Archpriest was divulged doth make many to feare, least the secrete intention yet not perceiued of all of these wch weare the principall seekers to erect a sodalitie or other superioritie & subordination was either ambitious or seditious. ffor havinge nowe that verie thing wch they sought for (although imposed on other persons then they had designed) to reprehend or impugne the same must needs make men suspect, that they doe it either because they them selves are not chosen, or because such weare not chosen as might deale peremptorilye wth those wch they ought to tender. Both wch affections sheweth them dubllye vnworthie of government. ffor what is so vnfitt for honor as ambition. And what have we done that all should not affect vs. Yea by gods greate goodnes so it is, (as we thinke) that if any affect vs not, the fault is in them & not in vs. So that if they would have them selves or others that doe not affect vs, though otherwise seeminge never so vertuous, to be chosen heades, let them first affect vs (so farre as in vertue they ought) that they may be worthie of government. Then you see (good sir) it wanteth not probabilitie that if any geue out that yo{u} wronge vs; it is because yo{u} are thought to drawe backe from yor Archpresbyter, wch yo{u} knowe whether it be so or noe. And althoughe I verilie perswade my self that moste of these speaches never proceded from yor mouth; yet those that wilbe parte of a discontented companie of force must be contented to bear the reproche of many things wch are done or saide amisse by a fewe, it beinge impossible, that all men should distinguishe, and applye everye particuler to the true author. And verilie, as it greiueth me oftentymes to heare, & I reprehend it so often as I heare it spoken, that such a one, or such another, who is not ioyned to the Archpresbyter, is condemned as opposite to the societie, and condemne such manner of speach for a fallacy wch we call (as yo{u} know) non causa ut causæ: for in verye deede I would not have them reprehended because they are opposite against vs but because they acknowledge not their lawfull superio{r}; so on the other syd must I neede acknowledge that it is, & by gods grace will I alwayes procure that it shall alwayes continue: that those two things are so annexed one to the other, that whosoever is opposite against o{r} Rd. Archpresbyter must of force be consequentlie opposite against vs. And therein will we gloriari in Domino: if any be thought opposite to vs who are opposite vnto him. Therefore (good sir) there is nothing I more desire, there is nothinge can be more honorable and profitable for yor selfe, than that yor vnite yor selfe vnto him whom god hath made yor superior: who like vnto him wch is Princeps pastorum is in this o{r} particular

47, f. 292b.

churche lapis qui factus est non in offensionem, sed in caput anguli, qui medium parietem maceria soluat, qui faciat vtraque vnam, is the onlye meanes to ioyne vs all together, in perfitt love & vnion: wch we had long since inioyed, if his authoritie had been admitted as at this p^rsent, there is no hinderance at all of vnitie, but the refusinge of the same. So that we fynd true, that wch moste worthilie saide S^ct Paule : Non tenens caput ex quo totum corpus per nexus et coniunctiones subministratum et constructum crescit in augmentum Dei.[a] And the cause of this refusinge the heade, he expressed before, frustra inflatus sensu carnis suæ. W^th this heade therefore muste I houlde, to him must I be vnited, to him must wee cleave, qui illi coniungitur meus est: qui cum illo non colligit spargit. And vnfaignedlye I affirme vnto yo^u, y^t I continuallie praye in particuler for yor vnion vnto him, in respect of the love I have borne and doe beare vnto yo^u, wch shall not decaye, although yo^u woulde, wth never so greate contrarietie of iudgments & opinions. And thus wishing yo^u to followe that wch is moste to the glorye of god & yor owne soules health : I ceasse, 11º. Nouember, 1598.

Yo^r plaine frend
as yo^u wished
HENERY.

8. *From John Maister.*

47, f. 118.

9, Dec. 1598.

The faire hope yor cosin intertained that we shou^ld ere this have injoyed yor presence ever stayed my penn, other wise willinge to have redubled this office manie a time. The difference sleepeth not, but rather all means set on worcke howe most to prevaile, as the inclosed shewes. Mr. Mushe wrote a letter from the northe dated the 3 of november, where in he giues us to vnderstand of an epistle brought to the pristes theire to have theire names there vnto

---

[a] Ephes., iv., 6 : "ex quo totum corpus compactum et connexum per omnem juncturam subministrationis . . . . . augmentum corporis facit in ædificationem sui in caritate."

but of an vnlike tenor in part. first, for that w^t them is dedicated to the cardinall protector, this to his holiues, the pointes wch this toucheth you see the other thancketh (to set downe the wordes of [t]his letter w^t out any change) the protecter first for his care and tendernesse ouer the students at Rome that he vsed them so frindlie and myldlie and mercifullie they beinge so disobedient and dissentious etc. And secondlie, for his great care and wisdome in procuringe and providinge vs an Archpresbiter of so singular talents as this is for stayinge and ouerthrowinge the like envie and discord here in England. Thus yo^u see, good sir, a kind of dubble dealinge if m^r Mushe weare not too too much mistaken, and if there be different epistles of the purport aforesaid. I coniecture (for further I would not willinglie goe) the one hereof to be for sooner drawinge of many handes, and hereafter that epistle or exemplar to be preferred ether to the protecter or his holines wch shall appeare fittest to father Parsons or his agent, w^t the subscription of all theire names, as m^r walleis letter on the backe side of the leafe gaveth cause to suspect. I haue received a letter from father Whalley, and to my owne seeminge of a very good tenor. I meane not to send my answere till I maie conferre w^t yo^u ethire freelie by letters or (wch I much more desier) by speache. A frind of myne saluteth yo^v w^t the token enclosed. Advertise yor further wantes and god willing they shalbe supplied.

47, f 118b.

This kind of epestelinge is the direction of father Parsons, as one told me, and from the knowledge of his own eye, seeinge the letter where in he wrote the said direction.

We heare nothinge from o^r frindes, nor have done since theire departure, but if the newse weare [ill] it wold be soone sent ouer and bruted. wch putteth some co[un]sel on vs that all laughtes not on them.

I praie advertise the termes of yor . . . . libertie, and whether there be saiftie in repayringe to any other prisoner for meanes to see or speak w^t yo^u. fare yo^u well wth most assured good will this 9 of december. [*in another hand* 1598.]

If yo{u} please yo{u} maie returne the coppie of the epistle . . . .
yor opinion there of.

Endorsement : John Master how the priests in the north labo{r} to gett hands for thanks to the pope for the appointing of so worthy an Archpresbiter.

9. *Letter from " Ed. T,"* [a] *in the Clink prison, to Dr. Bagshaw.*

[13 Jan. ? 1599.]

47, f. 131.

Ihus :

Right worshipfull,

if you haue occasion to speak wth Mr. Wade [b] I pray you on my parte to yeld him most humble and harty thanks for the fauour and benefitt wch he hath graunted me in yelding at my first petition to let me haue the libertye of the house. I know it to be a very extraordinary curtesy and graunted to few preastes besides myselfe in London. I am sure I might fil a whole quier of paper wth petitions to Mr. Blackwel and that route an lye at the sute a whole yeare for my facultyes wch they haue less reason to denye me al thinges considered, and be neuer the nigher neyther, and I assure you I find true that pointe of our grauamina in the college now in my selfe that their persecution is more greauous and hurteful then the hereticks. I pray you imparte vnto me what newes you haue from Mr. Deane. I vnderstande he is very desirous of my speedy retourne, but that I am affrayed is dashed. heare be of both sides of people frinds and foes, but we agree well enoughe, yet let me haue some lines from you somtimes when you haue any good newes I pray you and let me vnderstande if, and what talke,

---

[a] Apparently Edward Tempest, the recipient at the Roman College of the several letters from Dr. Gifford, referred to in the Chief Heads of Accusations (*supra*, p. 7). He was sent into England, Sept. 16, 1597, and was arrested Jan. 5, 1599. On the 15th of the same month he wrote a letter to the archpriest from the Clink prison (Foley, *Records*, vi., 182).

[b] William Waad, clerk of the Privy Council. Bagshaw had been summoned from Wisbech by the council in October, 1598, and remained in the Gatehouse or other London prisons until the following February.

you haue had wth Mr. Wade aboute me, eyther while I was abroade after I departed from you, or since I was taken, for I was coming to you to learne when I was taken.

Comend me hartily to Mr. Anthony. I wish y^r company hartely or you mine for I can like wel enoughe of imprisonment if I haue good company, but I coulde rather wish you heare by cause I know that y^r Thomas is very much in chollar wth vs al for thear 2 escapes, but if we cannot enioye one anothers presence let vs yet communicate in prayers one for another, I assure you I wil not be forgetful of you, our lord preserue you from the clink this 13 of Januar.[a] read and bierne.

yours vnfeinedly Ed. T.

Endorsed by writer: To Mr. D. Bagshaw.

In another hand: E. T-t. to D. B. that Blackewelles and the Jesuits persecution is more grevous then the Heret[iques].

10. *Blackwell to John Colleton.*[b]

March, 1599.

S^r,

I admonishe yo^w to reflect yor eye once againe vpon modestia vestra nota sit omnibus hominibus. Yo^w haue vttered too much bitternes against yor betters, whome in regarde of their callinge yo^w ought to reverence, of their learninge to esteme, of there vertue to imitate, of their benefites to love, of their care for the profitt of o^r countrie to favo^r, of their writinges & admonitions not to revile but to thanke in a moste humble and dutyfull manner. But

47, f. 115.

---

[a] Mr. Macray reads "June."

[b] Father Garnet, in a letter to Colleton dated March 7, had roundly denounced him as guilty of schism and of tempting his spiritual children " to carry away poison in lieu of medicine " from his masses and sacraments. Colleton remonstrated, and thereupon Blackwell takes up the defence of the Jesuit in the following letter. Some sentences from Garnet's letter and from this of Blackwell are quoted in the Appeal of the Thirty-three Priests, Nov. 17, 1600. See the Latin text in Colleton's *Just Defence*, 182, or the English translation in Tierney, iii., p. cxxxiii.

yo^w make little reckoninge of thes respects, and therefore as careles of yor creditt, yo^u will exemplifie in yor selfe the truthe of this Axiome: Nihil iusti rectique per iram et furorem fieri potest. Surelie (S^{ir}) yo^w haue vrged me excedinglie to give a restrainte to yor boldnes. I have spared yo^w vpon this counsell of Seneca: y^t, Dilatione fervor iræ elanguescit, et caligo mentem premens, aut decidit, aut minor fit. But nowe I perceave, that tyme can geve no temper to yor whotte fitts, and that our Lenitives have driven yo^w into the greater rages. Seinge then o^r patience hath so little profited yo^w, I must hereafter make a tryall whether o^r correction can give a staie to the fiercenesse of yor stile. If wrathe in yo^w had not overgrowen all discretion, this advice of the wyse might haue overruled the libertie of yor penn: Potentioris iram nunquam sapiens provocabit: imo declinabit non aliter, quam in navigando procellam. Yet that yo^w maye see in vs læsam patientiam non verti in aliquam immoderationem, I will deferr to chasten yo^w for a while vpon hope of yor recoverie, and of the recall of yor rashe, daungerouse, & offencive designements. And therefore this shalbe to yo^w but as nuncius penæ pro contumacia vestra: and as an advertisement to view advisedlie howe ignoraunce, error, pride & obstinancie hath drawne yo^w within the compasse of schisme to yor great discreditt and disturbance of o^r catholike vnite. Yo^r maistershipp proceeded not from vniuersitie, and therefore no marvaile yo^w espie not howe deservinglie yor tribute is cowched. Ne quid mimis: omne nimium vertitur in vitium. Similitudo satietatis mater.

So manie of yor letters have the exaction of tribute, that the multiplication is offensive, if the maiestie of the terme be not vnsemelye, for one of yor mediocritie. It appeareth yo^w had not Lynceus his eyes, who coulde not espie this yor Barbarisme, lynxis eyes. But yo^w haue as S. Augustine termeth them inflatos oculos, wch are an impedyment that yor sight will not be carried vpon the humilitie and charitie, wch as yo^w desire, & thinke requisite, so are the same verie evident in the partie, & in his open practise to all o^r comfortes. As for yor last letter, knowe yo^w that yor exaction of o^r othe aboute yor demaundes is in præiudicium et contemptum ecclesiasticæ authoritatis. Nam Episcopi commissio dari potest vivæ vocis oraculo, absque alia scriptura. Et in electione vicarij per Episcopum facienda non requiritur consensus capituli : imo assertione Cardinalis S. Rom. Ecclesiæ tanti viri, credendum esset absque literarum ostensione. His accedit quod tale iuramentum nobis deferre non potestis sine mandato speciali superioris, quia istud iuramentum est meri imperij. Ea vero quæ sunt imperij meri non possunt expediri per vicarium sine speciali Episcopi mandato. Howe then can yo^w havinge no title nor tittle of authoritie vrge vs to an othe aboute yor specialties, wch are so extreme, y^t euerye one of iudgement doe crye out against them. Cease to tyranize over o^r consciences, content yor selfe wth ordinarie procedinges, challenge no more then the approved canons wch are nowe in commune practise doe allowe vnto Clergie men of yor qualitie & condition. Read over, I praie yo^w, y^t treatise of S. dyonise ye Carthusian concerninge the endes of suche as haue gonne out of his religiouse order. In timore et tremore salutem vestram operamini obedite præpositis vestris et subiacere eis. And for a conclusion looke consideratelie vpon this sentance of S. Iræneus : qui schismata operantur, immanes sunt. Our Swete Jesus give yo^w grace to knowe yor selfe & yor betters and thos that haue bynn yor speciæll benefacto^{rs}, & to note in your selfe ye decaye of many graces since yor departure from them & their directions. Reuertere, reuertere, sulamitis, reuertere, reuertere vt intueamur te. Interim orabimus pro te vt dominus te conuertat.

Yo^{rs} albeit yo^u will not see the bande
G. B. A.

Endorsement (in another hand) : A letter of Mr. Blackwells to D^r. Bagshaw^a threatning hym verie sharply.

---

^{a} Notwithstanding the endorsement, this letter is evidently addressed not to

11. *Unsigned Letter* [*by Mr. Heborne?*]

47, f. 117. 8 May [1599].

Good Sir, M^r. Bl. taking me to be the author of the lesser letter because it came to his sight in my hand, both caleth it and acompteth it an infamous libell, and therevpon faceth wth me as you see, peruse I pray you his letter and retorne me your opinion of the cannons he auereth to be antiquated, whether here in he speak tru or no. I must nedes haue the letter againe for this bearer and at leasure you shall haue a coppie thereof. I send you the composition made between father Persons and the scollers, and if you thinck it necessarie you shall also haue his letter written in that behalf, and answer the contrary letter to that, the originales I haue not, that of M^r. Champnies wch you desire and beginneth 'college,' when I haue it, it shal be sent you, but as yet I never did see it. I pray you deliver this bearer yor coppy of (olim dicebamur)[a] to transport, for I cannot gett the other, for that M^r. Jhon is forth of the towne. Hasten your answer to the letter you intend, and thus remembering yourself and your neighbor I ended besiching you to deliver this bearer all such poyntes as the third person ther wth you hath opened, if any may benifit to our busines, to morow must all depart and therfore delay no time. This 8 May.

Bagshaw but to Colleton. "Yo^r maistership proceeded not from universitie" could scarcely refer to Bagshaw, who took his master's degree at Oxford and his doctor's cap at Padua. The advice to read the warning of St. Denys, the Carthusian, against those who should leave his order could have meaning only for Colleton, who, for reasons which he fully explains in his *Just Defence*, had left that order before completing his noviciate. Colleton, indeed, seems to allude to this letter of Blackwell when he asks (p. 300), "What cause hath father Parsons or our archpriest to twite me with leaving the Carthusians?"

[b] The "Olim dicebamur" was the letter addressed to the Pope (8 Nov., 1598) in thanksgiving for the institution of the new hierarchy of archpriest and assistants. It was printed by Bagshaw in his *Relatio Compendiosa* (pp. 33-35.). A copy in the Petyt MSS. (xlvii. f. 119) is signed by four Jesuits and seven secular priests.

I was not the author of that letter that M^r. Bla[ckwell] so much disliketh yet this wuld I be informed of from you, whether the coppie passing in my hand may be termed a libell ether in respect of the subiect or that it wanted the authors name.

     Yours, as yow know,
       Mr. HEBURNE (*in another hand*).

Endorsement 1:
 Mention is here of a writinge against the Jesuits it seemeth wch M^r. Blackwell tearmeth a libell.
 Parsons hath written two contrary Letters concerninge the scollers it seemeth at Rome.

Endorsement 2 (*in the hand of the writer of the letter*):
 Mr. C. letter and the letter not subscribed.

12 *Letter to Bagshaw, unsigned.*

May 9.

47, f. 171.

for yor better vnderstandinge and to the end yo^u maie returne me yor fuller answere and advise I have here in sent yo^u the coppie of my letter to Mr. Blackwell and his answere verbatim. I meane to answer, but here I wold first learne of you. and ear I send it yo^u shall have the pervsinge. His answere to the libell wch he willeth me or rather commandeth to deliuer to Mr. Smithsonne is in my opinion the fondest pennde thinge that ever I reade in my life coming from such a person. Mr. Smithsonne hath it, and I make scruple to showe it but to pristes onlie. He dealeth liberallie there in against me, in one place especially, and oft wrongfullie, as I hope and my conscience giveth.

by ye libell he meaneth ye letter I sent yo^u a coppie of, wch was not penned by nether of vs.

I have willed this bearer to goe first to Mr. Smithsonne and take it of him and so bring it yo^u to reade, but I praie give it to him againe after readinge; hereafter yo^u shall [have] a coppie there of if yo^u please but wth yor leave the originall shall still remaine in my custodie, soe in truth I wold not have it lost for a pounde twise tolde.

I litle feare all theire threats, albeit I stand very assured, the most they can do wilbe executed against me.

I have sent 11s. to the partie in newegate Ralfe Yewne [?] and shall remember him as I can, but to begge for any my credit will not now happelie serve. Let the prisoners writ, a gods name, to the societie who have, as I take it, the whole or most collection out the realme. Touchinge yor motion for loane of money for a monethe space, I praie writ the summe yo^u wold have, and the time against which yo^u wold have it, and I will assuredlie do my best to procure it. in veritie I am tenn poundes in debt, nor hath I one frend who hath money at this time.

This bearer is to deliuer yo^u 10^s for Allen, whose case yo^u pitied in yor last letter vnto me. I recommend two living parties to his remembringge. 9 of may.

Endorsements: 1. [*Original*] To Mr. Doc [*rest obliterated*].
2. To Mr. Dr. Bagshawe of Mr. Blackwells answer to his letter. the most of the collection in England cometh now to the Jesuits.

13. *Watson's Thirty Reasons.*

Jesus Maria.

47, f. 93.   That we can not in conscience, policie, nor equitie admitt of Mr. Blackw. archepresbiterie : probatur.

1°. His eleccion was withoute o^r consent, knowledge or acceptance.

2°, He was not palam, sed fraudulenter, secreto, et animo decipiendi, as may be proved, ergo contra canon^{es} et vid^{at} etiam casum excom . . . . .

3°. Noe example of ye apostles actions neith^r yet of any Infidels composition can free them from the decrets of the ord. observed in all eleccions becaus o^r countrey had from the beginning of these chevesies sundry prelates wth the laity y^t nunquam ante Baal etc., ergo, being continually ex parte catholica whatsoever doeth bind for eleccions in other cathol. countries byndes here etc. ergo, Black[well] contra canon.

4° Noe lawe, divine, humane, of nature or naccions alloweth a forced gouernor intruded, especially to tyranize as his autority (by the words in his bull corrigere, castigare etc.) is none other, not a word spoken of charatie equitie or iustice.

5°. It is opposite to all order in heaven & earthe : a Michall chosen as head of the principales quia unus ex illis & not a Raphael of an other order etc. & as the chapter of canons choose their Deene & not the priests dispersed in parishes; the priests of each bishoprick their bishop & not the inclused monkes of that Diocese ; the Dominicans their prior & not the ffranciscans : the Jesuites their provincall & not the Benedictines, the Aldermen & city of Lond. their maior & not the Justices etc. onely in hell and amongst heritics, ordo negligitur, ergo the Jesuits apointing vs a superior imitate one of these, videant ipsi.

6°. His letters to Rome against his brethren & æger defence of ye Jesuits convince him to be unus ex vel subditus illis, ergo contra ius imponit^r nobis etc.

7°. He publickely professeth partiality as in his bitter letter to Mr. Benson & others & y^t he mainteins them in all things, ergo vt iniquus & inustus iudex deponendus.

8°. His autority was vnhonestly procured because we were never made acquainted therewth, having e contrario friendly imparted o^r minds vnto them etc. vnlawfully confirmed because bie the Cardinall at Parsons suite both o^r enemies & vniustly apointed bycaus by iudges of their own cause & therefore all. 3. Card[inal] Pars[ons] & Blackw[ell] intrusores into o^r haruest, vsurpores of his holines autoritie, & tyrantes of vs & o^r countrey.

9°. That it was directly by & for the Jes[uits] to expell or bring all priests vnd^r them, probatur ex bulla quia instituitur præcipue vt pacem habeamus cum Jesuitis ergo ad interitum omnium aliorum etc.

10°. That it was foysted in by Parsons procurem^t onely vpon a pointe of extremity to colour his impietie & to stop the discovery of his treacherous minde towards his countrey probatur for it came in . . . at that time when bothe in Spaine Italie & the lowe countreis his dealings began to be odious for his tyrany against all priests & lay persons y^t consented not to his Jappon kingdome & in England his bookes & all their dealings being by cathol. generally disliked & by Sem[inarists] condemned & reiected as full of ambition, bloodshed, infamy & crime intended to o^r whole countrey. it was time to set vp such an archiprate or els had the Jappon bene quite pulled downe for evr wch thoughe he have but a blinde name of autority, yet it suffiseth to hold tacke till by invasion or oth^rwise ye Jappon may worke. Ergo vtterly by all English to be deiected.

11°. That (setting Blackw. private life aside wch now I omitte) he is vnfit (yt such autority were lawfully granted) to be chosen for a heade over soe greate a multitude of singular fine wits, ancient & learned especially in times soe dangerous & full of diuersities & differences in all things (besides religion & learning) it is most plaine for that he is well knowen to be a man of noe reache ; onely he hath red many autho^rs whereby he can speake or write sentences oute of others, not of himselfe : he never knew what gouernment ment : having had charge onely of a widow gentlewom[an] wth whom he lived, he never conversed wth any to learne eyther experience : or to behave himselfe in company, discourse or otherwise to syfte out any matter or to know how to doe iustice in his office. Ergo by Dolem. rule of deposing or choosing gouerno^rs Blac[kwell] is vnfittest of an 100. consequitur to be deposed yf he had autoritie etc.

12°. That Black. simplicitie & vnfitnes to governe sheweth plaine the greate mischeife & ruine of o^r countrey intended by choosing of him. Probatur for whoe in policie wolde attempt that wch the the Jap. goe aboute by any suche as wanting witte to enter into their drifte shold think every word to be gospell they speake & then vpon this grovende rather having tender consciences must think it a sin irremissible to resist etc.

13°. That the Jappon policie was marvailous dexterous in choosing one by profession a Secu[lar] & not a knowen Jesuite & consequently none fitter than Blackw. Probatur 1° otherwise they had opend their owne ambition to all ye world. 2° they could not in honesty & wth any face have spoken for themselves as others may doe for them. 3° they may hereby colour all their treacherie for yf it faired not well, ye heade is a Sem[inarist] if it hap to their wishe, he is by them set vp, ergo at their apointment. 4° they may (as they doe) more stoutely defend him then themselves.

14°. That a great^r persecucion is & must ensue by Bla[ckwells] archipresbiterie than ever came to cath. by the protestant civil magistrates 1° for y^t it opend the way to all rebellion freeing euery one to speake or do what they lyst or can against any except Jes. & all vnder pretence of zeale in taking (forsothe) ye popes parte by defending Blackw. autority & calling & esteming of vs all y^t resist it to be schimat[ic]or worse. 2° whereas before some few were infamed by private opposing against ye Jes. nowe all that obey not Blackw. are soe persecuted by these Dolemanists rayling & slanderous tongues as none can live free. 3° it bredes that contempte as every boye & gyrle are in manner of esteme of priesthoode becomes Wisemanists to put noe defrence but all secul^r etc. 4° it makes vent for invasion both of Scot. & Span. the archpriestes 12 assistants being dispersed in every corner w^{the} the laity to work by north & by south persuading it to be for ye Scots good to ioyne wth Spa. ergo mightely he is to be resisted.

15° That the plotte was laide long agone for this archpriest probatur by their olim dicebamur & oth^r forgeries of theirs. 1° to brede comiseracion of Jes[uits]. 2° to make Sem[inarists] odious to ye laity as iniurious detracto^{rs}. 3° to give scope by this to defame whom they wold wch were all y^t mighte seme to stand in their way : & this done then suche defamed persons being vnfitte to gouerne, none but Blackw. (supposing one must be chosen) cold be founde fitte euery way : a notable stratageme.

16°. That all whoe defend the Archpriest are eyth^r Jes. or liue vnd^r & by them, or are nowe put in autority for them, or have the collections of the money throughoute Engl. for cathol. to depend vpon them or their substitutes for the sacraments or live in expectance of mountains at ye Span. invasion by their procurem^t all wch none y^t hath sene & knowen ye state of thinges abroade but may easely discerne : & therefore of all well wishing to their countrey are these Dolemanists w^{the} their archpriest to be resisted & in noe case ev^r to ycalde to his false autority.

17°. The expostulacions manages & minaces of Blackw. autoritie shew plaine how impiously pharisaically and iniuriously they have dealte herein. 1° for y^t they have nothing to shew but ye Card. authorizing of him whoe is known to be o^r adversarie. 2° they never could bring any testimonie but of their owne companie to certifie soe muche as y^t the pope ever yet heard of this mans chosing or any such matter. 3° their excuse of a popes bull is vaine, y^t wch they have being all one & ye same, yf anything worthe, as confirmed by ye pope. 4° their pretence of the Card. feare in y^t he durst not grant it wthoute ye popes privitie is ridiculous & for babies (as ye Dolem. compute vs) his answeare being ready (yf called in question) y^t he apointed Blackw. onely as a prefect or some such one amongst a multitude to kepe good ord^r but noe farther, & not then but as he was informed or that he was fittest to appease contencions, etc. 5°. their comparison of the Card^l. w^{the} a L. Chancelo^r or L. Keper, etc., is simple & impertinent for it onely (yf soe much) holds in a priest or a iustice of peace v. g. the L. Chancelo^r or oth^r may apointe & make a iustice of peace by his generall autority given him from ye prince but to make a lord president or create an Earle or L. baron by that autority he can not, ergo ye Card^{ls} autority to giue faculties to priests, extends not to giue a supreme autority to any one priest more then himselfe hathe yf here amongst vs. 6° their color of charity to have vs yeald for ye time vntill we heare to ye contrary is flat hypocrisie, feyning pitying of vs to bolster oute their owne abuse of vs all & having by Parsons meanes (noe doubt) stopt all complaints or put a demur vntill he heare hence yf now they git these hands his conscience will stretche them to an absolute consent & acceptance of this vsurper. 7°. their excuse of noe ticket nor testimonie from the pope or oth^r whom we may trust is nothing by ye example of priests for euery one knowes the faculties of priests are generall, ergo nede noe oth^r testimonie but notice given by any that there they had them : but this arch-priest is a particular thing never heard of befc ɔ. ergo iniust vnlawfull & most to be resisted.

18°. The peveshnes, simplicity & vnfitnes of Blackw. the ambicion envy & machiavelisme of his electors & the ignorance, lightnes & ever blindly weyghed affeccion of ye mobile vulgus all considered: this archpresbit^ry wilbe ye bane of Engl. yf ever accepted of. 1°. for yt his autority extends to all Engl. Scotl. & (vt ait) Ireland, wth many agents in them all, ergo once confirme & up starts ye Jap. Monarchie. 2°. it derogates from all priestly autority. Probatur, by ye liberty of euery Jacke & gylle to defame vs w^thoute satisfaccion; by colling laymen to controlle vs or leave vs disgraced as Blackw. ordinarily speak^th not to any of vs but must have some of ye laity to heare the case by their generall maxime y^t they may & doe vse layty to defame, controlle, and direct priests they being not able to be in all places at all times themselves : & by the generall examples of their free speach had of all priests, monkes, fryers bishops & ye pope himselfe. 3°. it arrogates all supreme autority to ye Jes , probatur, by making it a sin most heynous, not to yeald to them in all things : or a signe of heresie to thinke they may erre : or malice & loosenes of life, to charge them wth any favlte : also by sending forth trumpeters to sound oute their & Blackw. vertues, concluding hereby neith^r them to be spoken of nor him to be refused as fittest of all etc.

as though inherent iustice depended vpon externall signes of virtue: Thus once yeald to them & farew^l etc.

19º. Their malice & evil meaning towards priests is in nothing more plaine, then managing oute y^t vsurpate archpriest. probatur by their ostencion of a most horrible sin to resist his autority, ergo we are (by their detraction) all fooles, vnlearned, conscienles, provde, malicious, infamous detractours, etc., & yet by the same acts they on the contrary are wise, learned, vertuous, & zealous, etc. O notable hypocrites!

20º. The causes moving them thus vehemently to vrge o^r consent must^a . . . . . shamefull abuses wch wold be called in question yf we had an equall iudge, 2º their cruelty vsed towards priests, 3º their vnhonest proceding in this eleccion, 4º their vnlawfull autorizing of him w^thoute comission, 5º their forging, facing, & coyning of letters, messages, etc. to git consents, etc., 6º the generall esteme simple people have of their pharis[aical] virtue, honesty & sincerity; soe as yealde o^r consents: we occasionate their sin to increase hold backe o^r yeald & their impiety is streighte knowen & they quite overthrowen, ergo.

21º. We can not in conscience yeald to it becaus that it is: 1º to yeald to ye slander raised by them of vs all. 2º an iniury to those y^t are gone. 3º a contradiccion to o^r owne doings. 4º an opposiccion against one an oth^r. 5º a breache of all order. 6º a participation, consent, associacion, combinacion or sodalitie w^the the Jappon to ouerthrowe o^r countrey & make all o^r posterity curse vs.

22º. That Blackw. is but a cipher for the Jap. to put what figu[re] they lyft vnto, prob. by ye addicions & sotraccions affirmacions & negacions, etc., of the particul^rs of his autority; ergo, parte the figure & the ciph^r & the best is but little, etc^r.

23º. That they have indiscretely marred their owne market in their violent covrse taken for confirmacion of his autority, prob. 1º by giving oute such & such to be excommunicated, suspended,

---

^a Line obliterated.

etc., wch he can not obtaine. 2° by constituting assistants to whom as yet he can not giue autority, they having come to Lond[on] 3 sundry tearmes for it & he answearing that it is not yet come. 3° the Jap. laity refusing to come at o^r service, to receive vs into their houses or to giue vs any maintenance : &, giving oute y^t we are schismat[ics], etc., all wch shew Blackw. to be most greedy in affecting of hono^r y^t can not have patience vntill we have an answeare or the Jappon to be most impudent in their dealings. y^t will turkise ov^r vs to vrge our consent by violent force & bothe to be voide of conscience, shame, religion or honesty to have set a worke a breache wh^ch to maintein they must nedes be desperate or els are quite overthrowen.

24°. This simple mans choosing the Jappon being his councello^rs all things drawing to a heade for invasion, soe as the plots are like to be discoverd shortly throughoute Christendome it stands them vpon to vrge dentibus et ensibus for Blackw. whom yf we yealde vnto we set up the Jap. kingdome, yf we resist we save o^r countrey & ouerthrow them for euer, ergo noe true.

25°. The very word Archipresbiter is anomalum abolendum quite oute of vse in gods churche at this day, ergo an innovation, never like to be allowed of by the pope yf he knew it.

26°. It was but a politie of Parsons to giue such a syllie man a poore tittle w^thoute an effectuall title to blere o^r eyes w^the his care of o^r countrey because (for sothe) the name of a bishop wold have raised persecucion as thoughe this be not as greate & greater cause of persecucion, but ye reason was (in dede), 1° for y^t the Card. nor he could not compasse such a matt^r. 2° for y^t the pope must then have bene bothe privie vnto it & ratified & confirmed it. 3° most of all for y^t then he must have bene aboue all Jes. too whereas he is now but vnder them. 4° the Jappon Iland could not then have bene gouerned absolutely by them as is intended by excluding all bishops & other autoritie.

27°. It is iust agreing w^the the Puritanes to have this kind of

Archipresbitery & Dolemans private rules of gouernment tende to noe lesse in morall matters thoughe in religion he yet braves it oute w^{the} ye most zealous y^t are.

28º. It was of purpose to kepe all gouernment from amongst vs therby to settle his Jappon monarchie, ergo to be resisted.

29º. It is contrary to ye custome of all countreis ages tymes & persons to have such an archipresbiticall gouernment, ergo, etc.

30º. It was invented of policie sent over w^{the} unnaturall hate towards o^r countrey, & will be mainteined wth greate blovdshed yf not prevented.[a]

38, f. 406.

14. *The Condicions of Yeldinge.*[b]

[April or May, 1599.]

Allwayes we haue beene readie, soe by these presentes do we all offer our selfes fourthw^{th} to admitt this authoritie of ye Archp^t. yf any Authenticall Instrument of his hol^{es} shalbe shewed unto vs wittnesshinge the same to be instituted by hym.

Moreover yf that can not be shewed for avoyding slanderouse reportes and more peaceable practizing of our functions we are well content voluntarilie to obay this forme of gouerment wth these condicions and not otherwyse.

1. first, that we mae be sufficiently advised how fare this authoritie extendeth particularly and that we may have a coppie therof.

2. secondly, that yo^u and the societie will consent wth vs to the sending over of certayne who may herevpon have the freer accesse

---

[a] The whole of this paper, in the minute and cramped hand of W. Watson, is written on two sides of half a folio.

[b] These are probably the conditions referred to by Mush in a letter written to Bagshaw on Friday after Ascension Day (printed in *Jesuits and Seculars*, p 147, from the Petyt MSS., xlvii., f. 204). Mush writes: "We offered to yeald upon verie reasonable condicions, wch all were refused. And Mr Collington, myselfe, & Mr Heberne suspended ab omni usu facultatum."

and leave to speake to his hol^nes for his further information in o^r cause & for our better assurance of his determination therein. Allwayes provided that yf theire audience be preuented directly or indirectly by yo^u or the Societies meanes that then we fullie revoke all obedience here offered.

3. thirdlie, that whereas too of o^r brethren imployed in this bussines have beene by information from hence discredited and imprisoned our desire is that we may receyue from yo^u notice of the crimes or misdemeanoure laid agaynst them or have yor testimony for their good carriage and behavio^r whereof they lyved here or at lest that yo^u knowe no defaminge ill by them.

4. fourthly, that whereas we all in generall and diuers particularely haue bene deeply iniured and defamed by a treatise of schisme[a] divulged by one of the Societie the same may be reuoked as false and we have o^r credites restored by an other contrarie treatise published to that ende by those parties and allowers of the former.

5. fiftly, that yo^u let vs have yor accord and letters over for procuringe that hereafter neither the Archps^t. nor his assistantes mae be chosen otherwyse then by the consent and voices of our owne bodie.

6. sixtly, that eueryone that shalbe made Archps^t. or assistant shall affirme by the word of a priest that he neither is, nor throwghly for the present determineth to be a Jesuitt.

7. seauently, that for asmuch as the state is alreadie merwelously incensed against vs by meanes of bookes letters and plotts towching state matters, and thervpon nothing belonging to our function our request is that all proceedinges of this qualitie may be disalowed and forbidden.

---

[a] Father Lister's treatise, *Adversus Factiosos*, declaring that the malcontents were guilty of schism, and had incurred excommunication. It was first printed by Bagshaw in his *Relatio Compendiosa*. Blackwell formally approved of this treatise in a letter dated March 26, 1599.

At foot (in other hand): These offers weare made by ye priestes about London as Mr Collington & ye rest. Blackwell tooke this in great scorne, & writ accordingly to them.

Endorsed (in same hand as above note): The conditions wch Mr B. & Mr Charnock weare to have required, &, those graunted, to have yealded.

III.

THE TWO DEPUTIES AT ROME.
Dec., 1598—April, 1599.

Out of M^r. Docter Had[dock]^s letters, novemb.^{a} 19. 47, f. 123

The 11 of this present heare arrived one Mr Bishope and Mr Charnock and wer courtesly entertayned in the college vpon condicion they should not seeke to disturbe the same, being now in so good order & quiet, & so free from all thoughtes of such as these men bent theire busie braynes abowt as that none of them would vouchsaf to speak wth them saue one or to excepted, wch by appoyntment of theire superiours and wth one in theire companye were licensed to talk wth them for some acquaintance wth them in England, and this mortification hath ben no litle one vnto these men, who seeke to disquiet booth college & contrey, & contemn all order, wch to their grife they see so florish at this present in o^r college, god allmightie the author of peace and louer of concord and order be praysed. In the morning folowinge our Reverend father f. rector send for my frend m^r. martyn, and declared vnto vs the will of o^r Re^d Archepriest and his assistantes that together wth hym we should deall wth these men in this bussines, and so that day we gave them theire welcome in such sort as I suppose theire formere bragges, wch as we have vnderstood they haue vsed in such places as they have ben in by the way, are pretely abatted, for we so syfted theire intentions and answered theire friuolous reasons, and bysyd bestowed such documentes vpon them as that they remayned

---

^{a} "Novemb." is a clerical error for Decemb. The two priests arrived at Rome on the 11th Dec. (Parsons' *Briefe Apologie*, f. 121 ; *Relatio Compendiosa*, p. 75.)

melancholy all that night, as we learned by those whoe have care of the pilgrimes. The next morning my old camerado had an other about them and found them much more calme then they had ben at their first arriual, and afrayd to talke wth hym alledging that they had been coursed & aduantage taken of theire speaches. Theire meaning was that we had termed them mantayners of former factions and dispicers of authoritie, wch though they sought to cleare them selfes of in theire first speaches, yet befor we had ended wth them we proved booth vnto them; And by such particulares as they could not avoyd we exhorted them to cease of to rune so shamefull a course and to deale as becomed catholicke preistes, other wyse they should fynd that we would answere them and defend the graunted authoritie to their confusion. they promysed they would not deale without our rector, and by our protector; but men of their schole regard litle what either they promyse or what shamles meanes they vse to manteyne so impudent a cause as they and their complices have in hand, for by syd the^{ir} manifest lyes & false rumours wch we knowe they have spred & sowen by the way in diuers places they have attempted wth theire lewd informations to abuse one of the schollers, a substantiall preiste, who had care of them & serued them, who being discreete and of no small judgement to discerne where at they shott, informed his superours, wherevppon they were discharged the colledg where they had ben wth all charitie & courtese interteyned 5 or 6 dayes. and the same day they went to Card^{all} Burghese (for our protector was out of the towne but is returned this night) whome they thought, as I suppose by Edward Bennets secrete directions, to have found fauorable, but booth they and their secret instructor must learne that the world is changed. I was wth Card^{all} Burghese, for that I belong vnto hym, and informed hym of the cause and he tould me he had remitted them vnto our protector w^thout further ceremonies, and he tould me that his opinion was that his holines would punish them according vnto their dimerites wch he would not faill to procure when his

47, f. 123b.

hol. returneth, wch wilbe the one and twentie of this present,^a so that I hope they will repent their iourney and wish them selfes sicke ^b in their beedes in Ingland.

I am sorie as I tould them y^t any of their profession should make such a voyage in so bad a cause but you knowe the sentence of the propheticall Apostles, oportet hereses esse, wch they will not think well applied, but assuredly if we either regard the latitude of the signification of the word or the harme they bring vnto gods churche and catholick religion in these hereticall tymes they will not easely avoyd the name for theire crosse & contradictiouse spirites wth the effectes they striue to produce where they may prevayle deserue no better a name. And god graunt that not a worse, seeing that all the heretickes in the world are not of force to endanger our cause so much by many degrees as these our brethren and felow laborers who, by the name of Catholicke priestes, have more credite and fredome to perswade, and vnder the cloake of zeale may more easely peruert the myndes of such as are not of judgement or experience to discerne theire fraudulent desigmentes wch are grounded vpon ambitious licentiousnes and auarice, from wch qualities I wish these good men were free. These men played that there is great iniurie donne vnto the other & contrarie part, wch I tell you is a shame to speake of that theire should be any part makinge, and they would confesse y^t yf they would looke into their vocation & attend vnto there profession. They extold greatlie their ringe leaders D. Bageshaw and Mr. Collingtonne and bragge of theire eminent qualities, all wch I could be glad were true and greater then they are or can be, and that they would consider vnde et ad quod finem hæc dona, and seeke to direct them ad ædificationem & cease to imploy their wrangling wittes against men of better qualities of more zeale and pietie and of higher fauoure wth god then they are desirous to

47, f. 124.

---

^a "Of this present" *i.e.* December. See preceding note. The Pope, in fact, returned from Ferrara on Dec. 20.

^b So it is written; perhaps, for the obsolete *sicker*, sure, safe.

attayne vnto, wherin it seameth vnto me that they discouere to
much their malace and enuye for in men of their profession and
talentes, ignorance it can not be wch M^r. Collingtone will easely
yeld me to be true, having attempted as I knowe, to have entered
into religion ^a wch he prefered at that tyme. And seing his bodie
would not serue his will, at the least me thincketh he should not
become an enimy vnto the state because he did forsake it vnlesse
he will allso preferre hym self vnto f. Campion, for that he escaped
the execution of such sentence of death as he should haue receyued
at one tyme wth hym.^b A more commendable & more meritorious
way y^t were in my judgement to retayne his old opinion of the
pre-eminence of the estates, and seing for such causes and he
findeth in hym self he is not apt for the best vocation, at the lest
y^t would much better become hym to commend and honor that, in
others, wch he can not but preferre in his secret conscience, and
yf by any humane frailtie any thing change, not so answerable vnto their humors as they desire, the counsell of the blessed
apostle were fitter to be folowed in fleing contention then, wth their
accustomed pertinac[it]ie, to impugne theire friendes and masters
in what goodnes they chalenge in any kind, wherin yf they
deame me partiall as they have ben wonte. I would they had
our B. brethren, f. Sherwyn, Kyrby, Ford, Shert and the
rest of that ranke ioyned wth the happie company of their leaders
in tyme past, D. Bristow, Licentiat Martyn, and the like by
whome they should quicly be enformed though hardly taught
(their prid is so great) from whence our spirituall goodnes, yf we
have any, first did spring, and to whome next after god we are
cheefly beholden. the case is to clere vnto those that are contented

---

^a He had entered the noviciate of the Carthusians, as has been said, but was
found unsuited to the life.

^b Colleton was put on his trial with Campion in 1581 for an imaginary con-
spiracy said to have been hatched at Rheims, but was acquitted on its being clearly
proved that he was in London at the time. He had, indeed, never been at Rheims.

by humilitie to be gratfull and for gods cause would wth Sem and
Japhet hyd theire [e]yes yf any fault were in their shamed
fathers rather then wth wicked Cham seeke to make them manifest. And in this it greaueth me infinitely to see these companions so farre to exceede that graceles child. as they do in
dyvising and thursting to puicke quarels wth those to whome
they are bounde, yf no way els for the best qualities they
have, and so vaunt of. And many of them allso for their temporall sustenaunce from no smaule tyme, yf the apostle exhorted
the Corinthians to quietnes & to leaue their strifes before infidell
Judges, exclaiming Quare non magis iniuriam accipitis, quare non
magis fraudem patimini, what may we thincke he would say vnto 47, f. 124b.
hym who can not deny the dutie he oweth vnto these whom he
persequuteth and yet will not desist from his vngratfull & iniurious
calumniations. I would to god these men would well consider whence
these dissentions spring wch yf they know not, or contemne to heare
I remitt them to the fo[re]said apostle to learne wth the Corinthians
the place and effect of carnis opera wth wch they shall fynd Inimicitiæ, contentiones, emulationes, iræ, rixæ, dissentiones and how
contrariwise do proceede pax, patientia, benignitas, bonitas, longani-
mitas, mansuetudo, as fructus spiritus, of wch they seem looth to
be partaker, but wth what sequell I am sorie to thincke but they
vse to quarell. And these mens long iourney doth showe yt they
thinke all men blynd but them self, and impudently accuse all that
will not yeld to there madnes wth no lesse reason then Fimbria
accused Scevula for not receyving into his belly the whole weapon
wherew{th} Fimbria wounded hym. These men have bragged much
as I touched before of the Auncientes, qualities and sufficiencie of
D. Bagshaw and Mr. Colingtoune wch I enuie not, yet was I somethinge bould wth them when they entred into comparisone wth our
R{d} Archipriest and his assistantes whome I defended for all these
pointes and would yeld in non excepting yt I would yeld vnto these
for wranglinge natures & contentious spirites, wch I have ben
acquaynted wth in one of them for 30 yeres and others here no

lesse tyme wth thother. And for such rare and pearlese qualities in hym whome I know I marvayile by what extraordinarie meaus he should come by them for ordinarie I am reasonablely priuie that he can fynd none. but for these matters I wish booth them & these men had a little more humilitie & so I comend them to god to whom they are to yeld accompt of booth the receipt and vsage of their bragging qualities. And so I leave them. And request yo^u to remember me in humble manner vnto our most Rend Archipriest and his assistantes whose wisdome I knowe and presume so fare of thire discretion for geving advantage vnto these wranglers that I shall make smaul accompt of Answering for them and hope wth ease to overcome such stormes as now can be raysed, having throwgh gods healp passed over more perilouse tempestes when I had lesse ayd, and our adversaries more force, than nowe they shall fynd in this place, for the world is well amended, god be thanked, and so kyssing their handes I commend them all & yo^u vnto our bleassed Sauour & my self vnto all yor good prayers.

Endorsed :

A letter : how Mr. Parsons appointed this writer and an other to be Mr. Blackwells procter : of ye Emb[assadors] just intertaynmt of ther discharg from ye college w^thin 5 or 6 days.

How the writer hereof & his fellow coursed them.

How they are theire found after a sorte heretiques.

He is verie bitter against Dr. Bagshaw & Mr. Collington.

47, f. 146.

2. *Copy of Letter from Cardinal Cajetan to Blackwell on the arrival of the two priests at Rome.*

Jan. 12, 1599.

Admodum Reverende in Christo vti frater.

Superioribus diebus literas ad te scripsimus^a quibus significamus aliquid nos mandasse (ipso etiam S^{mo} Domino significante) de duorum

^a The letter referred to (dated 10 Nov. 1598, and enquiring into the character and conduct of the priests in question) is printed in Tierney's *Dodd*, vol. iii., p. cxxv.

sacerdotum vestrorum Romam versus itinere vt authoritati et iurisdictioni vestræ S^{tis} suæ iussu per nos institutæ reluctarentur, rem valde S^{mo} bonisque omnibus nationis vestræ amantibus displicuisse quod post veteres tumultus saluberrime sublatos nova iterum paucorum hominum contentione (nam maxima sacerdotum pars iam antea literis tam nobis quam S^{mo} perscriptis assensum gaudiumque suum ex hac Hierarchia constituta attestati fuerant) non sine gravi scandalo excitari videbantur, vnde S^{te} sua constitutum plane fuerat si Ferrarium (vbi tunc morabatur) appulissent seuerius forte castigandos iubere. Illi vero cum diutius in itinere propter viarum difficultates hæsissent existimatum est sapientius consilium cepisse vt domum reuerterentur sed initio huius mensis Romam appulerunt meque post aliquot dies adierunt, quos libenter quidem vt gentis vestræ homines quibus maxime cupio libentius etiam vt istinc ex Illma Christi vinea venientes amplexus sum, subinvitus tamen, in istiusmodi causa. Itaque auditi[s] primum quæ referebant omnem animi mei sensum candide eis exposui, displicere nimirum tanti itineris tam inanes aut non necessarias causas (nihil enim afferebant quod alicuius mihi momenti videbatur) notandam fore gentem vestram de inquietioris naturæ atque ingenij condicione quam ad causæ vestræ honorem expediat genus regiminis ecclesiastici quod S^{tas} sua in Anglia pro rerum temporumque presenti statu instituerat facillimam atque commodissimam rem et non nisi cogitatione magnaque deliberatione delectam fuisse, tum vt episcopalis nominis invidia apud hereticos vitaretur tum etiam vt presbyteris pie laborantibus auxilium inde solamen ac directio præberentur : si quid incommodi successu temporis accideret (quod speratur non futurum) ei tunc erit medendum, cum acciderit, veræque causæ perspectæ fuerint vnde incommodum et impedimentum nascatur : ab initio vero non fuisse reclamandum quod seditionis cuiusdam speciem summo domino aliisque viris prudentibus vehementer odiosam præ se ferebat. Cumque illi nescio quod præferrent de acriori vestra disceptatione cum aliquibus ex suis ac de conventibus literisque prohibitis, dixi videndum esse quænam fuissent; ita nam, si pauci, agendis conventibus ac scribendis literis id notitarint vt aliorum corda ad Hierarchiam a sede apostolica institutam impugnandam sollicitarent merito fuisse hæc a vobis prohibita. Denique jussi vt scripto pararent quæ proponenda haberent, me acturum cum sanctissimo ut omnia, quoad fieri potest, clementer et benigne transigerentur, offensam esse suam sanctit[em] maleque rem accepisse non esse dubium, sed si humiliter ac pacate se gererent facilius fore placandam. Postea tamen sua sanct[as] id censuit non esse (ab initio saltem) audiendos sed custodiæ potius tradendos quousque rerum suarum rationes reddidissent, cui examini officialem quendam suum præfecit. Ego vero id obtinui vt non publicis carceribus sed cubiculis potius collegii anglicani committerentur vbi amice et benevole tractati minori animi molestia negotia tractent. neque deerunt partes meæ ut cito et humaniter expediantur quamquam difficile fore video vt Sanctissimus consentiat vt hi ipsi tam cito ad vos reuertantur nisi magnæ admodum mutationis argumenta præbeant quod spero facturos, quia viros bonos existimo magisque errore quam maleuolentia deceptos. De rebus vero alijs pro quibus intercedit dominatio vestra vt facultates restituantur Tempestio nimirum, Bensonio, atque Hillo, etsi non ea hactenus de eorum emendatione audiuimus quæ cupimus quæque sanctitatem suam ad hoc ipsum concedendum inducant quia tamen d. v. spem nobis facit de futuro tempore, sanctissimus arbitrij nostri fecit, ego vero [rem] omnem promitto, ea tamen conditione vt sufficientem vobis satisfactionem de præteritis præstent ac promissa de futuris, quod si non obseruarint vestri judicij erit easdem facultates vel auferre vel restringere prout æquitatis rationi diuinique seruitii obsequio magis expedire in domino judicabitis, ad quam etiam regulam cætera omnia dirigantur fortique animo sitis neque fatigari vos patiamini, erit nam merces operi vestro, dominusque ipse, eiusque in terris vicarius vobis adest aderitque. Attendite vobis, vestroque gregi super quem sedes apostolica vos constituit pastorem, bonos ac quietos consolamini. Inquietos patientia et benignitate (si fieri potest) lucramini sin minus reprehendite ac corrigite : secundum eam potestatem quam S^mus D^ns ad hoc ipsum vobis [. . .]^a meque orationibus vestris omniumque vestrorum quorum literas habeo, quosque omnes ac singulos nominatim ex me salutari cupio, nostro D^no commendandum queso curate. Romæ pridie Idus Januarij 1599.

D^is vræ R^dæ   vti frater etc.

At foot: In another hand.

Ex literis R^mæ D. Octavii ep^i Tricaricensis Nuncii apostolici.

Quemadmodum commenta et falsa sunt quæ de nobis referuntur vt [quæ] patres Societatis istuc agant, quemadmodum vivant, inquirendi cuidam sacerdoti iuueni, . . . ^b nomine, potestatem dedissemus, longe quidem ea a nostris sensibus abhorrent. Si quidem is vel aliquis sit qui hanc sibi audeat potestatem vendicare eam curet R^ra V. authoritatem qua fungitur exhiberi, nullam profecto inueniet, propterea ne patiatur tale verbum in me falso conferri, nam a pueritia semper et hoc tempore maxime Societatem obseruamus et diligimus. valeat, etc.

3. *A third Letter from M[artin] A[rray].*

Jan. 18, 1599.   47, f. 133.

My good frend, this is my third letter that I wrote to you about yor two ambass[adors] Bishop and Char[nock]: my last ^c was of the second of this presente, wch related vnto you howe his holynes had given order to haue them restrayned and shutt up, and how our good frend nowe Rector ^d procured wth the Card. Protector, that it might be rather in the Colledge than other where; and so it hathe ben. And they are and have ben verie curteouslie treated as I learne for certeyne: and hitherto theire examinacions haue

---

^a Some words wanting here.
^b The name cut out.
^c This second letter and the fourth (referred to, p. 115) are unfortunately not in the Petyt collection.
^d Father Parsons.

indured by the popes Comissary, and so none of vs abroade could speake wth them. Nowe I heare that matters drawinge towards an end they are like to haue some more libertie : yet I vnderstand there is like to be a great difficulty to obteyne them licence of the vice-gerent to celebrate : for that they bring no letters pattente from theire superior there wth you, nor other of creditt, that they are free ab omni impedimento celebrandi, to witt excomunicacion, suspencion, Irregularitie etc. wthout wch clauses no man is per‑ mitted to celebrate by this newe reformation of his holynes. And seinge they haue brought wth them letters of far lesse moment, and of no lesse daunger then these, greate difficulty is like to be made herein, if the creditt and labor of our frend (who will doe no dowbt for them in this point what he can) doe not procure particuler dispensation, as I presume at length it will. And truly I doe bothe prove in myself, and see in other men dailye, a greate greefe of mynde, that they are forced by the necessitie of our common cause, and for conservation of vnion in our body to oppose themselves to these men and theire doinges in this action, whom otherwise for theire vocations sake, and other respects, they would bothe honor, cherishe and interteyne wth all kynde of curtesye most willinglie. But seeinge that these men and theire fautors indevors are to divide our bodye and mainteyne sedition in the same, no good man is there in the world, that doth not abhorre the same, as they will bothe finde and feele. And here already they haue found suche vnion peace and zeale in all those of this college, from the highest to the lowest, against theire attempts, as they haue alredie disclaymed vtterlie from divers of theire cheife points they had in comission, and are found in their papers, namely for changing of this, and all the rest of the Semin‑ aries from the ffathers to priests of theire faction, for changinge the protector, for havinge an englishe Card : of the same faction— for advauncinge some 4 or 5 of the same faction, who came also named in particular to be Bishops. All whch points smellinge of manifest ambition, and faction, these men nowe doe say, they

allow not of them, but doe lay them vppon theire fellowes that
sent them. Seinge further, that they are not bound to stand to
any thinge, that the others have sett downe in theire scrowles
& ticketts (for suche only they bringe) and yet can shewe no
authoritie at all that they may deale of theire owne hands. Nor
doe they bringe (as I vnderstand) any other letter of credence
worth the lookinge vppon, but litle scrowles and ticketts, as before
I said, w^{t}h w^{c}h I heare say, the Comissary that examineth them,
was wonderfully offended, sayinge that he would not goe to a
Pothecary for drugges w^{t}h suche papers. And nowe I heare that
whereas they bringe are not aboue [twenty] one or 22 of this
sort of letters, yet 16 or 17 of them doe appeare to be written
before the Archepriest was appointed in England, and they demaund
only some superiour wch nowe they haue, and consequently they
make nothinge for these men but rather against them, for that they
produce them against the meaninge of the writers. The other 4
or 5 that be properly of these mens fautors have verie fewe names,
not aboue a dozen (as I suppose) and the half of these out of one
house. And I heare say, that these men here beinge prest vppon
theire oathes to say how many they knewe assuredly to be of theire
parte in England and will stand to all they treate of here, they
answered, some twelve they knowe, but presumed of more, w^{ch}
made the Comissary to laugh, and yet to be angry also, to see
such perversitie of a fewe, and still he retorneth to the old principle
tha nowe is over common, questi cervelli ynglesi. And this our
nation and cause gayneth by these contentious people, who for
satisfyinge theire owne humo^r of contradiction and contention, care
not what infamie they bringe vppon our Nation, and when it
breakes out to be knowne reprehended, or punished, then they will
needes lay the blame vppon good men, that resiste theire follies and
furies.

Greate disputation I vnderstand to haue passed betweene the
Comissary that is our canonist, and these two Ambass: about the
newe forme of governement they would have there amonge yo^u,

47, f. 133b

and the mislike that they and theire fellowes have of the governement present, and of the manner and causes thereof. ffor that theire newe devised governement of 2 Archepr[iests] of equall authoritie to live in one place, or a sunder as they list, and to have voluntary subiects by choice (for to this point only have they nowe restrayned them selves giving over all theire other pretences as impertinent, or impossible) semeth to the Comissary a mere Chimera, not practicable any way for many arguments that he hath alledged against it And for the second point, it seemeth they haue no other reason to alleadge against the present Archep^rsbiter but only that some doe feare partialitie at his hand. To wch the other answered that by this reason the[y] might change the pope also, and all other magistrates in the worlde, and vrged muche, if they have brought any thinge in particuler, and lawfully proved against him, wch they deny to haue done, and do say moreover, that they came not to accuse him, and muche lesse the Jesuites, but only the humble peticion to request, that respect may be had of a fewe mens infirmities, y^t will hardly be contented, except they may have some man of theire owne parte over them, at least some assistant or two, wch I dowbt muche whether his holynes will graunt or no. ffor perhaps it will seme more reasonable to him, to remove them out of England, or punishe them there that are so infirme, as they cannot live quietlie, and obey theire superio^r appointed, especiallie seeinge the obedience required there wth yowe at this day is so easie, and required in so fewe cases as litle or no vertue att all is thought needfull to performe the same excepte only not to impugne the superior or otherwise not to give publick scandall. ffor in all other cases it is presumed that the Arch. appointed will have nothinge to doe wth them; but willingly lett them alone, and consequently, yf they be vnquieted, it is only of them selves: and so no necessitye of changinge matters already stablyshed for theire quiett or for curinge theire infirmities. And this is all I haue to write of this affaire at this present: as more falleth out, more shalbe written. I hope all will end well, and

47, f. 134.

alredy it appeareth, that it was a good providence of god for them selves, that they were restrayned by his holynes, vntill theire affaires are examined. ffor if they had gone vp and downe fillinge greate mens eares wth false opynions of matters (as they begone to doe) in the end they would haue proved nothinge of substance as nowe it is found, it would have served but only to haue infamed more our Nation of sedition among ourselves, and have procured more offence and punishment against these men in particuler, who nowe I hope will escape wth litle, excepte theire restrainte for retorninge into England and losse of theire faculties, wch most men thinke is like to ensue, if nothinge more. And wth this I end, wthout entringe into any other matter for the present. this 18th of January, S. p. Bab.

Towchinge the faculties that were taken from the three, to witt Benson and his fellowes, I can assure yow that our frend here, hathe labored much wth the protector to deale wth Clement for the restitution, who at length is contented to remitt the matter to the Arch. and, as I heare say, the Protector himself writeth of it. I praye god they vse them well, and knowe theire true ffrendes, that wishe them best.

Yo^r loving^e ffrend
M. A.

I had almost omitted one particuler wch shall not be evill for yow to knowe, and that is, that amonge other pointes of Comission delivered in writinge to these two Ambass. one principall was noted in all theire latter letters, that no bookes should be admitted that offended the present state of England in matters of state, or exasperate the adversaries. Wherevppon they beinge examined what bookes or booke they ment in particuler, said it was the booke of succession. And, beinge demaunded further, whether any particuler persecution had been moved hetherto by that booke, or any man put to deathe for havinge it in this 3 or 4 yeres since it was written, they sayd that they knewe of none. Then was it asked them, why there was more grudginge then and complaynt against this booke that had moved no persecution,[a] then against D[r] Saunders Monarchia and book de Schismate, and D. Bristowes motives (for w[ch] diverse in particular have ben put to deathe) [b] as also against D. Allen late Cardinall his booke contra iustitiam Britanicam, D. Stapletons Didimus,[c] M[r] Renoldes against Whitacres, and suche others, who are muche more ernest against the present state then this other book of succession, w[ch] speaketh so myldlie, and indifferently, as he can iustly offend no parte. And howe our spirituall masters, beinge not able to answere, discovered them selves and their fellowes vnder pretence of spirit and religion to be Scotists in faction, w[t]hout any respect of religion at all there but beinge to sett vp a knowne heretick, and thereby also to meddle more in matters of state and to offend nowe the present state then by any other waye that is yet knowne. So as in this they have neither reason, religion, nor state w[th] them, but only emulation, follie, and faction. And so I vnderstand that the elder of these two hathe vnder his oathe since that tyme recalled this proposition of him self, sayinge that he alloweth not thereof, but rather

47, f. 134b.

---

[a] The Conference about the next Succession, by N. Doleman (*i.e.*, Parsons), was published in 1594. Parliament in the following year made it high treason to possess a copy.

[b] The writer may mean that the Six Questions on the deposing power of the Pope, extracted from, or based upon, Sanders' *De Visibili Monarchia* and Bristowe's *Motives*, and proposed to priests on their trial for alleged treason in 1582, contributed to the death of those who were then executed. No instance is known of anyone being put to death for the possession or dissemination of Sanders' books. His *De Schismate Anglicano* was not printed till 1585. But William Carter, a printer, was hanged in 1584 for reprinting Dr. Gregory Martin's *Treatise of Schism* (see *Lingard*, vol. vi., Appendix, note QQ.); and Alfield, a priest, and Webley, a dyer, suffered the same penalty in 1585 for importing and distributing copies of Allen's *Modest Defence*. The handling of Bristowe's *Motives* was fatal, indeed, to both James Duckett, the printer, and Bullock, his binder, but this was in 1602, and therefore after the date of the present letter.

[c] Apologia pro rege Catholico, authore Didymo Veridico Henfildano (*i.e.*, Thomas Stapleton of Henfield), Constantiæ [1592].

THE TWO DEPUTIES AT ROME. 115

thinketh that the said book of succession hathe done more good then hurt in England. And so you see howe these matters goe. ffare yow well hartily and comend me to all o^r ffrendes wth yowe.

Yo^{rs}
M. A.

Endorsed : Mart. Arrayes letter, 1599.

4. *Fifth letter of the Proctors (written by Array), with account of their Pleadings before the Pope's Commissioners.* 47, f. 135.

In another hand : M^r. Blackwells proctors in Rome. What they obiected against ye embass. Much against D^r. Bagshawe. The Emb. were hard, 17 Feb., 1599.

Most dear frend. I promysed yo^u at ye first aryvall of our embass. here to aduertise from fournight to fornight how matters went and so have I donne punctually by foure seuerall letters vntill now y^t I have expected 3 weekes to see what would be the issue of the matter committed by his holines speciall commission to Card. Caiet. & Burgheses to be examined and hard deligently by way of congregation as befor I have written at the English college y^t self, and so it was vpon Wensday 17 of this moneth when, after sundrie informations had from Monsig^r Acarionio,^a fiscall of his hol. congregation of reformation, that had taken there seuerall examinations, vpon theire othes. And after they had read & vewed such letters memorialls & papers as the Embass. had browght withe them they cam ioyntly together to the colledg vpon the forsaid day & wth them the said fiscall, and there, having a convenient seate & tribunall provided in forme of judgment they hard the whole

---

^a Acarisio. Parsons calls him "Signor Acaritius Squarsiontus, Canon of St. John Laterans" (*Apologie,* f. 121).

cause. And first ech of Embass: confession and declaration seuerally reade by the notarie of the cause, wch were long, & euery one of more then an howres reading. And then was ech of them willed to say yf he had any thinge to adde to his declaration more then he had theire sett downe. And after this ther papers & letters browght wth them were sene agayne by the said Judges, wher of the most part were translated into laten and, bysydes that, were allso f. persons Rector of the college and f. henrie Tichborne prefect of the studies willed to be present to interpret any thing that should be needfull. And after this agayne were booth Embass: called in ioyntly, as allso M^r. Doctor haddock and myself as procurators of the Arch[priest] and of the clergie vnited vnto hym appoynted by letters from thence and allowed here by his holiness wth whome we had ben and had audience particuler about this affaire befor, and being come in we were willed as procurators to speake what we had to say in this behalfe. Our speache in effect was that albeyt yt greued vs much to be drawen to accuse or plead agaynst our own brethren preistes that had ben of the same college and nurserie here in Rome and gone hence into England ioyntly to laboure and aduenture our lyfes for the same cause of the Catholique faith (thought we before them), yet that there manner of proceding had bin and was so preiudiciall to our comon peace & vnion and soe scandalouse to all good & modest men, that either wee must oppose our selves against them in the nam[es][a] of our head & of all the rest of our Catholike bodie in England & abrode, or else wee shoulde see[m] to betraye the same cause impugned by them. Wherfore wee prayed their graces not to be scandalized to see this division amongest vs, for that these were the moathes that breede [in] the best cloathes & the wormes that were commonlie fownde vnder the barck of everie tree y[f] they were not looked vnto in tyme. And that this happened also in ye verie primatyve church permitted by God for the better proofe & exercise of

---

[a] The edge of the MS. for a few lines hence mutilated or discoloured.

good men. And that this was a verie heresie in manners &
actions, as the other of protestants was in faithe & religion ; and
that this woulde breake into that in tyme if it were not looked
into, as in dyvers it had donne alredye and must needes doe,
for that it was contention fownded vpon ye same growndes of
emulation, envye, ambition, hatred, covetousnes & libertie of
liffe as the other heresie was & wrought a spiri[t] conforme
to that in all respects. And then wee gave vpp a wrytinge
wch before had be[n] exhibited to his hol. and was remitted
hether as it seemeth; and the notarie red it openlie & it conteyned in effect to this sense that followeth: That these men
came hether onlie to . . . . the peace of Englande and to renewe
styrrs in Rome, and that of their owne heads as . . . . seemed
for that they had brought noe one letter of credence wth them of
superior or othe[r to] his holi: Protector, or other men in rome.
They shewed no commission nor anie accord [. . . .] consent of
preestes to stande to what they shoulde treate, nor woulde they
stand to all [that] was sett downe by particuler persons in cer-
teyn open scrolles that they had brought wth them, wch scrolles,
beinge to the number of 23, sixtene of them were found to be **47, f. 135b.**
agaynst them for that they were written before the Archp^t was
appoynted by his holines and they demaunded only a Bishopp or
some that showld have like authoritie, wch allso being graunted
they remayned content, as by their later letters and subscriptions
did appear, wch we shewed, and that they had submitted them
selfes to the Archp^r. the other six or seuen scrolles or letters that
were in in deede of the principall authors of this embasige did not
agree amongst them selfes, and the embassadors did disclame
openly from the principall pointes demaunded therein, as namely
the makinge of many Byshopes or at least two archpreistes one
opposed to the other, the changing of the protector, the changing
of the gouerment of this and other colleges, wherin they protested
that they were now fullie of an other mynd and had found this
college in so quiet and good estat and had seene such matters by

readinge over the last visitation of Card. Sega and other authenticall writtings as they had vtterly changed theire judgement abouut these affayers and stures in Rome in such sort as they never meant more to open theire mouthes in lyk demaundes nor in defence of the late demissed or of others that had bin trowblesome here.

We alledged further how these men would not obey ye Archip^t. in Ingland and others by their example, had followed the like course of disobedience, and that it was a plaine Schisme that they sought to make, confessinge them selfes vpon their othes that they knewe not abouc twelve fourtene or fivetene preists in all Ingland that would take theire partes against the rest whome they seemed [a] to thincke to be neere three hundred. And the protector said well neer 200 had written to hym agaynst this sedition. We towched more over breefly the singular ingratitud these men and theire fellowes vsed agaynst the fathers of the Societie in going abouut everie way to sclander imbouge [?] in common obloque in recompence of theire great laboures for vs in all countreyes and procuringe vs so many seminaries and maintenance for them and breeding vpe so many preists who afterwarde by insitation of these seditious spirites were made enemyes to them to the notorious infamie of our nation wth all princes that knewe their merites and benefitts towardes vs, wherevnto the Cardinalles did seeme greatlie to geve consent and one of them reported that agayne afterwarde.

Finally not to hold yo^u more in leght we charged them wth five or six great scandalls and publicke damages offered to our common cause by this iourney. As first the iust offence and iniurie offered to theres and our superiours the Archip^t, protector, and his hol. in this willfull acte of theirs, and namely theire seeking to disgrace that man of our nation for whom all the whole bodie of Catholickes will testifie agaynst them. I mean Mr. Blackw[ell], for whom we had many graue testimonies here allso reade as well of principall persons in Ingland as of flaunders and other partes. And

---

[a] Or perhaps "faind." The writing is not clear.

as their abuse of the protector we would not vrge, as well for that he was present, as allso for verie shame of our Inglish ingratitude, he being the best and most louingest noble man lightly that lyueth, and most affectionate to vs all, as yo{{u}} in part do knowe. And secondly y{{e}} offence and iniurie offered to all the bodie of quiet priests ioyned to their superiour, their Archip{{t}}, in all whose names these men would have it thought at the beginning that they cam seing they still said they dealt in y{{e}} name of the priests w{{t}}hout distinction. Thirdly the scandall geven to lay gentlemen that are Catholiques who before thought our clergie to be vnited. fourthly y{{e}} conforth and cause of lawghture and triumph geven herby to heretiques and specially to the councell. fivethly the iust occasion geven to the fathers of the Societie to retyre them selfes from us in all places, wherby our whole cause would fall to the ground, none of these seditions havinge credite, wisdome, or autho- ritie to susteyne the lest peece thereof. And lastly the universall scandall to all men in fraunce, flanders, Spayne and Italie where these Embass. have passed or their iourney hath ben knowen or written and specially here in Rome making men to weene therby that all is in sedition and diuision among vs in Ingland and we are intractable natures and that most of mens sufferinges there is rather of contention and willfull obstinacie then of vertue w{{ch}} is most false and opprobrious to our cause, wherfore we desired remedie in this behalf and exhibited diuers letters of the Doctors of Doway and of Mr. Wright y{{e}} Deane of cortrek and of other grave men of our nation to this effect.[a] Against all w{{ch}} the Embassators were able to say litle & willinge to say lesse, but only excused their own intentions and asked pardon if they had geven scandall by theire maner of proceeding more than euer they ment. And in truth I vnderstand of certayne that they are verie sorie and ashamed of there iourney and do further say they were deceyued & evill informed there in Ingland and that by considera-

47, f. 136.

---

[a] These letters are printed in Parsons' *Briefe Apologie*, ff. 125-127.

tion and reflextion they perceyue that diuers contentious & dissolute spirites would shrewed them selfes vnder this cloake of ther partie & that diuers are like ynought to proue heretickes in the ende.

The two Car^{alls}, after all this was said, made seuerall speeches vnto them shewinge first how much his hol. was offended wth this their iourney and attempt, and that of hym self he had caused them to be apprehended and had so determyned in Ferrara, yf they had arrived there, that this contention was dishonorable to our nation and caused that all men did see the groundes thereof to be naught. And they [sic] ingratitude offered by vs to the fathers of the societie to be great, they laboringe for vs in all partes as they did. And that f. Persons had much at the beginning to have bishops in Ingland and caused the protecter to speake abount, not only to his hol. but to all the Card^{alls} of the inquisition, to whome his hol. had remitted the consultation, and that his holines would not yeld to it at the end for diuers particulare considerations for the present. And this did Cardinall Burgheses allso, being one of the inquisition, avouch in particular and added more over the great myslik that he had of the troblesome schollers while they were here and he vice protecter calling in Italian discoli et seditiosi, and saing that his hol. meant seuerely to haue layd his hand vpon them had not the matter ben ended sweetly as it was by the industrie of others. And finallie booth of them exhorting the Ambassators to a new course of proceedinge and that they should persuade the same to theire frindes. They said they would relate the whole processe to his hol. who showld geve sentence what was further to be donne, and so they departed leavinge the Embassators to be deteyned as before.

Amonge ye letters and papers y^t they brought wth them I vnderstand that principall were from D. Bags[haw], three or foure in number, but such in qualitie and spirite as made men wounder, hearing otherwyse that he was in prison for the cause he is, some of them were in latin wherein were certayne quicke pro-. positions as is cito indignabitur confratrum nostrorum libertas si prematur.ᵃ And Agayne, Hierarchia solis et liberis seminariorum suffragijs instituenda nobis est, and other such like sownding only to libertie. Then was there a large invectiue against yᵉ superiour and rules admitted by the greater part of his felowes in Wisbich wᵗʰ many bitter scoffes comparing there Governor to the sewdicall congregation of Geneua and their rules to the lawes and customes of Anabaptistes & reuined arians especially in [this] that they appoynted hym only to sitt in highest place in the refectorie that was to say grace for that day & all others to sitt as they came. Against wᶜʰ order he inveheight most bitterly throughout all his large letter as though it had bin most uniust wicked and absurdest point in the world, at wᶜʰ the Cardᵃˡˡˢ booth laughed and marueled greatlye inquiring of the tyme of his being in this Roman College, yt was found regestered in the comon book that in the moneth of Januarij 1585 he was put furth of the said college by Cardinall Boncompagnio ye protector for his vnquiet behauiour.ᵇ And others here that had knowen his affayers in Oxford could testifie of his like behauiour there & of his turbulent dealing for geting the heedeshipe of Glocester Hall and missing thereof he cam over so as men marueyled not so much of his maner of writting and dealing now suteable to the same humor. And further I must tell you that sence that tym letters are come from yoʳ partes and from flaunders relatinge further of the said D. that vpon his late being at London foure good men whome he most mysliked were called from Wisbich and some of them sent to the Tower and new seraches haue ben made, more priestes taken, And the Archpᵗ in daunger yf not taken. All wᶜʰ together wᵗʰ the circumstance of the keper of Wisbich his good speache of the D. and others like hym selfe & that the D. wth other of his crew are to goe to dwell in place of the other remoued do make matters verie suspicious. And at this verie instante I haue sene a letter of yᵉ 3 of Januarij

47, f. 13 b.

ᵃ Compare Puncta Principalia, *infra*, p. 126.

ᵇ Upon this matter see "An Answear of Mr. Doctor Bagshaw to certayne pointes of a libell," &c., printed in Dr. Ely's *Certaine Briefe Notes*, p. 331.

fro Doway of the principall ther who do say that 3 dayes before there passed one Browne that way and was newly come out of Ingland and had a messanger for the said D. to his frind at Lile willing hym to writt a letter of defiance to f. Persons and charge hym to have suborned f. Walpoole to send in one squire to draw the said D. and his frindes into suspicion of killing the Quene and this he will prove to the whole world. And others from other places do writt that he should [have] geven owt in Ingland as delivered by word that the said f. Walpoole writt to hym in the name of Nicholas fitchherbart by the said f. Persons persuasion to counsell hym and some of his frindes to ioyne wth the Spaniardes when they should come.[a] All wch euery man seeth how childish fictions they be and were at the beginning to procede only from the heretickes (in wch sense allso I have answered the divise of Squire as shortly yo{u} will see, for I knewe the man in Spayne) but now it seameth that the said D : hath a hand in it hym selfe allso or will have, therby to vtter his stomake agaynst that man vnto whome all and our holl cause ys so much bounde as the world knoweth And the D. in particulare yf pride and passion did not blynd hym from seing and acknowledging the same, And I feare me that his end will shew (and that over quickly yf god have not mercy over hym) how grevious in the sight of his Devine ma{tie} these synnes of sedition, trouble, and diuision ar in such a cause as ours is and ye present exemples, Secheverell, Ithell and some others fallen that way to plaine Apostacie may teache us, yet lett vs be of good comfourt for all will proue to god's glorie in the end and to the meritt of good men. And this is the last pushe of ye Divill as I suppose and hope, & wth this I leave yo{u} and send yo{u} the hartie com-

---

[a] The affair of Squiers' plot and his alleged connection with F. Walpole is fully discussed by Dr. Jessopp in his *One Generation of a Norfolk House*, pp. 290-297. Squiers declared that he had a letter from Walpole for Bagshaw but that he (Squiers) had thrown it into the sea. The Council, believing that Bagshaw was implicated in the supposed plot, summoned him from Wisbech to London for examination, Oct. 1598. See also *Jesuits and Seculars*, p. lxxix.

mendacons of all yor good frindes from hence where all goeth as well as yo^u or they could wish especially for ye blessed state of ye college, where nothinge but vertue peace & confourt ys seen, wch god continew & preserue ever, this 20 of februarij 1599.

5. *From William Bishop.*   47, f. 125.
20 Feb., 1599.

Jesus Maria.

Good Sir, As well to certifie yo^u of o^r affaires as to satisfie the rest of o^r brethren I have thought it expedient to writte vnto yo^u this breyfe of all o^r negotiation. Arriving at Rome somewhat late by reason of many lettes by the way, we found the citie as it were fullie possessed wth certification and exclamations from all coastes against vs as seditious persons sent from a few tumultuous & restles spirites to the scandall of the good in England, & euery place els & to the great contentations of o^r aduersaries here in Rome to trouble the court yf they would admitt vs, & to renewe the old stirres of the colleage yf we were lett alon, wheruppon his holines, who was so much troubled wth the former tumultes that he may not abid to here of any such other, condescended vnto their petitions that also further enformed hym that yf we were lett alon he should never want some such as should alwayes hereafter trouble & molest the courte & citie wth english striffes & contentions. And so we were not long after o^r comming to Rome apprehended, & had gone to prison had not f. Parsons, to saue o^r credites, spoken for vs & taken vs into the colleage, where we haue now bin almost eight weekes shutt up in chambers, as Mr Charnocke hath (as I vnderstand) more at large declared vnto yo^u, during wch tyme by reason of o^r examinations I haue had

---

ᵃ The letter of Charnock here referred to did not reach those to whom it was addressed until after the receipt of the papal Brief confirming the appointment of the archpriest and compelling the submission of the malcontents. Bishop's letter had arrived "some 17 or 18 days" before the Brief (Colleton, p. 76).

much conference concerning all the pointes of o^r message, the some wherof I will write vnto yo^u breifly. first towching Byshoppes the matter hath bin allreadie (to vse Card. Burgetius termes) most diligently discussed in the congregation of ye inquisition & found not meet for the present estate of o^r contrey, and to joyne next o^r last point of the colleage it is by comon report so quieted and all things ranged into so good order that f. Parsons therby hath not a litle encreased his creditte w^{t}h his holines & in the whole courte, so that there was no dealing in yt matter. Concerning o^r Archipresbiter he hath so plentifull approbat[i]on out of our own contry, such high commendacons out of all coastes abroad, soe mightie support in this place, that it had ben but meere follie for vs meane men sent but from a fewe to have opposed o^r selfes agaynst hym. especially having not any great matter lawfullie proved to alleage for exception agaynst hym. as for that point of free election it hath place where there is Deane & Chapter, wch faylinge w^{t}h vs the right of election reuolueth vnto hym that hath charge of the flocke. A long tyme I stood in defence of o^r sodalitie intended; but at last perceaving that o^r superiour not being subordinate vnto the Archp^r he must needes be as it were an other head of hym self, And so there should be continuallie two equalles together, wch would be a perpetuall mayntenaunce of debate & contention, ech syd in favoure of his owne part & vnder hope of his superioures supporte more boldlie & freelie contradictinge & resistinge the one thother, wch is taken of the wiser sort not to be tollerable in any good gouernment, to this yf we adde that wch vppon better aduice I have more deptlie considered I thincke that yo^u will scarecelye like of that diuision for all be it you my self, and manie more wch I knowe have a verie good meaning in this separation & would behave our selfes soe that noe honest man should have iust cause to mislike of vs: yet there would some such (I feare) be of o^r companye for evill affected towardes some of sounder sort of catholickes & the best meanes we have to vpholde o^r religion that I, to tell you playnly, should as I thincke be ashamed of their companie, and deame it much more sure in the way of saluation to joine wth them who following o^r zealous and most prudent predecessors steppes do sowndlie go forward wth the holye worke of the conuersion of our contrey then to harke to others whoe tormented wth the spirite of contradiction can not soe well discerne the better way to draw vnto an end. I thinck we shall optayne the sacrament of confirmation and the consecration of oyles, and yf any further favo^r happen vnto any of o^r part it most be through the fauour of father Parsons, & by our lord protectors benevolense. all that is past shalbe pardoned, And great good will is promysed vppon amendment. Wherfor, good Sir, having donne our endeuoures to remedie matters as we thought, they should lett us now rest in peace as men that have discharged theire duties & conforme our selfes to the present gouernment, wch descendeth from our superiours. And then yf anythinge fall out othere wyse then well we shalbe free from the blame of it. And yf it happen to be better then we expected we shalbe glad for our countrey sake. Aud trulie I rather pittie those wch in this tyme be called to preferment then envye at theire aduauncement, for besydes the great charge they vndertake to gouerne well, whereof they most render a straight accompt vnto o^r just judge, They are as it were called furth to be better knowen & more narrowlie searched after by those that wyshe them litle good. Yo^u knowe how true that sentence is in o^r contrey, bene vixit qui bene latuit, wherfor desiring o^r most mylde Sauiour to send vs, in force of that his feruent prayer vt omnes vnum sint, etc., Jo. 17., the comfortable spirite of vnitie & myldenes, I comitt yo^u and the rest of o^r good brethren vnto his holie protection. I long to see [you] & the rest of my frendes there. I pray yo^u continewe yor prayers for our safe returne. At Rome the xx^th of februarij 1599.

47, f. 125b.

yo^urs in his prayers,

W. B.

I had forgotten an especiall point, wch is that our lord protector publickelie beinge assisted by Card^all Burgesio affirmed all this that had bin donne agaynst vs here, or was before donne towching o^r Archip^t., was by order of his holines,[a] the wch allso of diuers others we have credibly herd, so that they are too blame that will other wyse thincke of hym. Thus desyring you to do my humble dutie vnto o^r superiour the Archip^rt I byd yo^u once agayn adewe.

6. *Puncta Principalia.*

Puncta principalia et secreta quæ habent in mandatis duo sacerdotes inquieti ex Anglia venientes ut ex literulis et memorialibus patet quæ secum attulerunt 29 decembris 1598.[b]

---

[a] In reference to a similar postscript in Charnock's letter, Colleton writes (*Just Defence*, p. 79) : " When maister Charnoche wrote his letter unto us, by the appointment of the Cardinalls, for a finall end of their durance as father Owen reporteth, and father Parsons had the perusing thereof a night and a day, it was broughte againe unto him by father Owen, with order from father Parsons to adde that the subordination erected was the order of his Holinesse, who, answering he could not write so, because he knew it not, the other replied, that the Cardinall protector sayd it when he sate in judgement in the cause, and that father Parsons affirmed the same, and therefore he might well and truly write that to his knowledge the archpresbitership was the appointment of his Holinesse. Whereupon the prisoner, being willing to give the fathers the most contentment he could for his speedier riddance out of prison, promised him to write in so large a manner in that point as possibly he could with any truth, and accordingly signified in his letter yet not that he knew the subordination to be the order of his Holinesse, but that he heard the Cardinal to affirme it and also understood it by the credible relation of others. The like wrote Mr. Bishop, and not unlikely on the same persuasion." On the other hand Signor Acarisio, the fiscal, stated distinctly to both the prisoners apart that the new superiority was *not* instituted by the pope's command and that the pope himself had told him so (*Ibid.*, p. 34). In any case (as Colleton remarks) no one ventured to affirm that the unusual jurisdiction and faculties annexed to the archpresbytery proceeded from the pope's ordinance.

[b] This document is written on the third page of the preceding letter and in the same hand. The language is, however, not that of the appellants but of their opponents.

1. Vt archipresbyteratus S^{tis} suæ iussu per Card. protectorem in Anglia institutus revocetur eo quod ab istius factionis hominibus neque expetitus neque approbatus fuerit.

2. Quod talis Hierarchia sit instituenda in Anglia quæ solis et liberis seminariorum suffragijs (hæc enim verba eorum sunt) approbetur ex quo fit vt neque S^{mo} Pontifici neque protectori aliquid ea in re relinquatur.

3. Quod ordinatio $archip^{ri}$ per suam S^{tem} in Anglia iam instituta ideo non sit admittenda quod absque notitia presbyterorum istorum (licet paucissimorum) et contra antiquos, vt aiunt, ecclesiæ canones et contra Angliæ consuetudinem sit introducta, quod probare etiam conantur ex Can. nullus dist. 61 et Can. vlt. d. 63.

4. Quod nullus episcopus inuitis aut non petentibus clericis ordinari debeat a S^{mo} Pontifice in vllo loco. Atque eorum doctrinam disseminari per Angliam hoc tempore constat quo spes est conuersionis Regni ne tunc pontifex episcopos instituere possit sed ipsis relinquatur libera rerum omnium perturbatio.

5. Si huius archipresbyteri authoritas revocari non poterit tunc fiat ipsemet episcopus et alius vna cum illo ex horum hominum factione qui hanc partem foueat atque sustentet universamque Angliam inter se diuisam habeant.

6. Si episcopum suæ factionis obtinere non possunt, enitantur saltem aliquot assistentes ex suo numero habere qui factiosis immediate præsint.

7. Vt protector alius obtineatur nationi Anglicanæ qui magis huic factiosorum parti sit propitius.

8. Vt aliquis Cardinalis eiusdem Nationis illis creetur qui negotia ipsorum tractet.

9. Vt collegium Romanum a regimine Jesuitarum transferatur ad regimen presbyterorum Anglicanæ Nationis qui ex horum factione sint, quo, vt ipsi aiunt, liberior sit et Anglorum naturæ convenientior ingenuorum juvenum educatio.

10. Vt Associatio quædam istorum hominum a sua sc^{te} approbatur cuius regulas in scriptis se mississe vna cum his duobus

sacerdotibus dicunt asserentes insuper hos associatos paratos fore vt rebus Jesuitarum ac aliorum eis fauentium se opponant.

11. Concludunt tamen in quibusdam literis dom[in]ationum contrariæ sibi partis non esse vocandam pacem, sed vnicuique rei vocabulum suum reddendum esse sic sentire ipsos ac confratres suos quorum cito (inquiunt) indignabitur libertas si prematur. Vnde patet libertatem in omnibus ab eis quæri.

47, f. 126b.

Cardinal Cajetan to Parsons.
[*On the back of* Puncta Principalia, *and in another hand.*]

Reverende in Christo pater cum partim adversa valetudine partim alijs rebus impediti non possumus tam celeriter quam cupimus duorum sacerdotum Anglorum, Guilelmi Bushopi et Roberti Charnoci, causam quam nobis cognoscendam S^{mus} commissit expedire interim quia tam V. R. quam alijs referentibus intellexerimus eos Jubelæum hebdomada præterita percepisse atque inde ob omni censurarum impedimento si quas forte incurrissent, liberos esse, melius etiam isti . . [a] ac paratius se gerrere facultatem illis damus celebrandi sacra quoad causam eorum plenius audierimus et si quando et R. $V^{æ}$ expedire videbitur vt extra eorum cubicula per ambulacrum aliquod collegij ad tempus illis præscriptum separatim se recreent eius rei facimus licentiam modo in cæteris maneant vt nunc sunt quousque a nobis auditi fuerint, quod breui admodum futurum speramus. Ex edibus nostris die sexto februarij 1599.

Endorsement of Nos. 5 and 6 :
20 Feb., 1599.

The copie of a letter wch Mr. Bisshop, as it seemeth, or else one in his name, writeth to Dr. Bagshawe or some other of yt parte signifying that there is no remedy but that they must yeald to ye subordination :

[a] Blotted.

Here is also a copie of Mr. Biss: & Mr. Charnockes instruction what they shuld desyre.

The copie of a letter from Cardinal Caietan, as it seemeth to Parsons: y^t Mr. Bissh: & Mr. Charnocke, having receaved ye pardon of ye Jubilye, might haue liberty to say masse, & to walk out of theire chambers.

7. *Libell:* 47, f. 138.

Obiecta de Seditione S^{mo}: D: oblata contra duo presbyteros Bish: et Ch: per Rich: Haddo: et Mar: Ar: in causa Arch^{ri}: procuratores constitutos, die 10 *Januarij* 1599.

Cum S^{mus}: D: N: turbas, et tumultus in Anglorum collegio de Vrbe factiosorum quorundam molitionibus excitatos turbulentorum diuisione anno superiori prudentissime sustulisset, summamque pacem, vnionem, et deuotionem, quibus hodie fruuntur tam scholares, quam patres, pijssime constituisset, et ad eorundem dissidiorum reliquias ex Anglia quoque tollendas Hierarchiam quandam Sacerdotum secularium inter se sub vno Archipresbytero et 12 Asistentibus, seu Consultoribus per Ill^{mi} Cardinalis Protectoris literas ordinasset; boni omnes et quietj ingenij homines tam ex clero, quam Laici, non solum libenter, sed exultanter amplexi sunt; isti vero duo cum paucissimis alijs obedire nolentibus, ac factiones facientibus et calcitare cæperunt, aliosque contra suæ S^{ctis} ordinationem concitare, aliaque ad turbas, et seditiones spectantia moliri, provt hic dicetur.

2. Statim atque D: Georgius Blackwellus Archip^r constitutus, vir omni genere virtutis, eruditionis, ac grauitatis præditus, authoritatem quam Ill^{mi} Cardinalis Caietanj literis testatam Roma transmissam accepisset, sciens aliquos ex hijs proteruioris ingenij esse qui facile tumultuarentur, vocauit ad se perhumaniter duo Joannem nimirum Coll[eton] et Robertun hunc Char[nock] qui præcipui factiosorum Lo[ndini] commorantium sciebantur, iisque exposuit quid sua sanctitas instituisset, et quem in finem, nimirum vt pax

inter sacerdotes Capite constituto conseruaretur ; literas etiam Ill^{mi} Cardinalis legendas præbuit, rogans vt fraterne, ac pacate ijsdem obedirent, seque paratissimum esse, vt omnibus inseruiret.

Ipsi vero nihil credere neque acquiescere, sed hæsitare ad omnia, non admittere authoritatem, vocare in dubium num vera essent quæ literis illis continebantur, S^{mi} iussu hoc esse constitutum, et si verum id erat, dubitare tamen an Pontifex facere possit vt ipsis inconsultis ac inuitis superiorem ijs constitueret, quod postea etiam quam Roman appulerunt, dicere, ac sæpius etiam repetere non sunt veriti, vt per testes idoneos probare possumus, ex quo non tantum arrogantia, ac peruersitas, sed ignorantia etiam ostenditur.

3. Neque solum verbis contradicere cæperunt, sed conuenticula inter se agitare, et consilia inire de resistendo Pontificis per Ill^m Protectorem ordinationi vt ex literis ipsius Archipresbiteri constat, qui his rebus coactus necesse habuit hoc ipsum ijs interdicere ne grauiorem inde seditionem per Angliam concitarent, sed illi duo parere nolentes Romam quoque proficisci se velle contradicendj studio significabant.

4. Et quanquam non potuerunt non intelligere quanta scandala, et quam grauia damna causæ Catholicæ Anglicanæ ex hac ipsorum secessione sequutura esset: nihil tamen de contentionis studio remittere valuerunt, neque vllam publicæ vtilitatis, aut ædificationis habere rationem : itaque secutum est primo, vt omnes illi presbyteri qui cum suo capite (id est) Archipresbytero vniti sunt, grauiter lædantur, atque offendantur, vt ex ipsorum frequentibus literis ad Protectorem patet. 2º Vt Catholici Laici nobilesque qui hac ipsorum profectione dissidia inter sacerdotes animaduerterunt, vehementer inde scandalizati fuerint. 3º Secutum est etiam vt hæretici et persecutores audita hac seditione mirifice, tanquam re ad propositum valde vtili, lætentur. 4º Per Galliam, et Italiam, et Romæ præcipue, aures, mentesque hominum impleuerunt magnarum factionum et contentionum in Anglia vigentium opinionibus quod tamen falsum (quid enim sunt 10 factiosi ad 300 plus minus presbyteros pacificos et ad multa Laicorum Catholicorum millia cum illis coniunctissime niuentium?) tum etiam

causæ Anglicanæ valde ignominiosum, de qua ignominia, aliisque damnis hos accusamus apud suam Sanctitatem.

5. Accusamus eos præterea, quod ex suo capite sine vllis literis credentialibus ad suam Sc^{tem} vel ad Ill^m Protectorem, vel ad vllum alium Romæ existentem scriptis, quibus aliorum nomine se missos esse constet, profectionem hanc susceperunt. Tantum enim afferunt literulas quasdam, seu schedulas apertas Sacerdotum inter se ad inuicem pugnantes, qui si vllius authoritatis sunt, contra hos ipsos faciunt. Nam cum ad 30 plus minus subscriptiones presbyterorum contineant, maior eorum pars scripta fuit ante triennium priusquam Archip^{ri} authoritas per suam Sc^{tem} constituta esset, et hi tantummodo Episcopum postulant, aut aliquem Episcopali iurisdictione præditum quod jam per Archip^r constitutionem completum est: alia vero pars inquietorum est quorundam, qui tamen non eadem postulant, quæ isti neque isti approbare se dicunt, quæ illi suis literis proponunt; ita vt, neque cum suis, neque cum alienis vlla sit iudiciorum vel rerum tractandarum concordia.

6. Itaque affirmamus hos duos nihil quicquam afferre momenti præter contentionis studium, propriaque peruicacia Romam aduenisse ad pacem Anglicanam perturbandam, nullam autem ab alijs vel etiam factionis suæ authoritatem certam habere, neque vllam instructionem adferre de quibus rebus agant, vel quæ postulent; neque vllo modo constare, quod alij quorum literas ostendunt, stare velint ijs, quæ ab his proponuntur, vel promittuntur. Literæ vero scriptæ antequam Archipresbyter constitueretur, manifesta fraude nunc ab istis producuntur, tanquam si contra Archipresbyteri authoritatem essent, et pro illo potius sunt, quia vel Episcopum, vel Episcopalem authoritatem habentem sibi præfici tantum postulabant, quo iam ordinato illi libenter acquieuerunt, de hac igitur fraude hos etiam accusamus.

7. Præterea dicimus, quod licet hi duo ad vitandam manifestæ seditionis opinionem verbis dicunt se pacem quærere, et moderatiora quædam media ad illam promovendam afferre; re ipsa tamen tam ex verbis, ac memorialibus ipsorum, quam ex sociorum

suorum literis, quas secum afferunt constat eos alia multa in mandatis habere, quæ plena seditionis sunt, qualia videntur de Archipresbyteratu reuocando, de prouehendis ad Episcopatum aliquibus ex suis factiosis, nominatim de Cardinale aliquo Anglo procurando, de mutando Protectore, de regimine Collegij Anglicani de Vrbe ad presbyteros sui ordinis transferendo, aliaque similia, quæ totius Causæ Anglicanæ perturbationem continent.

47, f. 139.
8. Non paucas etiam habent in suis scripturis literisque expositiones, quæ eandem plane superbiam ac seditionem sapiunt, qualis est illa supra memorata, quod sua S^{tas} non possit, neque debeat dare ijs superiorem ipsis non petentibus, inconsultis, vel inuitis, quod diuersis etiam personis hic Romæ dixerunt. Item quod talis Hierarchia in Anglia sit instituenda, quæ solis, ac liberis Seminariorum suffragijs approbetur, quo constat eos omnia suis arbitrijs permitti velle. Item quod cito indignabitur libertas ipsorum si prematur, quo nihil arrogantius, aut petulantius dici potest, aliaque similia : ex quibus omnibus constat, quo spiritu ducuntur hi factiosi, et quo tandem prorumpant, nisi a sua S^{te} mature coerceantur.

9. Insuper spiritus eorum inde cognosci potest, quod cum in Castro ad 30 plus minus sacerdotes essent, accidit vt minor longè pars turbas non exiguas admonita a bonis excitauit. Vnus (viz. ex minore ista parte) scandalose mortuus est: Alius manifeste apostatauit: Sex qui remanent, quorum dux ob seditionem eiectus est ex Collegio Anglicano Romano Anno Dni 1585 publica Protectoris sententia, cum istis contra Archipresbyterum se coniungunt et mediam partem suffragiorum faciunt, quæ isti duo pro se afferunt, reliqui 19 pro Archipresbytero stant. paucissimi ergo sunt per dei gratiam inquieti, et ideo grauius castigandi, quod tantæ bonorum multitudini unionique tam peruersè se opponant.

10. Hoc etiam idem de spiritu discordiæ ac seditionis inde cernitur, quòd ipsummet pacis medium, quod isti proponunt, nihil in se habet aliud quam contentionem: Nam cum duo sint presbyterorum in Anglicana vinea hodie laborantium genera, vnum religiosorum Societatis Jesu sub vno sui ordinis Superiore degen-

tium; aliud sacerdotum secularium Archipresbytero subiectorum, qui omnes summa cum concordia, ac vnione inter se conglutinati cernuntur: isti vellent tertium genus institui, suorum scilicet factiosorum, quod cum nullo priorum conveniret, sed bellis perpetuis cum vtrisque digladiaretur. Si enim isti pauci, qui nunc sine capite et viribus molestias inferunt, S^{tis} suæ authoritatem haberent, simili affectu dissidiorum contra patres Societatis, ac Archipresbyterum suosque præditum,[a] (nullum enim alium sibi pro superiori nisi huiusmodi spiritus hominem admitterent) quis non videt quantæ inde turbæ ac tumultus statim excitarentur?

11. Preterea ex posterioribus ex Anglia literis vidimus rempublicam quandam novam recenter ab istis excogitatam, plenam ambitione, vanitate, ac seditione in qua insignis contentio est de Cathedris in Cænis, et de prærogatiuis, quorum 22 discrimina proponuntur; de expellendis etiam ab Anglia omnis generis religiosorum ordinibus agitur, et alia multa ad contentiones, ac seditiones spectantia decernuntur.

12. Quare cum haec ita sint, ut isti seditiosi ex Anglia recesserint, et Archipresbyterum suum, virum Apostolicum, ac totius fere nationis facile . . . .[b] eminentissimum, decessione hac sua plurimum afflixerint, aliosque, ne illi parerent, verbis exemploque suo retardauerint: cum Patres quoque Societatis Jesu homines innocentes, industrios, ac optime de Anglia nostra, nobisque omnibus meritos, qui sanguinem pro colenda Anglia fuderunt, multaque nobis Seminaria varijs in locis procurârunt, aliaque beneficia contulerunt, verbis, factisque suis ingratissimè violarint, ac in hominum obloquium susurrationibus suis tanquam malè se gerentes induxerint (cum nihil tamen contra eos legitimè probatum proferre posse ipsi fateantur) cumque tota hæc eorum profectio ad seditiones, et ad ea turbanda pertinet, quæ sua S^{tas} prudentissime tam in Anglia, quam hic Romæ pro pace stabilienda constituit, nos infra scripti Pro-

47, f. 139b.

[a] Something here must be incorrectly copied.
[b] Word obliterated by damp.

curatores tam reuerendi Archipresbyteri, quam reliqui Cleri Anglicani, ac omnium Catholicorum nomine petimus, vt pæna aliqua idonea in istos duos statuatur, ne alij simili exemplo insolescant: et vt in Angliam non reuertantur, saltem ad tempus, quo meliorem de se suisque ad pacem conatibus satisfactionem dederint. hoc enim non tantum nostrum est ac bonorum omnium, qui in Anglia viuunt, iudicium, sed grauiorum etiam virorum gentis nostræ alibi viuentium, vt ex subiectis eorum testimonijs constat:—

Exemplar literarum D. Rich: Barretti Præsidis Collegij Duacensis ad Ill^m. Cardinalem Caietanum.[a]

Intelleximus nuper pro certo, quod antea rumore quodam ad nos allatum fuit, duos sacerdotes, Bish: et Char: ex Anglia profectos ad S^m. D: N: ut perturbent communem pacem, et concordiam Ecclesiæ Anglicanæ sub hac specie, quod subordinatio illa, quæ sapientissime et saluberrime instituta est, et cum maximo applausu recepta, quibusdam non placeat, viz. illis, qui æmulatione quadam se prætermissos esse moleste ferunt, vel certè, quod peius est, ex studio factionis cuiusdam et discordiæ commovendæ. Satis sunt noti, et nobis, et in Anglia, et quidam in illo tumultu Collegi$^.$ Anglicani, qui et S^{mo} D. et Ill^{mæ} Dni Vestræ molestissimus fuit, et genti nostræ ignominiosus valde, quas habuere partes. Quare cum istiusmodi duo homines necdum quiescere didicerunt, nihilque nec aliorum malo aut infamia, nullo exemplo, neque periculo in quod et collegium Romanum et causam patriæ nostræ communem conijcerent, cum nulla re, aut remedio commoventur ad meliorem animum, cum vestram, ac S^{mi} D. N. voluntatem, et authoritatem non nisi coacte sequi velint : nostra sententia est (saluo semper meliori iudicio) vt exemplum aliquod severitatis, aut correctionis cuiusdam ostendatur in istos duos, quo facilius alij, qui sunt eiusdem factionis et audaciæ in officio contineantur. [Duaci ex collegio vestro Anglicano 25 Octob. 1598.]

[a] A translation of this letter was printed by Parsons in his *Briefe Apologie*, f. 125.

Ill^mae D. V. in christo serui
D. Richar: Barrettus Præses
{ D. Laurentius Webbus.
D. Gul. Harrisonus.
D. Mat. Kellinsonus.
Assistentes.

Exemplar Literarum D: Joannis Wright Decani Cortracensis ad Ill^m Cardinalem Caietanum.[a]

Spes quidem affulserat impositum iri finem seditionibus gentis nostrae tam in vrbe, quam in Anglia a factiosis hominibus excitatis, cum restaurato Collegio Anglorum Romæ designatus esset ac datus Archip^r: D. Georgius Blak: vir et pietate, et fidei confessione clarissimus: sed mirum, quam malum hoc omne occultis hæreticorum consilijs fulcitur. Serpit vt rancor, et hidræ instar, cum videtur extinctum, magis reuiuiscit. Duo quidem submissi sunt nomine reliquorum, qui in tota Anglia vix restant, qui refricatis querelis, novas turbas in Vrbe excitent; sunt autem Bish: et Char: notæ leuitatis et inquietudinis homines de quibus hoc affirmare ausim plus periculi, et molestiæ veris fidei propugnatoribus, ac propagatoribus a falsis istis, ac factiosis fratribus procurari, quam ab ipsis hostibus apertis.[b] Ego certe, vt de meipso confitear, neque ex calamitate, et exilio 36 annorum, neque ex angustijs carceris, quas

---

[a] The translation which Parsons gives of the greater part of this letter is curiously wide of the original. "Yet cannot we omyt to alleage," he writes, "one peece of a large, godly, and zealous letter which M. Licentiate Wright, deane of Cortrac, in Flaunders, a man of knowne learning and merits, who wrote about this matter unto the Protector in these words" [*Margin*, Nov. 10, 1591 (*sic*.)]: "Videt scio Illustrissima Dominatio tua quantum res ista perniciosa, etc. Your Grace, I know, doth wel se how great mischief this matter is like to bring unto our English church if it be permitted, and how great trouble and molestation it will breed unto your grace (in governing us) except as we hope remedy be put by diligence at the beginning. . . . ." (*Briefe Apologie*, f. 126.)

[b] This sentence, beginning with the words "hoc affirmare ausim," is rendered literally in Parsons' version, but he adds: "and no marvaile for that these men being privy to all their secrets are no less malitious against them then the very heretiks themselues." Parsons, in his translation, does not, however, name Bishop and Charnock, as in the Latin.

annis octo grauissimis pro fide catholica sum perpessus tantam percepi animi tristitiam, quantam mihi seditiones istæ pepererunt. Ego[a] Archipresbyterum 30 abhinc annis novi, virum doctum, pium, prudentem, pacificum, humilem, cui nulla vnquam inusta est lenitatis alicuius aut factionis notula, qualem non est in disgregato quamvis exiguo istorum ambitiosorum grege reperiri. Quæ cum ita sint, videt D. V. Illma, quam non sit horum querelis fides adhibenda, sed si tamen S^{tem} suam de rebus Anglicis vlterius informandam censeret, id non a turbulentis istis, et parvæ fidei omnibus, sed vel ex Anglia ipsa vel ab alijs fiat, qui his in partibus vitam fidei causa exulem sed innocuam, et ab omni ambitione, et factione alienam degant, vel ab ipso denique nuncio Apostolico, qui Bruxellis est, quod si obtineatur, evicta est causa.

Cortraci, 3 Idus Nouembris, 1598.

  Ill^{mae} D. V. cliens deditissimus Jo: Wrightus Decanus Cortracensis.

Multa alia grauissimorum virorum testimonia in hanc sententiam allegare possumus, qui vel ad suam S^{tem}: vel ad Ill^m Cardinalem Protectorem his de rebus scripserunt, sed breuitatis causa omittimus, quemadmodum etiam personalia quædam, quæ ex Anglia contra hos duos perscripta habemus; volentes hac in parte fratrum nostrorum honori, quantum in nobis est, quantumque causa communis patiatur, consulere. Quod tamen gladij, et pugiones, citharaque in istorum cubiculo atque aras [sic] hic Romæ inventa fuerint, nullam habuit ædificationem, neque spiritum sapit apostolicum, cum nulla hæc gestandi per Italiam necessitas esset, neque vtilitas habendi. Romæ 10 Januarij 1599. Hæc pro officio procurationis nostræ obijcimus, et siquid ipsi negent, probaturos nos esse promittimus.

      Rich: Had. S. Theol. Doctor.
      Martinus Array presbyter.

---

* From this point Parsons' English is in exact agreement with the Latin copy.

8. *Robert Charnock's Answer to the Libel.*

The aunswer to the lybell wch Mr. Richard Haddock D. of Divinity & Mr. Martin Aray both priests and proctors for the Archprest preferred to the two Cardinals Caetan & Burghesius 17 Febr., 1599, in the English Colledg. at Roome agaynst the two priests Mr. William Bishop & Rob. Charnock, at what tyme (nothwithstanding it was earnestly desyred by them that then they myght make this aunswere vnto it) they could not haue it.[a]

47, f. 142.

De turbis et tumultibus factiosorum molitionibus in collegio Anglorum de vrbe excitatis aliud erat Ill^{mi} Alani, R^{mi} [Cassanensis], nobilium etiam omnium Anglorum Romæ degentium, aliud Jesuitarum iudicium quamuis vt ignominian illam a se auerterent perpaucos eosque ex iunioribus in reliquos omnes incitarent atque in horum subsidium milites quosdam Hungaricos atque etiam Maritos [sic] vocarent qui in vestitu clericali decem piorum (vt aiebant) et quietorum scolarium numerum efficerent. De pace autem ibidem per p. Parsonum constituta qualis sit habenda aliorum sit iudicium, prudentioribus sane bestiaram catabulum videtur magis quam ingenuorum collegium. pax enim quæ ibidem prudenter facta dicitur non alia ratione præseruatur quam diligentissima custodum observatione ne qui in vno sunt cubiculo cum alijs qui sunt in alio conversentur eo fortassis consilio vt custodes suadere et persuadere facilius possint quidlibet et quos velint ad partes suas attrahere ant quietioris ingenij homines pro libito suo disturbare atque misere distrahere, quorum reliquiæ non tolli ex Anglia sed præseruari magis videntur, cum Jesuitæ authoritatem (quod ambiebant) artificiose satis in alio posuerint qui, ipsorum in omnibus parens mandatis presbiteros reliquos Jesuitare compelleret. Quod hic de pontificis ordinatione asseritur non constabat, sed contrarium magis (si D. Acrisio ex ore pontificis illud referenti fides sit adhibenda) antequam Breue quoddam obtentum esset quo viso omnes

47, f. 143.
ad primum.

---

[a] What follows is in a minute hand, the lines being very closely written.

138   THE ARCHPRIEST CONTROVERSY.

se ordinationi illi submiserunt. Si qui igitur ordinationi huic (nullis S^{mi} literis constitutæ aut significandæ) parere distulerint donec mentem eius intelligerent, quo iure vel qua potius iniuria factiosi, inobedientes, seditiosi vocantur? Sed ad 2um obiectum veniamus cuius difficultatibus enodatis totus plane scurrilis iste libellus euanescit.

secundum.   Quam sit omni genere virtutis eruditionis ac grauitatis præditus D. Georgius Blackwellus quantumque in hoc genere profecerit sub Jesuitarum gubernio sacerdotum seminariorum superior constitutus vrbs loquatur et orbis, cuius authoritas ab Illmo card. Caetano data non testificata literis, ex ipsismet literis contra libellatores istos manifeste convincitur etiamsi voluntatem S^{mi} in subordinatione aliqua instituenda alio quam suo de se testimonio se sequutum ostendisset. Cum enim execrandam illam omnibus sacerdotibus Seminariorum pijsque catholicis iniuriosissimam atque falsisimam suggestionem authoritatis huius basim his proposuisset verbis,[a] " Imo catholicos ipsos ac sacerdotes nonnullos Seminariorum, qui cæterorum duces atque antesignani ad omnem excelsæ virtutis laudem hactenus extiterunt aggredi Sathanas non dubitauit vt inter se collideret et vnionis murum (quo omnis nititur christianæ pietatis spes) dissiparet, cui hostis conatui Romam quoque nuper emergenti cum S^{mi} D. N. summa prudentia ac paternus amor remedium salutare per Dei gratiam diebus præteritis adhibuerit, etc. speciali mandato nobis iniunxit ut huic rei procurandæ omni nos qua possumus vigilantia impendamus, quod perlibenter quidem facimus," etc. postea ad institutionem huius authoritatis venit, quædam tamen præfatur quasi negotium hoc ab ipsis sacerdotibus actum fuisset, qui de eo ne somniarunt quidem. Sic autem ad verbum se habent literæ: " Cum igitur non parum interesse ad hoc ipsum nonnulli censeant si subordinatio aliqua inter sacerdotes Anglicanos constituatur, et rationes ab ipsis Sacerdotibus pro ea re

---

[a] The letter of Card. Cajetan (Mar. 7, 1598), from which the following quotations are made, will be found printed in full by Tierney, vol. iii. p. cxix.

redditæ, a S^{mo} D. N. probatæ fuerint, Nos S^{tis} suæ pijssimam prouidentissimamque voluntatem sequentes, hoc ipsum statuere decreuimus. Atque pro ijs quidem sacerdotibus Anglicanæ nationis dirigendis ac gubernandis qui in Angliæ Scotiæve regnis in præsentia versantur vel in posterum eo venturi sunt dum hæc Nostra ordinatio durauerit te delegimus cui vices nostras pro tempore delegamus, inducti relatione ac fama publica virtutis, eruditionis, prudentiæ ac laborum tuorum in ista vinea Anglicana per multos annos excolenda. Facultates autem quas ad hoc ipsum tibi concedimus hæ sunt: primum vt cæteris omnibus seminariorum sacerdotibus secularibus vt iam dictum est authoritate Archipresbiteri præsis, quoad S^{mus} aut nos eius mandato aliud statuerimus : Deinde," etc. Quis modo qui hæc et similia legit authoritatem Ill^{mi} literis testatam et non potius institutam contendat? Sed ad alia pergamus, quæ in hoc 2° obiecto ponuntur. Intellexerunt fortasis libellatores ambitiosissimos illos atque impijssimos Jesuitarum conatus Wisbicenses (quorum gustum aliqualem modo habet orbis) nobis non arrisisse, et protervioris propterea ingenij homines, quique facile tumultuaremur, præcipuos insuper factiosorum Londini commorantium fuisse nos calumniantur. Aliæ enim controversiæ in Anglia non erant, quam quæ occasione huiusmodi conatuum Jesuitarum ortæ fuerunt.

Vocauit quidem ad se D Georgius Blackwellus D Joannem Collintonium, virum de ecclesia tum in vinculis tum alias optime meritum, et qui aliquandiu ante adventum D. Black. in vinea Anglicana laborauerat, vocauit etiam D. Anthonium Hebbournum virum omnium testimonio in vinea domini summopere industrium, cum his me tertium vocauit sed eo humanitatis genere, vt tunc temporis alicuius rei pessime sibi conscius videretur, neque fefellit nos opinio. Cum enim ad ipsum in libello nominati venissemus, et literas Il^{mi} Cardinalis Caetani legissemus, ne iniquissimæ calumniæ contra Sacerdotes et Catholicos Anglos in literis præsuppositæ impietas aliqua deesset, instructiones quasdam tanquam literis commissionis suæ annexas, et Roma missas protulit, legitque, quas vt audiuimus fictitias comperimus et non sine maxima confu-

47, f. 143b.

sione hoc ipsum fateri eum compulimus. Ad alia tamen postea progressus est, ac si frontem omnino non submisisset et quod neque in literis, nec in instructionibus continebatur, potestatem excommunicandi habuisse se asseruit, et quos vellet ad vrbem mittendi. Obedientiam a nobis in omnibus expostulauit, et tandem adeo absolutam vindicauit sibi authoritatem, vt a suo tribunali ne ad sedem quidem Apostolicam potuisse nos appellare aliquoties contenderet.

Quis igitur nos iure reprehendat, quod neque crediderimus, nec ipsi acquieverimus, quod ad omnia hæsitauerimus et non admiserimus authoritatem taliter nobis promulgatam, quod vocauerimus in dubium num verum esset (quod falso dicitur in illis literis contineri), S^{mi} iussu hanc authoritatem fuisse constitutam, quæ tot et tantis indigebat mendacijs, vt effectum suum apud nos sortiretur? Quod autem attinet ad arrogantiam, perversitatem, atque ignorantiam quam superciliosi isti scioli clericis secularibus solent obijcere, et nobis maxime hoc loco quod dubitauerimus (vt aiunt) vtrum nobis inconsultis ac invitis superior a S^{mo} constitui possit, similibus convitijs respondere non libet. Neque modo primum dubitatur (si tamen dubitetur) an qui in persequutione viuunt saluti suæ consulere possint, aut alij liceat in vno loco aliqualiter securum, pro libito ex eo mouere, et ad alium pellere, quod sub prætextu maioris gloriæ dei, quemlibet[a] vel proprij lucri causa, vel Jesuitarum promouendi negotia in potestate est superioris nostri a Jesuitis electi.

ad tertium. Ex his ad tertium facilis patet responsio non sine iustissima causa nos inijsse consilia non de resistenda pontificis ordinatione (vt calumniantur libellatores) sed de cognoscenda S^{mi} voluntate super his quæ ab alio ordinata manifestissime convincuntur, et Romam ex Anglia venimus, quod etiam antea Archipresbitero significavimus non contradicendi studio (vti hic mentiuntur libellatores) sed melius informandi S^{mum} de rebus nostris, vt ex literis Archipresbiteri constare potuisset si voluisset, hoc enim fuisse negotium nostrum propria sua subscriptione testatus est,

[a] So in the original, but evidently misplaced.

quod Rome Jesuitas latere non poterat, inter alia enim scripta quæ S^{mi} nomine sub pæna excommunicationis ipso facto incurrendæ a nobis expostulabantur extortum est per D. Acrisium hujusmodi Archipresbiteri testimonium.

In quarto obiecto quatuor inferuntur contra nos. In prioribus duobus offensiones clericorum et laicorum scandala vrgentur, quæ ex superius dictis scandala phariseorum convincuntur. de tertio aliorum sit iudicium vtri maiorem lætitiæ causam hæreticis et persequutoribus præbuerint illine qvi ad sedem Apostolicam in prædictis constituti difficultatibus confugerunt, an illi qui ob dictas vel similes causas ad S^{mum} proficiscentes incarcerari, exulare et relegari fecerunt: contentiones autem et factiones in Anglia vigere (quorum ista erant initia) qui videt, quod in quarto dicitur falsum nimis verum inveniet. ad quartum. 47 f. 144.

Quod de decem presbiteris qui pro nobis starent adversvs 300 et multis milibus laicorum asseritur, fraudulenter asseritvr (quamvis ex falsissimis Jesuitarum suggestionibus aut grauissimis minis allecti quam plurimi aut territi illis subscripserint, a quibus corda illorum longe erant, nobis tum antea tum postea subscripserint) non poterat enim latere Jesuitas multo plures 10 fuisse, cum ex istis decem aliqui testarentur multos alios idem plane sentijsse in partibus illis vbi isti morabantur, sed quia comperit p. Personus plures nos non convenisse vel cognouisse ex nominibus, decem tantum aliquando, aliquando 12 tantum pro nobis stetisse audacter affirmat, qui si sub iuramento interrogetur de 300 istis presbiteris et multis catholicorum millibus fortassis de temeritate maxima argueretur, si pro pluribus iuraret, quam ijs, quos ipsemet probe cognosceret, et si ex sola aliorum relatione directe iuraret, sine dubio periurio manifestissime se exponeret. causam vero quare pauciores presbiterorum subscriptiones nobiscum tulerimus hic temporis istam dedimus, ne ex mora nostra acceptasse, vel acquievisse . . . . . pari falsitate suggereretur, qua proponebatur, et confirmaretur tanquam optimum consilium quod ex pessima informatione institutum apparebat.

Ad quintum mirum profecto in modum scrupulosi sunt aliquando ad quintum.

Jesuitæ et puri. Uni presbitero placentia ipsis nuncianti fidem adhibendam curarunt, quamvis ne unam quidem scedulam infimi alicuius ordinis hominis secum ferret quæ fidem faceret: quam sedulo autem querunt literas credentiales a duobus presbiteris Sanctissimum informaturis de ijs quæ falsissime a priore suggesta erant! Literas plurimas ad suam S^{tem} nobiscum tulimus, quas hic sub [literularum?] nomine fatentur libellatores, proprijs presbiterorum manibus subscriptas et ope multorum tulissemus nos ipsi instar literarum et ad s^{um} et Ill^{um} protectorem . . . . et (si quid ineat) literas etiam ad alios Romæ existentes ex Anglia tulimus, quibus constabat aliquos missos ad sedem Apostolicam quamvis fortassis nomina nostra ex rationabili causa in illis omitterentur. Quomodo autem literis scriptis ante constitutionem [huius] authoritatis episcopum poscentibus aut aliquem episcopali iurisdictione præditum satisfactum dici possit per Archipresbiteri constitutionem non constat, cum neque episcopus factus sit, neque episcopali iurisdictione præditus, sed authoritatem Archipresbiteri tantum habeat, et meram affligendi potestatem, vt in literis Ill^{mi} Caetani est videre, et cum speciatim in omnibus fere illis literis potestas consecrandi olea, et sacramentum confirmationis administrandi postularetur, et ad neutrum data sit, quam imprudenter literis presbiterorum satisfactum dicitur per Archipresbiteri talis constitutionem! Varia a varijs postulata miraculum non est, pugnasse autem scedulas inter se et ad invicem quas nobiscum protulimus asserere plenum malitia est, et si approbaturos nos ea omnia quæ in literis prædictis reperiuntur negaverimus, mirum certe nemini videri debet, cum in adversariorum nostrorum manibus iamdudum fuissent, et petiissent variis modis falsificari, et quæstio ista nobis proposita sub iuramento, An illis . . . . in literis nostris . . . stare vellemus non paruam dedit falsificationis suspicionem. ob hanc causam fortassis Jesuitæ literas alias finxerunt, quas ad S^m missas a nostris in Anglia p. personus intercepisse se asseruit coram Ill^{is} Card. Caet. et Burghes. et earum initum nobis præsentibus legit, in quibus petebant nostri vt nos duo Archiepiscopi consecraremur

tutius multo ratus huiusmodi aliorum literas nobis inscijs scriptas
huic temporis proferre, quam quas in privatis colloquijs Romam 47, f. 144
nobiscum nos tulisse etiam sub iuramento confirmaturum se
contendit ad nos sub episcoporum titulis a nostris in Anglia datas,
prout etiam postea in literis suis ad nos 19 octob. 1599 hoc ipsum
scribere non erubuit; has autem literas instantissime Romæ petentibus nobis ostendere verebatur manifestissimæ fallaciæ statim
convincendus.

Ad 6^m Respondetur temere valde iudicare libellatores non facta   ad sextum.
nihil iam omnino a nobis . . . .[a] ad iniquissima quæque patienter
ferenda, cum in carceribus coniectis nec cum invicem neque cum
quoquam alio loqui de re quaquam liceret; quod autem hic asserunt
manifesta fraude a nobis productas contra Archipresbiteri authoritatem literas illas, quæ scriptæ erant antequam Archip^{r}sbiter constitueretur, manifestissima continent mendacia, primo quia nullas
omnino produximus, vi enim ablata erant a nobis omnia scripta
nostra prima nocte incarcerationis nostræ; secundo (vt iam dictum
est) . . .[a] agere, multo minus coram aliquo coram quo literas istas aut
aliquas alias produceremus; tertio quando p. personus me examin-
abat super his literis ita distincta accepit quæ, quorum, quo tempore
scriptæ, et quare Romam tulerim, tam quæ ante authoritatem constitutam datæ erant, quam quæ postea, vt non sine maxima impu-
dentia ista hic inferantur.

Ad 7^m Respondetur libellatoribus excidisse e memoria, quod in 6º   ad septimum.
obiecerant, nullam scilicet instructionem attulisse nos de quibus
rebus ageremus—hic enim constare aiunt nos multa in mandatis
habuise, quæ plena seditione erant. rogasse debuissent vt harum
rationes a nobis redderentur, non autem vt libellus iste nobis non
traderetur, quando ad omnia responsuri coram Ill^{mis} Card: Caiet. et
Burghes. illum postulabamus. Et cum in libris quas nobiscum tulimus nonnulli ad dignitates promouendi nominarentur quos a   47 f. 144b.
Jesuitis stetisse pro certo habuimus, imprudenter certe objicitur

[a] Some words illegible.

nos in mandatis habuisse de provehendis ad episcopatus aliquibus ex nostris factiosis. et si vnquam eos qui pro nobis stabant illis prætulissemus qui erant a partibus Jesuitarum (quod tamen nunquam fecimus, qui nihil facere permittebamur) et doctrina et meritis erga ecclesiam catholicam longe superiores cæteris prætulissemus.

ad octauum. Quæ in octauo obiecto congeruntur nihil habent veritatis, quamuis enim potestas talis data videatur quæ dominium in vitas nostras supponere debet, vt in responsione ad 2^m obiectum ostensum est, non poterunt nisi perfidorum testimonio probare (quod toties inculcant) asseruisse nos suam S^{tem} non posse neque debere, nobis non petentibus, inconsultis, vel invitis, dare superiorem vel aliquid eiusmodi, sed contrarium potius, quod et in examinationibus nostris sub iuramento acceptis latere non poterat Jesuitas, quando et pro nobis et alijs socijs nostris testati sumus S^{mi} voluntati cognitæ omnes paratissimos se submittere, quod postea omnes præstiterunt. similis huic est impostura illa quod libertas nostra scilicet indignaretur si premeretur; dum enim scripta nostra apud nos manerent, hæc non continebant.

ad nonum. Ad 9^m cum opportunitatem habituri sint Wisbicenses, pleniorem daturi sunt satisfactionem. Sufficiat interim quod turbæ ibidem natæ, atque scandala ex Jesuitarum insolentia ortum et progressum habuerint. Qui scandolose ibidem mortuus dicitur, morbo lytergico[a] correptus, pijssime vitam suam finiuit. qui apostatauit, tempore Jesuitismi sui (fuerat enim per multos annos Jesuita) fortassis illud didicerat. Qui ex collegio Anglico romano expulsus dicitur, honorifice dimissus est, non tamen sine aliqua suspicione, quod pater Personus disturbatum illum cuperet, erat enim iste ex illis vnus qui patrem personum non religionis causa (vt pluribus tum Romæ tum alibi imponit) sed propter nequitiam ex collegio Balyolensi Oxonij in Anglia solemniter expulerat, et si maior pars in

[a] For *lethargico*. The reference is to the death of Dr. Norden.

castro Wisbicensi a Jesuitis decepta ipsis se antea subiecissent mirum non est si quidlibet admittere parati essent, quod ipsis arridere cognoscerent.

Ad 10^m cum in chartis nostris reperisset p. personus de alio Archipresbitero constituendo mentionem, interrogationem quamdam formauit quibus medijs pax in Anglia conseruari posset, cui responsum est (inter alia) vno ex his tribus. primo si ordinarius constitueretur superior. secundo si extraordinario constituto presbiteri possent cognoscere in quibus tenerentur ipsi obedire ne ad libitum suum quemuis disturbaret. tertio (neutro horum concesso) si alius in eadem dignitate constitueretur qui eos propulsaret si quando Archipresbiter, a Jesuitis constitutus in Jesuitarum causa (in quos et presbiteros erat controversia) alteri parti iniurias inferret. In hoc autem vltimo discutiendo (nam de duobus prioribus medijs altissimum erat silentium) si prius ignorantiam postea certe malitiam ostendit pa. parsonus. inauditum enim contendebat quod duo in eodem regno essent superiores, quorum alter alteri non esset subordinatus. contra hoc instabam in presenti Archipresbitero et superiore Jesuitarum, quorum alterum alteri subordinatum non debuit fateri, sed rogauit vt omnino hoc tacerem. secundo instabam in Archiepiscopis Cantuariensi et Eboracensi. horum alterum alteri subordinatum contendit p.parsonus. et ex ijs quae in comitijs quibusdam Henrico 2° in Anglia regnante contigerunt probare voluit, cum vero tandem aliquando persuasissem (quod aut ignorauit aut in re tam seria malitiose dissimulauit) contentionem illam non fuisse vter illorum subordineretur alteri, sed vtri superior in comitijs deberetur locus, vt inter regum Galliarum et Hispaniorum legatos aliquando Romæ contingit, scribere iussit Jesuitam (qui notarij vices supplebat, et ipsi in omnibus parebat) et quæ ipse proposuisset, et quæ me respondisse voluisset, donec multoties reclamassem scribendo quæ respondi, aut nihil me postea ad quicquam responsurum.[a]

Ad 11^m respondetur, ostendisse nobis p. parsonum literas quasdam ex Anglia (vt aiebat) ad S^{mum} D. missas in quibus discrimina

[a] Some words wanting here.

ad decimum.

ad undecimum.
47, f 145.

quædam dignitatum omnium in dei ecclesia et in Academijs christianis obseruata ponebantur, quibus Caluinistæ atque Anabaptistæ ambitione, vanitate, et seditione plenis calumniari solent. In collegio Anglorum de vrbe locum suum in mensa habet rector, vicerector suum, Jesuitæ qui presbiteri sunt suum, qui non sunt suum, presbiteri seculares suum, prefecti cubiculorum suum, dispensator, magister domus, celerarius, cocus, lixa suum, et omnia hæc discrimina humilitate, grauitate, pietate sunt plena, ea sola irridenda a Jesuitis et condemnanda sunt quæ antiquissima catholica ecclesia recipit et colit.

ad duodecimum. Ad 12^m respondetur potuisse patrem parsonum huius libelli authorem maiore cum modestia ab istis suis suorumque laudibus abstinuisse. iamdudum enim ipsorum intentiones in Anglia nostra excolenda longe alias esse apparuerunt, quam quæ religiosos deceant. Seminaria quibus Anglia plurimum debet, pene desolata iacent, et nova quædam ædificia in Hispanijs erecta sunt nunc Anglis aliquali, dehinc maiori multo Jesuitis futura vsui. His quidem initium nonnullorum Hispanorum charitas sine dubio dedit, ad instantiam non Jesuitarum, sed quorumdam sacerdotum nostrorum facta quamuis ad istam molem iniquissimis suis artibus perduxit ea p. parsonus dum prædicta abusus charitate regna integra pro vno vel altero collegio permutandi potestatem sordidissimus homuncio sibi arrogauit, gladiumque principis nostræ acuit, quæ inter regni proditores et presbiteros religiosos nesciens distinguere omnes eadem plectit pæna. Quod autem hic adijcitur fassos nos nihil legitime probatum contra eos proferri posse, falsissimum est, quamuis nos fortassis non haberemus quod tunc temporis contra eos proponeremus. petitio præsens libellatorum vt scilicet ad tempus in Angliam non reverteremur tantæ impietatis convicta non fuisset, si adiecissent quod interim aliquid ad victum et vestitum nobis suppeditaretur, sed nouis his antiquorum christianorum charitas numquam arrisit.

De literis grauissimorum illorum hominum gentis nostræ non est quod quicquam hic aliud dicamus quam (quod omnes norunt) primas ab eo scriptas qui promotionem aliquam Jesuitarum opera expectabat, subscriptas vero ab ijs, qui huic parebant, et datas antequam aliqui eorum cognoscerent quid Romæ acturi essemus, secundas autem a quodam scriptas, qui non solum nihil de negotijs nostris nouit, sed neque nos, contra quos tum imprudenter scripsit. non possumus tamen satis mirari quod incarcerationis suæ fecerit mentionem in suis literis contra eos, qui quomodo se in carceribus gesserit facile possent cognoscere. Si præsentem Archipresbiterum tot ab hinc annis virum doctum, pium, prudentem, pacificum, humilem, cui nulla unquam inusta est leuitatis alicuius aut factionis notula cognouerit, quid de Jesuitis censendum est (in quorum gratiam hæc scripsit) cum quibus aliquando bella intestina habuit vir iste tantopere laudatus? et si nos ex Anglia Romam iniisse, aut nec solos, nec omnes veridicos esse, quos ipse innocentes atque ab omni ambitione, et factione alienos prædicat, aut Nuntium denique Apostolicum ex revelatione diuina non habere veram Anglicorum [et] perfectam notitiam constiterit, quam inepte homo iste leuis armaturæ causæ, nescit cuius, promittit sibi victoriam ?

Concluditur tandem libellus et honori nostro consuli prætenditur, cum plus quam omnia in libello hoc congessissent libellatores. personalia quidem ex Anglia quotidie expectabant (ad hunc enim finem iamdudum scripserat Ill^{mus}Caetanus, vt informatio de moribus nostris ad vrbem mitteretur) sed cum ipsorum spes fefellisset eos, tacere non poterant quæ dici poterant, gladios scilicet et pugiones, cytharamque submisisse nos in cubiculis nostris, quod (vt aiunt) nec aliquam ædificationem habuit, nec ideo fortassis spiritum sapuit Apostolicum, quia cum duos haberemus gladios in nullo percussimus, quando cum gladijs Jesuitæ nos comprehendere nocte venirent.

Quando libellum istum Ill^{mis} Card. Caeta. et Burghes. petebamus, vt illi responderemus, impetrabant procuratores a prædictis cardinalibus vt vobis non traderetur, qui in calce libelli pro . . . . se spondebant si quid a nobis negaretur.

Hæc[a] absque præiudicio causæ communis sit responsio mea particularis ad libellum quem Rr. DD. Richardus Had[dock], S. Th. Doct., et Mart. Aray presbiter, obtulerunt Ill^{mis} Cardinalibus Caet. et Burghes. in collegio Anglorum de vrbe, 17 februarij 1599, in causa, vt aiebant, Archipresbiteri et cleri Anglicani procuratores constituti contra R. D. Gul. Bysh. in theologia magistrum, et me. omnia . . . . S. R Ecclesiæ iudicio subiecta hæc esse volo.

Rob. Char. presbiter Anglus.

38, f. 403.

9. *Rough Draft of a Letter to the Deputies by Bagshaw.*

IHS.

Quam Deus in cordibus vestris dedit sollicitudinem pro communi Angliæ bono multis indicijs vestris, desyderatissimi fratres, intelligimus et gratulamur. Eorum quæ suæ sanctitati intimanda censemus, præcipua capita subiecimus omni cum humilitate petenda.

Archipresbyteratus domini Bla: vtpote nec expetitus nec vtilis futurus revocandus, etc.

Assignentur aliqui qui sacramentum confirmationis inprimis necessarium administrent.

Hierarchia aliqua quæ solis et liberis seminarianorm suffragijs approbetur est instituenda. Visitatio canonica in Anglia, præcipue pro scandalis in Castro Wisbicensi exortis, est procuranda. Prohibendum ne Romanense nostrorum collegium sit terra quasi scandalorum.

Alumnorum Romanensium educatio sit qualis esse debet ingenuorum, et sponte pro fide exulantium.

Infamia nulla impune publicetur, quæ absentes, inauditos, et indiscriminatim innocentes etiam involvat, nec libris nec rumoribus

---

[a] This last paragraph is written cross-wise in the margin, ending on the inside of the flyleaf.

nec molitionibus invtiliter status temporalis contra religionem irritetur.

Alia quædam sunt, quæ inscijs nostris commisimus, vestris relinquimus pertractanda arbitrijs: nos cum Beato Hieronymo ad Theophilum Alexandrinum dicimus Volumus pacem, et non solum volumus sed et rogamus sed pacem Christi, pacem veram, pacem sine inimicitijs, pacem in qua non sit bellum involutum, pacem quæ non vt adversarios subijciat sed vt amicos iungat. Quid dominationem pacem vocamus, et non reddimus vnicuique rei vocabulum suum? Sic ille, sic nos, sic fratrum nostrorum plurimi sentiunt, quorum cito indignabitur libertas fr[atris] prædicti vestri.[a] Valete et pro nobis pedes suæ sanctitatis de[vot]issime osculamini. Vestræ nos Deo orationes commendent. nostræ vobis non deerunt.

Albanus Dolmannus sacerdos publica ludibria in vesti sacerdotali Londini insigni constantia perpessus, ob incarcerationem non semel fortiter toleratam et quadraginta annos in excolenda vinea Domini Anglicana egregie impensos, nobilis fidei confessor, idem sentit.

Endorsed :
Dr. Bag:
pointes to be reformed by ye Pope, the subordination.

10. *Copy of a Letter or portion of a letter to the Pope in Bagshaw's hand.* 38, f. 404.

IHS.

Pro instituendo in Ecclesia Anglicana Archipresbyteratu quodam qui soli aut præcipui laborarunt obnixe Patres societatis invitis aut inscijs alijs omnibus, pro eodem iam (vt aiunt) instituto, idque tuo, B. P., motu et authoritate, litteris congratulari satagentes, P. Parsonio præeunte, monstrantes alijs viam, sibi ipsi ducatum vendicant. Qui nomina subscribunt, experientia plerumque in

[a] These last three words very doubtful.

rebus Anglicanis carent, vtpote nec ætate nec iudicio provecti, quique pondus diei et æstum cum nondum in vinea nostra portaverint, non ita amplam et cum alijs strenuis operarijs parem mercedem expectare possent, nisi ad Jesuitarum, quibus operas suas præstant, patrocinium confugerent. Ab illis enim dona et munera sibi promittunt, penes quos rei pecuniariæ et in publicos et in privatos vsus insumendæ distributionem perspiciunt. Quam vsu iam confirmatam facillime sibi Patres in initio arrogarunt, cedentibus Angliæ sacerdotibus et deferentibus omnia illis, quos ad cooperandum secum invitarunt, et Christum non sua quærere obligatos voto etiam intellexerunt, ideoque temporalium, quæ munificentissime pro more nostræ gentis in pauperes conferuntur, dispensatores religiosissimos fore crediderunt. Quid quod ipse Archipresbyter ante novum quem attribuunt titulum de paupertate conquestus, iam ad arbitrium Jesuitarum, (qua illectus spe nescimus) se totum efformavit, et assistentes suos ascivit. Qui cum vix vnquam in arenam descenderit, non liquet an præficiendus sit exercitui prælianti prælia domini. Alij, propter aculeatas nimis litteras (vt non dicamus quod vere dici posset, contumeliosas) contra sacerdotum nonnullos quos revereri oportuerat, Alij propter minas censurarum non innocentibus solum sed et optime de Religione et patria meritis, intentatas, Alij, propter inconcinnas quasdam opiniones suas et excommunicationum allegationes, Alij propter electionis canonicæ (vt cætera taceantur) defectum, Alij quod authoritatem suam iustissime refutantibus, adeoque post legationem ad se missam ea de re et provocationem furtam [sic] obtrudat, indignum censent qui Ecclesiam Anglicanam gubernet. Accedit quod statui temporali, quia Jesuitis obsequitur, sit inprimis modo et in posterum vt apparet, magis ac magis futurus sit exosus, vt diurnæ et horariæ Catholicorum propter odium contra Jesuitas conceptum quia titulorum et Regnorum negotijs se immiscent, vexationes declarant. Nos istis et alijs plurimis incommodis provocati et adacti, sine irritatione sæcularis magistratus, commune Angliæ bonum, et Ecclesiasticam Hiararchiæ formam, nobis ipsis proposueramus.

Sed ne Cathedræ Petri quicquam decederet authoritatis, aut ad eam perfidia accessum haberet, fratres duos multis nominibus dilectissimos, et omni (vt speramus) favore excipiendos, ad V. S. direximus qui et observantiam nostram singularem, et veritatis studium eximium, amplo testimonio confirmarent. Quod interea tanquam inobedientes et refractarij male audiamus parum movet. Qui prælaturas indigne sibi aucupantur, alijs et vt plurimum melioribus detrahant necesse est. Nos conscientiarum nostrarum securitate freti, et vestræ sæpe sæpius erga nostrates demonstratæ Apostolicæ sollicitudini, prudentiæ, Humanitati, innixi, non moramur aliorum quomodocunque specioso prætextu velatas machinationes.

[*At foot, in another hand*] by Mr. Biss. & Ch.

Dr. Bagshaw to ye B. of Rome, [to have bene sent by ye 2 y^t shuld last have gone thither: *erased.*]

Endorsed:

P^t of a letter supposed to be written against the intended government of the Jesuits, by Bagshaw, eyther to the Pope or to the Cardinall protector, wherein he sheweth both the insufficiencye of Mr. Blackwell to be the Archp^{r}sbiter and the badnes of his courses allready undertaken.

11. *Faculties for the Clergy communicated by Blackwell to his Assistants.*   47, f. 137.

Feb. 2, 1599.

Dilectissimi coadiutores. Jam tandem a superioribus deducta est ad me potestas communicandi facultates. Quæ ergo ad certam meam notitiam pervenerunt, volui quamprimum facere vos earum omnium participes, quas particulatim notatas et hic nunc inclusas recipietis. Has vobis defero, communico, et do ad commune commodum ecclesiæ et Catholicorum allevamentum. Et si ampliores in me derivatas esse deprehendero, eas statim vt perfluant ad vos non indiligenter curabo. Interim hisce facultatibus refectos, cupio vos in instituto regiminis vestri cursu convalescere. Et ne confratres nostri earundem indigentia elanguescerent in officio, volo eas omnes proficisci ad compresbiteros nostros, quorum obedientiam, consignato publico testimonio satis expressam in literis ad sanctissimum Dominum perspexistis. Illis ergo (queso) mittite has omnes facultates, et significate me eas tribuere illis, et impartiri, vt qui necessitatibus pressi sunt inter Catholicos, hi possint erigi tanto beneficio, et plurimum recreari. Non dubito, quin omnium contradicentium obstinatæ voluntates facillime iam ad nostram moderationem traduci velint. Vident enim iam, quod in edificatione Babilonis in vanum laboraverunt. Det illis Dominus sanam mentem, vt desinant effundere se ad inania. Et discant (vt loquitur D. Gregorius) desideriorum temporalium grave onus abijcere, et leve iugum Domini libera servitute portare. Valete in Christo charissimi consultores, et orate pro me. In festo Purificationis 1599.

Facultates concedendæ Sacerdotibus in Anglia euntibus, cum remissione ad Archipresbiterum.

1. Facultas absolvendi ab omnibus Casibus et censuris in Bulla Cænæ reservatis, in regnis Angliæ, Scotiæ et Hyberniæ.

2. Vt possint illis quos reconciliaverunt dare Apostolicam benedictionem, cum plenaria indulgentia. Catholicis vero congregatis ad concionem, vel ad Sacrum in festis solemnibus Apostolicam benedictionem sine plenaria indulgentia.

3. Vt possint dispensare cum illis qui contraxerunt in tertio et quarto gradu in foro conscientiæ tantum.

4. Vt possint commutare vota simplicia, exceptis votis castitatis et Religionis, in aliud opus pium cum causa.

5. Vt possint restituere ius petendi debitum coniugale, quando ex aliqua causa amissum est.

6. Vt possint benedicere vestes, et alia omnia quæ pertinent ad Sacrificium missae, preter ea quæ requirunt Crisma.

7. Vt possint dare facultatem Catholicis legendi libros controversiarum a Catholicis scriptos in vulgari lingua.

8. Quando non possunt ferre Brevium, vel recitare officium sine probabili periculo, suppleant dicendo aliquot psalmos, vel alias orationes quas sciant memoriter, si alijs facultatibus indiguerint vel dubia circa harum vsum occurrerint remittantur ad R. D. Archipresbiterum Angliæ, vt illis satisfiat provt ipsi in Domino expedire visum fuerit, eique in omnibus obedire teneantur. Quod etiam se facturos promittant priusquam hæ vel aliæ facultates eis concedantur.

Henricus Card[lis] Caetanus Protector.

Endorsed (in different hands):

1. 1599. Cardinal Caietans faculties graunted to suche priestes in England as submit them selues to the newe Hierarchie: Festo purificationis 1599.

iuxta computationem Romanam et novam.

2. Smyle take copy & send to hyme.

IV.

RENEWAL OF THE CONFLICT.

June 1599—June 1601.

47, f. 132.

1. *Letter signed R. B.*[a]

June 7, 1599.

My discourses are nothinge of ioye or comfort, but of sorrowe and lamenta[tions] because entringe into concerte of thes daingerous and vnaturall complo[tts] I beforehande see the ruyne of o^r Countrey, and a bloudy pryze of o^r Nation. The monster that beforehande hath made sale of his Natiue soyle and people, being composed of all Nations kingdomes and provinces in the worlde, and him self chainged into an vnnaturall condition, cannot be satisfied w^t a litle bloude, but must haue our landes and houses also to seate his patched body of all elements as a Nurcerye to replenish other countries w^t their swarme. This, though it be foreseen, as yet hath no way of remedye but to fly to him by humble prayer that remedyeth all things and saie Deus misereatur nostri. Holcorne hath ben at Ofchurche, to establish that syllie man in his conceited opynion of their cause, as he will to the gallowes vi et armis. Some good men haue required restitucion of their good name by him who wounded them w^t report of schisme and excommunicacion or to satisfie them so far forth as to discouer the partie that perswaded him therein. But he answereth that god almighty tellinge him thereof, he will accuse none other, so as one of the said good men obiectinge that then he had the spirite, & so had the puritans, for they much bragged of their spirit. The sylly gentilman chargeth him that he called him Purytane and threatneth to com-

Fra: Grey.
(In margin in other hand.)

[a] Addressed to one of the prisoners at Wisbech, probably to Bagshaw, who had now returned from London, and had made his submission to the Archpriest.

plaine to his head of him, saieng that his wourde is to be creadyted, and to that end prepareth him self towardes London.

I have here expected the arryvall of Mr. Collington but as yet I heare not of him. I can doe no good for Mrs. J. the gent. being of opinion that her callinge & other bringinge up will not answer their expectacion, because an overseer must haue a iudgement in those thinges belonging to her charge, and a ready hande to instruct whome she shall comptrol in any such matt^r as shall apeare amysse. Thus much, S^r, for this time, commendinge me to yor self, Mr Bluet, Mr Caluerley, Mr Tailer, Mr Theules, and whom els yo^u please, and to all yor prayers. This corpus Christi Day, 1599.

yo^{rs} ev^r to be commaunded,
R. B.

2. *R. B. to Bagshaw.*

Very good Syr, I commende me right hartely & was in expectation to heare from you or now but ere long I hope I shall : I perceaue ou^r newe ffrends houlde on ther oulde course as this bearer is able to certify you whoe hathe bene at liberty this monethe (though to his greater coste) fyndinge as harde measure abroade as when he was in houlde, not receauinge a penny or meales meate of any, albeyt yt hathe bene a custome to relieve suche poore men & to collecte for them when they weare discharged, I refer hym therfore vnto you^r charity beseechinge you^r helpes wht you may, for I assure you yf I weare in case I could not but take compassion vpon his long continued misery : where he had some interest he is discountenanced by slanderous reports. Where he wente aboute to preferr hym selfe for a tyme he was preuented. hope was giuen hym of greate helpe & not any thinge performed, in fyne yf he stay here longe he shall be forced to serue where he would not, sterued for wante of foode or clapped vpp againe for wante of countenance . m^r Wade commaunded hym of late (being a sufficient pen man) to write for Mr. Watson, vnto whome he repared a weeke together, wch hathe made hym more odious then before soe y^t he is homo perditus emongest these curious carpers, but to giue you some taste of my owne estate, howe at this presente y^t standeth wch me since my submission, I doe assure you, Syr, wth out all exaggeration I fynde myselfe in worse case then before, for nowe I doe not onely wante my faculties as I did then (althoughe I was borne in hande vpon my submission I shoulde reccaue them) but alsoe y^t meanes of maintenaunce wch I had before, such as were my ffrends perchaunce thinkinge y^t vpon this generall accorde of submission all partiality & supposed inuiries woulde be layde asyde & forgotten on the behalfe of ou^r newe ffrends (I will not say newe foes) & y^t therefore I shoulde neede noe more of ther helpe. well, syr, yf the case standes wth you & the reste of ou^r ffrends wth you where you are I see noe other remedy but wee muste needs in patientia nostra possidere animas nostras.

Vpon Mr. Brusters firste comminge vpp the newes was very hott, for a while, y^t wee shoulde to Wisebitche out of hande, but nowe me thinkes y^t beginnes to coole. I pray god his comminge vpp this tyme take not as greate effecte as his laste did. other certayne newes wee haue none, wherfore in haste I take my leaue, thankinge you for all curtesies, committinge you to the protection of the higheste & commendinge my selfe to you^r good prayers.

Yours as his owne
R. B.

Endorsed 1. To Mr. D. Bagsh: giue these.
" 2. one of . . . . since his submission at Blackwell.

3. *Letter by Francis Clark.*

June 20.   47, f. 240.

My very lovinge frende,[a] whereas you write vnto me concerninge certayne rumors spread abroade of some vnnaturall and disloyall attemptes pretended heare at home by suche as shewe themselves more vnnaturall towards theire cuntrie, then either discreete or conscionable in their actions and endevours; whereof you desire to knowe my conceit, and what I can say therein: I answere you: ffirste that I ever held all suche practizes and attemptes, as bothe vnnaturall because againest our lawfull prince and natif Cuntrey, and also vnlawfvll, because grounded, and proceedinge more vppon passion, and hedlounge affections, measured only by theire owne disordinate and ambitious desires, then vppon any true iustice at all. Secondly concerninge the particulars; it is true that Mr. Oldcorne[b] dealt wth a gentleman, & my frende, to haue ben on of a certeyne smale number as I take it 25 or 13, all wch as he sayed shoulde be gentlemen or gentleme[n]s fellowes who should vppon a soden surprise the Tower of London. the mann^r should haue ben (as M^r. Oldcorne sayed) that the sayde parties should so dispose of themselves, as that some of them beinge entred under some pretence or other, the rest should sodaynly sett vppon the warders, knocke them downe & slay them, & then takinge away the keyes possesse the reste of the wardes, & so maintayne the sayde Tower for some moneth or 6 weakes, untill ayde should come frome the Spanierd; This attempte was to haue benne practized, yf theire designes had taken place, muche aboute the tyme of the investinge of this o^r newe Archprieste: But when

---

[a] It may perhaps be addressed to Thomas Bluet. Compare Bluet's note to a letter of Bagshaw, Petyt MSS., xlvii., f. 227, printed in *Jesuits and Seculars*, p. 150.

[b] Father Edward Oldcorne, S. J., afterwards executed for alleged complicity in the Gunpowder Plot. Francis (*alias* William) Clark, the writer of this letter, was himself executed, together with his friend William Watson, for the plot known as "The Bye," Nov. 29, 1603. Some of Clark's letters are signed: "Francis *alias* Will. Clarke."

the good Jesuit perceaued that this gentleman, in whome, as I dare bouldly affirme, neuer scintill of disloyalty towards his prince and cuntrie did once lurke, altogether mislyked such courses, as disloyall and trecherous in themselues, and foule & tainty to the actors: he gladly would haue intreated secresie therin ; wch assuredly had not falen oute yf this plott had not bene lett fall, by reason of contrarie successe, as I suppose, to theire expectations in the Spanishe attempts.

As touchinge the bostinge speache or words spoken in bravery by m^r Jones vppon occasion of talke had by the sayde Jones in the hearinge of some of his favorites, (at the leaste as he then conceaved) it is true that he sayed he had 60 or an 100 tall fellowes in Wales at a dayes wornige to be redy when tyme should serue, wch words he vttered vppon occasion of talke what might happen in our cuntrie hereafter, either by invasions, civill mutinies or deathe of her Matie. As for yor therde poynte concerninge ffa. Parsonnes discourses had before the schollars in the Colledge at Rome concerninge suche practizes, and his vsuall speache of (haue at state & all I referre you vnto suche as weare presente at his discourse (of whome I suppose you knowe somme) they can informe you therof more at large. Thus leavinge to holde you any lounger, hauinge satisfied your request herin, I take my leaue this 20 of June.

your euer faithfull frende
FRAN : CLERKE.

4. *Letter signed Ratclife, i.e. Mush, to Blackwell.*

47, f. 198.

March 2, 1600.

R. D.

I haue received two from you & one from fa: Walley, all 3 the 28 of feb.

Yo^r first dated in Novemb. came open to me, & had been tossed through many handes as it seemed by the muche soyling thereof.

I humbly thanke you, for bestowing the faculties of Mr. francis Robinson, for certifying the complantes of them that wanted in prisons. truly S^r I did it not in any sorte to afflict or trouble you but writt some parte of that wch I hard many waies, & by sondrie persons. that you assure me, it is otherwise than was reported I am verie glad & will do my best to hinder suche odious matter.

Touching Mr. Knight, bothe I & others had delt w^t him aboute temperinge his tonge. but I found much more to be said of him than he had given occasion of. At tymes & in places when commyng to some houses, he was either not admitted in suche sorte as common charitie required, or doubt made of him & question putt whether he was a right or lefte handied man, an appellant & one of the faction, or on the other side, in thes hard occasions he was moved to speake in o^r defence, & of [the] iniuries we had suffered. wch he had never mentioned but vpon this fond vsage of Catholickes that had adhered to yor side in the late controversy, & now after his Ho : haue ended all, contynewe in their offensive peruersitie to make exceptions & I know not what. I doubt not but he will do & speake as becommeth him, & so as may rather cause peace & loue, than contynewe old contentions. And so shall all do w^t whome I can preuale.

For the cauling of me away emong the rest, truly I can not but doubt false measures in some too familiar & too confident w^t London, etc., for I am lett to vnderstand by one that haith received yt from the mouthe of a familiar w^t London, that I procured my selfe this enmitie of the staite, & some others that should not haue disliked that I did w^t you; by that conference & agrement Mr. Col. & I made w^t you. And yett I thinke you say truly, that the ambition of some, & a stomake they carrie against all, not of pleasing humor to them in what they do, haith caused some particular exceptions to be maid against me. but be all as shall please God. I can not but dislike of all suche as ar familiar & in fauour extraordinarie w^t o^r common aduersaries. And againe I can neuer brooke the humor of them that delite in wrangle & contention to my smale abilitie I must euer be a blocke in the way of suche disposed persons. Touching the lo: protectors letter that no satisfaction shalbe demaunded on either parte, his Ho: & his Grace may command what they please in this case, & I wishe all to obey specially at thes tymes, for the common good, but yett you knowe, this commandment of theirs can no way loose them from the bond of making satisfaction, wch haue done the wronge. Vnlesse the iniuried freely forgiue no power on earthe can secure the offendors conscience. And therefore I could wishe for the good of bothe yor soules & o^{rs}, we had conference touching remission of all past. The carier will lett me write no more. I shall answere further Wal. w^t the next. Thus resting yo^{rs} in whatsoever may be for the common good, I humbly take my leave this 2 martij.

Yo^r R. to command,
J. M. Ratclife.

I. *Endorsement* (*original*):
To the right Wor^{ll} & R^d his loving frend
Mr. Georg Black:

II. *Endorsemment.*
Mr. Mush to Mr. Blackw.

5. *Copy of a Letter from Arthur Pitts, Dean of Liverdun, to Blackwell.* April 11, 1600.

My deare frende, this bearer Mr. Charnock beinge confyned to Pont.[a] as you know, Doctor Ely, F. Darbishire & I, employed the best frendes we had, to provide him meanes to stay there. And findinge none, he wrote to his frendes in England & to Rome to the same effect, in hope whereof, I haue received him in my howse whilest I was able, & seinge no good answeare from any place, necessitie enforced him to retyre him self into the Countrie. So soone as he found here noe provision of maintenance, he appealed

[a] Pont-à-Mousson, in Lorraine, whither he had been banished by sentence of the cardinals in the preceding year.

before me: a gravamine, & goeth to the Bishoppes Vicar generall to doe the same at Toul. I thought good to signifie thus much vnto youe, lest you should thinke that he departed hence, either of disobedience against the sentence, or of contempt of the Censures. This I can assure you moreover, that he haith lived in my howse these neene monthes vertuously and peaceably though he haith had causes to doe otherwise, & goethe towarde you with the same minde to prosecute with all peace and charitie his vocation. The longe and aunciente experience that I haue had of yor vertue and prudence, maketh me presume, that you will further both there, and with your letters to the Superiours his charitable intention. wch I besech you to doe for his sake that gave his life for vs all, Thus most humbly commendinge my self to your praiers, I committ you to God to assist you with his holie spiritt. From Liuerdune, the 11 of Aprill 1600.

Your lovinge frende Arthur Pittes Deane of Liuerdune & Chauncelour of the Legation in Lorraine.

To his verie frende M^r. Blakwell.

6. *Copy of a Letter from Blackwell to Francis Clark.*

47, f. 166.

27 Feb., 1600.

Reverend sir, I mervaile y^t yo^u will trouble me wth busses either bredd in yor owne braines: or els blowen vpon yo^u by some contentious breathe. I knowe not of any courses about ye abrogacion (as yo^u tearme it) of yor faculties. Such blasts woulde be restrained, wch trouble the water, wch woulde be quiet. I woulde not have yo^u rove in generalities: but if you have any particular wrongs yo^u have there wth yo^u my reverend assistant, to whome yo^u maye haue remedie, & sufficient releife. But I feare yo^u take that to be a wrong, wch in myne opinion I take to be yor right. As I woulde not haue any to speake of yor state heeretofore, so I cannot thinke but that it was schismaticall. Neither doth this opinion cast vpon yo{u} any discreditt. ffor all good catholicks do make accompt of yo{u}, as yo{u} are: not as yo{u} have beene. The ioye wch they take of yor returne to yor fathers house hath suppressed all the grieffe of yor prodigall errors. The recouerie of the lost sheepe hath yeelded such comfortes, as yor disobedience heeretofore hath not depressed yo{u} into the depthe of discreditts so much, as yor submissive behavio{ur} to lawfull authoritie hath lifted yo{u} up to ye height of good opinion in the conceites of all good men, & a verie commendable reputation. Maintaine therefore this yor creditt, & runne not vpon the losse thereof by iustifying yor former disobedience. Yo{u} knowe how myldlie I haue dealt wth yo{u}. Quo indulgentior liberalitas, eo inexcusabilior peruicacia. Cease to rest vpon yor owne iudgments: follow yor superio{r}. If yo{u} like not hereof, then as I haue to Mr Mush already given; so I give yo{u}, & all yor adherents this finall admonition, that if ever I can fynde hereafter, that either by worde, or wryting, yo{u} iustifye yor enormous disobedience as void of sinne: this being a signe of want of grace, et defensio peccati, wch is an highe pryde, I will suspend yo{u} from yor function, as vnworthie to exercise the same. I hope I shall not neede to put this in practise: neither are yo{u} to thinke this to be an over hard proceeding. Qui vere diligit, non quæ mulceant, sed quæ prosint, cogitat. You shall haue me carefull for yor profitts. Deus pacis sit vobiscum.

27 Februarij
Vester seruus in Chr̃o
GEORGIUS BLACKWELLUS.
Archip{r} et Protonotarius
Apostolicus.

To his very frend Mr. ffrancis.

Marginal notes:
- Their course was schismaticall.[a]
- Former disobedience.
- Rest not upon yor owne iudgments, follow yor superior.
- A gallant threate.

[a] The marginal notes appear to be in Bagshaw's hand.

7. Letter of Clark in reply to the foregoing.

April 5 [1600].

R^t. R^d.

I am very sory that the advertisements proceedinge from me in all sinceritye and charitye for the common peace as I thought have any wayes discontented yor reverence: and I am no lesse grieved that yow shold suspect them to be buzzes of myne owne brayne. ffor I must needs conceave thereby yor to to hard opinion of me as eyther a rayser and inventor of lyes, or a spreader of dissentions. ffor reproofe whereof I apeale to all wth whom I converse of whom many know how much I have laboured to stoppe false whispered suggestions, and to keep unknowen o^r late vnpleasant affayres till the earth itselfe did ring thereof, though o^r concealinge thereof for conscience sake so longe was cause of litle ease vnto vs: as by experience sithence we have found. 47, f. 167.

Deare S^r, the things I write vnto you of diverse others can and will witnes aswell as my selfe: and that yor reverence may know they were no buzzes of myne owne brayne, even then I imparted them to m^r Oldcorne one of the societye, and where they were whispered: But sithence they have displeased yor reverence, pardon me, I pray yow, I shall no more trouble yow in the like; but arme myselfe wth patience where I see small hope of redresse.

As for my case, R^d. S^r, wch still yow iudge to have been schismaticall, why hath not yor Reverence corrected it in me and others, if not for o^rselves, yet at the least for the good of so many poore soules as have been deceaved by vs whilest we were such as yow affirme: all which insteed of sacraments receaved nothinge els at o^r hands but sacrilegious abuses: neyther could ignorance excuse them that have dealt wth vs vnto whom the controversy was knowen as well as to o^rselves, and could ignorance excuse them from sinne, yet were they no whit nearer the benefitt and graces of the sacraments they receaved from vs. ffor where no authoritye was, there no dispensation of graces could be, and by consequence all confessions heard by vs voyd and irritat and to be reiterated, wch none yet to o^r knowledge have done: neyther can that we now doe in o^r functions be currant because if we were schismaticks we consequently lost all iurisdiction and facultyes wch yet never receyving againe to o^r knowledge we remayne in statu quo prius, deprived thereof and disabled to any sacramentall function. Wherefore deare S^r if the case be thus wth me lett not yor lenitye towards me be cause of so sacrilegious a hurte both to myselfe and others. I desire not in yor favo^r to abuse god his sacraments and servaunts: wherefore, deare S^r, if I runne astray as a father convert me and as a judge compell me to the right: felix necessitas qua cogit ad meliora. I had rather by compulsion worke iustice, then by freedome offend: where yor reverence sayth, Catholicks accompt of me as I now am, not what I have been, ioyinge in the retorne of the prodigall childe and lost sheep etc.: these phrases, R^d. S^r, are wonderful hard still mainteyning o^r discreditts? what shall the world iudge of me if yor reverence pronounce so hard a sentence of me. If my superior accuse me, who shall protect me. If my iudge sentence me who will not condemne me? And yet I stand and must stande vpon myne owne innocency therein: neyther life nor death shall make me accuse myselfe vniustly[a] .... testimonium habeo bonæ conscientiæ. And wold god I could in all the ac[tions] and periode of my life apeare so litle towched in my soule and conscience as in this pretended schisme. God and my soule know how farre my will was from disobedience to Gods church: and my diligence I vsed to be rightly resolved therein may sufficiently beare testimonye thereof to the worlde. Quapropter non recedam ab innocentia mea. If by yor authoritye yow list to strike, yow may: I am yor subiect, and will obey, though my soule cannot yeald to yor conceyts and opinions in ye matter of schisme or mortall dis-

[a] Mutilated.

obedience therein pretended against me: yet shall I beare wth patience the burden of yor censures god assistinge me howsoever preiudicall vnto me vntill god otherwise dispose of me to his best pleasure. Thus leavinge all to gods sweet providence humbly I take my leave. Aprill 5.

Yo^r subiect and servaunt in all iustice,

FRA: CLE:

8. *Letter by "Mr. Clarke" with Narrative of proceedings in the controversy to the time of the Paris Sentence (May 3, 1600).*[a]   47, f. 267.

20 Dec. [1600]

Very worshipfull Sir, the request yo^u demaund at my handes concerneth so unpleasinge a subiect, that had not the great discretion I suppose to be in yo^u as muche moved me thereto, as the extraordinary curtesie I owe yo^u: Certes I had not condescended so far fourth vnto yor desyre herein, syth that in performance thereof I shalbe inforced to lay open suche proceeding and of suche men, as bothe in regard of the persones as also of the proceedings I conld wyshe they were buried in perpetuall oblivion: yet to satisfie yor so ernest and importunate request presuminge bothe of yor charitable construccion and also yor discrete concealment hereof, I will truly and playnely sett downe in as breef manner as I can the whole processe of that yo^u require, not to incense you against any partie but to informe yo^u arighte in the cause.

You shall vnderstand, wor^ll Sir, that some of vs beinge desirous wth the good likinge and consent of the rest of o^r brethren, and not otherwise, to conbine and vnite o^rselves in forme of a sodalitie or association, to live vnder certeyne prescript rules of government such as might be pleasing and convenient as well for every one in particular as for the common good : And hauing proceded so far

[a] This document is much injured and in parts indecipherable.

therein to the good likinge of all, yea of the fathers themselues beinge made acquainted wth o^r purposes and intentions in these busynes, that there rested nowe no difficultie or dowbt at all of effecting our designes. It pleased them, I meane the ffathers, contrarie to theire faire shewe of applauding o^r endevours spedely to transporte a messinger or factor to the sea apostolick, there to attend the retorne of ff. Parsons from Spayne and wth him acte a newe conceyved pollicie to prevent and crosse what was or might be pretended of vs for that they thought it not convenient (as should seme) that any newe strength by waie of vnion or incorporation should arise or increase amongest vs, wch happely mighte deminishe or preiudice some sparke of theire greatnes and popularitie, and thereby in tyme be able to worke some countercheck to the exorbitant actions of suche working heads as presume to plott beyonde the circumference of their comission. This policye (forsoth) was that the messinger being a preist, should wth the countenance of the Cardinall protector Caietane and diligent seco[nding] of ff. Parsons, sole Polipragmon in these fine policies, be broug[ht] vnto his holy^s: and there in a grave and solemne oration in the nam[es] of all his brethren, humbly and instantly desire some superioritie and subordination for the endinge of suche quæstions and controuersies as should happen to arise amangest vs; leaving the manner thereof and nominacion of the superior vnto holy^s: There Mercury having thus finished his parte of Embassy, further information therein and discussing of the meanes and person was to be lefte vnto the Protector, informed and directed whollye (as is evident) by ff. Parsons. By whose meanes the erection of an Archepresbitery amongest vs was procured of his holy^s: yet not absolutely neither (as should seme] but condicionally vppon o^r likinge, for that his holy^s (as it is reported) at suche tyme as he graunted thereto, vsed this speche, that he would not impose anythinge vppon the good priestes in England but suche as them selves should like: yet not w^thstanding his holy^s sincere intentions and fatherly love towardes vs, a letter was presently

47, f. 267 b.

addressed from the Protector wth comaundm^t from his holy^s specified therein, that wee should forthw^th w^thout demurre admitt for o^r superior this o^r nowe present Archipresbiter, in wch letters also were nominated sixe of his assistants, one of them beinge their proctor in this busynes,[a] and other sixe to be chosen by the Archepresbiter himself or rather in very deede by ff: Walley w^thout whose counsell direccions and consent no one of them was elected. A strange accident this semed vnto vs, and to passe (in some sorte) the bondes of civile curtesie: that Jesuites beinge incorporate to a different body or societie in religion from vs should prescribe orders, chose governors, and erecte monarchies to vs who by no lawe or other ordinance whatsoever are subiects or belonginge vnto their charge, especially they being men vowed to obedience, wee not so. No marvaile then though wee were a little discontented to see these theire preposterous procedinges, tendinge in verie truthe to no other end but to keep vs in awe and subiection to them as either children to their parentes or schollers to their masters, by wch o^r oppression all actions and direccions in all matters might have a more free passe at theire wills and pleasures w^thout controlle of any: But to them that these intentions and all other procedinges hereafter might be the better shadowed, and yet theire designes effectnally proceede, all must be covered forsoth under the cloake of a superiors commaund, but suche an one (as being theire creature) shall stand at theire sole direccion, so that when they liste he shall commaunde, and when any thinge happeth amisse whereof complaint shalbe made, as of any wrong or iniury don to any thereby, they may disclayme as ignorant of his proceedinges. And that yo^u may have some taste hereof consider I beseche yo^u the late handling of the matter of schisme pretended agaainst vs and yo^u shall easely perceyve thereby that tnis wch I speake is not a mere supposall, but founded vppon more then probable, if not evident reasons. for as yo^u well knowe the first authors thereof were the Jesuites, one of them to that effect writing

[a] James Standish.

a whole tracte or discourse thereof, besides other letters and messages sent by diverse of them to many theire frendes and o^rs concerning that subiecte, yet when they came to be towched therew^th they disclaymed as not guiltie of any suche action, laying all vppon the Archepriest his neck as the only promulgator and maynteyner thereof against vs. What I pray yo^u is this but to play wth bothe handes, nowe out, nowe in, as though they could daunce in a nett, and not be seen. Who in wisedome indifferently considering these moste indirecte and sinisterous procedinges can condemne vs for standing only vppon o^r owne righte beinge thus abused and made youngelinges by them. The wronges we have receyved at theire handes by these theire procedinges are not I suppose vnknowne vnto yo^u, not w^thstanding o^r moste milde procedinges towardes them behaving o^rselves only passively in these affaires not impugning theires but defending o^r owne righte.

ffor first wee desired at the coming ouer of the Cardinalls letters but that o^r two agents elected in o^r former busynes and even then to departe when as the Cardinalls letter were presented vnto vs, might wth their consent yet proceede in o^r former determinations to make his holy^s acquainted therew^th, and if after information made to his holynes of o^r estates and desynes it should better please him to confirme that order nowe taken then thother wee should propose, that then forthw^th wee would submitt and accepte thereof and in the meane season behave oure selves towards him whom they had caused to be elected as towards o^r superior: yf so that his holy^s vppon more mature considerations and better or further informations should preferre o^r petitions that they would likewise remayne contente; but they by no meanes condescending vnto this o^r reasonable mocion wee were inforced in o^r owne righte to appeale rom the Cardinalls order, holding his letters as insufficient bycause not iuridicall notice to bynde vs vnto any suche newe and strange manner of subordination, And thereof [a] . . . . . . these letters or there disclayming wee sent over . . . . . . to followe o^r pretended

---

[a] At this point the edge of the MS. is torn off for the space of several lines.

busynes. Hinc illæ lachrymæ. Noe sooner were oure agents
departed but that greate fear, it would seme, invaded o^r opposers,
least that by . . . . . . theire cunning plotts mighte be descovered
and their actions and endevors reuersed. Wherupon . . . . . .
newe policies, and as a preparative . . . . . . caste out generall 47, f. 268b.
busses of schisme [that those who] refuse (for sothe) to subscribe vnto
the newe erected authoritie were *ipso facto* schismaticks and rebells
vnto godes churche. W^{ch} vniust accusations they so stiffly main-
teyned against vs that bothe by messages, letters, informations,
and tracts, to that end spred abrode, they omitted no occasion to
terrifye suche of o^r ffrendes as shoulde deale wth vs in matters of
sacramentes and to intangle fearefull and scrupulous consciences wth
a certeyne religious fear of no lesse offence then sacrilege. By w^{ch}
theire vniust accusacion many of both sortes were drawne into
dowbtfull suspence howe to behave themselves towardes vs, theire
love on the one side drawing them still to affecte vs, and feare of
doing ill on the other side pulling back from vs others that were
indifferent, yet ignorant of the iustice or iniustice of these accusations: thinking to take the securer parte, forbare to deale wth vs.
A thirde sorte wholly devoted vnto the ffathers, not only forbare to
communicate wth vs, but also wth mighte and maine running theire
masters course, maynteyned the same staine against vs, alyenating
by all the meanes they coulde as many from vs as they mighte.
And the more to helpe forwarde this action, priviledges of larger
faculties were distributed to such of the clergie as woulde subscribe.
So that between favo^r, perswasions, and feare, no marvayle that
many were distracted from vs of bothe sortes: yet was not this the
end aud sole drifte of theire intentions. A further matter was yet
aimed at, wch was to procure subscripcions for the confirmation of
theire late procured subordination. ffor procurement whereof a letter
was framed, somewhat in an obscure stile by way of congratulation
or thanksgiving vnto his holy^s. for the order of goverment erected
amongst us, wch letters, as you knowe, were spedely sent flying into
all partes that a sodayne dispatche therein might be made and a

spedy . . . . . . thereof vnto his holynes. Vnto these congratulations . . . . . . many and the moste parte easely subscribed, partly for favo^r, partly [through] feare, partly in polycie, thinkinge they would compasse theire designes howsoeuer wthout them, and partly thorouge ignorance or inconsideration, not vnderstandinge or not perceyvinge that a thansgivinge importeth a consent. Neither was this the meanest policye they practised in these affaires (yf yo^u will consider it) for havinge first desired this subordination in the name of all the priestes, no one priest witting thereof, and informed his holynes that o^r two agents in the way towards Rome, came but from some fewe discontented persons: what better polycie could be devised then to procure subscribcions vnto a thansgiving whereby his holy^s. must nedes be perswaded by the multitude of consentes that the former petition and desire by them made in the priests names was current, and that o^r two agents were indeede messengers but from a fewe discontented persons (as they had informed). And this their polycie fayled them not, for even so it fell out as they desired, that not only his holynes was confirmed in theire former informations against our messingers and cause, but also therevpon was easely drawne by other theire suggestions of feare to incorage theire discontented spirits and to give the like scope or occasion hereafter of newe broyles and sturres wherewth to trouble contynually his holy^s. not to admitt them to audience, as men factious wthout any iuste occasion. So that the whole managinge of all their sutes was comitted over vnto the Cardinall protector and Cardinall . . . . his hearing, the one of them and chiefe wholly at the direction of ffather Parsons (as all the worlde knoweth) and the other perhaps vnwilling to countercheck the protecto^{rs} courses in any thing. And before they shoulde be called before these two princes . . . . . . provided that they should be arrested by the . . . . . . officers for that purpose, and raunsakt and . . . . . . theire papers of informations they brought . . . . . . them and shutt up close, and seuerally in two chambers never to speake or conferre wth one an other about theire affair[s] or to knowe what

47, f. 268c.

was done or said by eache other . . . . . . was a strange strategeme, yet such a one as . . . . . . served for theire purpose, for by this 47, f. 268d. meanes they mighte give oute what rumors they would of them and theire busynes or of theire papers and informations they brought wth them, as in very deede most vniustly and vntruly they did, bothe of the nomber of names consenting to theire actions, as also theire answers and weak behavio^r in o^r cause. After theire long imprisonm^t and examinations, had before the foresaid cardinalls, they were wth faire wordes dismissed but consyned vnto two seuerall places in ffraunce and debarred from their entrance into England, to this end only that wee should remayne ignorant in theire affaires what had hapned, and that the whole cuntrie mighte be fedd wth theire reports alone. While these thinges were thus in handling and that theire devises had currant passage wthout suspicion of any indirecte or cunning dealing therein, easie perswasions prevayled wth his holy^s. suspecting no circumvention in all this processe to graunt his breef or instrument of confirmation of the proiected authoritie , before the cominge whereof, many thundering reports were spred abrode against vs as contemners of the authoritie of the sea apostolike, and that o^r expectance of his holynes further absolute resolution was but a shifte, neither would wee yelde thereto. But when they sawe that at the receipte of the briefe wee presently admitted his authoritie Saluo nostro iure, though gotten by indirecte meanes, they were content to come to some indifferent agreement; wch contynued but a while, for when they were towched wth the matter of schisme wherein wee had receyved wronge (as then appeared by o^r submission to the breef) that we might have o^r creditts repaired by the authors of that imputed crime by some publick testimonye to the contrary for the satisfaction of suche as had ben scandalized therby, they were so farre from doinge vs any 47, f. 269. righte of satisfaccion that they burst out a newe the defence thereof: and bicause no colo^r of faul[t] . . . . . . shoulde seme to have ben committed by them against vs . . . . . . sought to bringe in a newe founde conceipte (forsothe) at the least of mortall synne in vs: for that as they affirmed by o^r contradictions the Cardinall protector was discredited, the ffathers iniured, and oure Archepresbiter him self drawne into daungers; and there they not only buszed into the lay catholicks eares, but also sought by perswasions and all other meanes to drawe vs to acknowledge. Wee at length seeinge their procedings, suche as there was no hope lefte to vs of any indifferent course to be had at their handes, were at the length constrayned to send over the case to Paris, there to be discussed and determined by the whole facultye, by whose iudgement we were not only freed of all suspicion of schisme but also from note or touche of synne. This censure was (as yo^u well knowe) nothinge pleasinge vnto theire humors, and therefore least happely it mighte perswade th . . . . . . sorte of o^r iuste procedinges, and the wronges wee . . . . . . receyved therein, first, the credite of the Vniuersity [was] . . . . . . called in question: secondly dowbte of the true . . . . . . proposing of the case, and last of all a flat . . . . . . from the Archeprieste vnder payne of censure to all who should manteyne the iudgement of Paris therein: Thirdly . . . . syr, have ben there hard and vniust procedinges from . . . . . . against vs debarring vs of all meanes of iustice . . . . . . attribute generally vnto them, bicause the actions of th[e archpriest] (as is moste apparant) procede not wthout their . . . . . . advice. Judge nowe indifferently wthout preiudice . . . . . . any I beseche yo^u, whether wee have not cause . . . . . . and to appeale from so apparant iniurious proceedings . . . . . . wishing yo^u all felicetye I take my leave, 20 december.

You^r most faithfull,
. . . .

[*Signature torn off.*]

RENEWAL OF THE CONFLICT. 173

9. *Copy of Blackwell's Order for the Examination of William Clark, priest, in the Clink.*

Feb. 28 [1601].

In dei nomine Amen. An⁰ dni 1600, secundum computum Anglicanum et 28 februarij.   47, f. 209.

Nos Georgius Blac : Archip: Angliæ vobis R^{dis} Dnis Rob: Baroesio et Ant⁰. Rousio committimus facultatem et potestatem examinandi dominum Gulielmum Clerkum presbyterum in vestro Castro Clinkensi detentum. 1 Vtrum subscripserit aut nomen suum fecerit apponi litteris illis datis 17 Novemb:[a] et prætensæ appellationi præfixis, quæ plenissimæ iniuriarum contra me et alios ecclesiasticos, et etiam non vacuæ a pravibus contumelijs evagantur insolentius, et propterea probro libelli famosi notari deberent. 2 Vtrum iudicet omnia in eisdem litteris vera esse, et adeo iusta vt declinare in proposito, et deflectere sententiam illam, et mutare nullo modo voluerit. Hec præcipimus in virtute obedientiæ vt confestim et sine mora faciat. Si se præstiterit inobedientem aut si vos deprehenderitis illum confidentem et defendentem subscriptionem illam, tunc illud in scriptis vestris volo vt mihi quamprimum renuncietis. Sed si negaverit quod illis literis consensum, et subscriptionem præbuerit, iubeo vt illud manu sua propria notatum et suo iuramento stabilitum ad me percitissime transmittatis. Hæc actutum et sine dilatione, hæc serio et syncere perficite : et videte diligenter ne aliquam moram falacijs concinnandis, et respirationem concedatis.

Ex hospitio nostro 28 febr., 1600.
Vester servus Georgius Blackwellus.
Archip^{r}sbiter Catholicorum Anglorum.

Endorsed :

Reverendis D. D. Rob. Bur. et Anth. Rous and because these names are [?] this would be concealed.

[a] William Clark's name appears among the thirty signatures to the Appeal of Nov. 17, 1600. On Dec. 17 Blackwell had suspended Robert Drury, another appellant, afterwards martyr. March 10, 1601, he suspended and interdicted Colleton and eight of the prisoners at Framlingham. See *Jesuits and Seculars*, p. 93.

Copy of Blackwell's Suspension of Clark.

10 March, 1600-1.

R^{dis} Confratribus suis et compresbiteris salutem.

Quoniam seditiosis quibusdam literis 17 Novemb., 1600, ad nos directis affixum fuit nomen D: Giulielmi Clerki presbyteri, Isque ex mandato nostro in virtute obedientiæ interrogatus, an ipse subscripserit illis literis, aut nomen suum fecerit apponi, etc. Ad hæc directe respondere recusaverit; sed (quæsitis falsis, et callidis effugiis) aperte ludificari, ac sciens calumniari voluerit: Propterea nos illi omnes facultates iurisdictionis abrogamus: eumque ab omni ordinum executione suspendimus, donec vel se sufficienter purgaverit; vel ad nostrum arbitrium congruam satisfactionem præstiterit.

> Datum ex hospitio nostro 10 Martij anno 1600 secundum computum Anglicanum, Georgius Blackwellus Archipresbyter.

Concordat cum originali.　　　　　Robertus Baruis.
　　　　　　　　　　　　　　　　Antonius Rous.

Endorsed:

R^{dis} D. R^{to} Baruisio et Ant^o. Rousio.

10. *C. R.*[a] *to John Smith. Low Sunday* [1601].

Good Mr John. We wante Mr. Blackwells first letter, non est quod quisque concaleat stomacho: & his decree against Paris.[b] We would gladly see yours wch he sayth be like to owrs. I pray you lett vs heare at & wth as much speed as may be for matters

---

[a] Mr. Macray says: "no doubt Rob. Charnock."

[b] The decree of Blackwell condemning the censure of the Paris University in favour of the appellants was dated 29 May, 1600. It is printed in Bagshaw's *True Relation*.

proceede. We have sent Mr. Blackwell an answere to his suspension & interdicte [a] wch I pray you see sent vnto him.

In any case, good S^r, fayle not to certifye vs vppon what grounde he excepteth againste Mr. Button, Mr. Potter, & Mr. Cope[b] & what issue that sorteth vnto. & what hath passed synce from him. Our wants ar suche as present relief must needes be hadd wth gods assiatance, & therfore ether by requeste or creditt some way sende some trusty body hyther wth mony to poore suspended men. It would grieve you & it maketh me lawghe & disdayne, to see how some of his seditiouse lay men ether of feare or simplycyty looke at vs as if yt were true, wch John a greene[c] wrote y^t we were to be avoyded as men havinge the plague soare.

We ar so vnsetled & vnfurnished y^t we can scarce do any thinge. Beare wth vs a while. Willingnes is not wantinge. I am gladd you & we be come both to sownde alike in Mr. Blackwells eares. The more indignities you suffer the greater your merite. Commend vs to all our brethren & theyre prayers, whome we dayly remember. Dominica in albis.

Yours not to fayle
C. R.

for godes sake so deale wth Mr. Bluett as he may be assisted & cownsayled by you & the rest from time to time.

Endorsement (by writer):
To his approved good friende Mr. John Smithe.

---

[a] Perhaps that of March 10. 1601, directed against a number of prisoners at Framlingham.

[b] Richard Button, George Potter *alias* Transham, and James Cope, signed the Appeal.

[c] Perhaps John Greene, a prisoner at Wisbech on the Jesuit side, in reference to whom Bagshaw wrote to Bluet (April 1601), "The pride of Bickley, Green, and Bramston must be rebated or else our estate is not tolerable." (*Jesuits and Seculars*, p. 151.)

47, f. 186.
also
54, f. 324.

11. *Letter to a Lady, from Father Richard Holtby, alias Duckett, S. J.*

June 30, 1601.

Holteby ye Jesuite against ye secular priests answered by Mr. Collington.^a

Good Madam, though of late I haue in writinge delivered vnto you as breeflie as I could the true originall and progresse of all these contentions in oure Clergie, wherein I desier no further trust at yor La : handes, then the verie triall of all matters shall deserve, and am content wthall to hazard my whole creditt wth you so farre, that if in any substantiall matter or circumstance of the same I be found to doble, forge, or, dissemble, or to vtter any thinge otherwise then truth and that wch I will take in hand to convince either vppon my oathe if neede were or other sufficient proofe that you give me lesse creditt in the rest. And herein I will ioyne wth yor frend M^r. Rat:^b or any other of that sort whatsoeuer if it shall please you in any matter to take the triall of oure honest and faithfull dealinge. I am more forwarde in this manner to satisfie yor La : perhaps then neede dothe require yet the weightiness of the cause itself, and the perill of these dissemblinge and more politick then playne dealinge men, together wth some further occasion offred, dothe vrge me to ymportune yo^u for yor good, and also exacteth the more discretion and warynes att yor handes, there is no wisedome for yo^u in so greate a difficultie after a blynde manner to be ledd away wth to much affection or to give credite peremptorily vnto any one or a few persons in theire owne cause, neither is it convenient for you nor any to cast lottes for yor soule by exposinge the same wthout iudgement vnto either partie in a sedition vppon a meere presumption of the right of the one side, when the other hathe no lesse showe of religion and honestye, more weight of reason and authoritie and as of equall iudgement learninge and æstimation, if not more, then those vppon whose trust and sincerity you repose yo^rself : but rather you ought first

^a Colleton's *Just Defence*, printed in 1602, was in the main an answer to this letter. *See* pp. 77 and 92 of that work.
^b Ratcliffe *i.e.* Mush.

to take the ordinary meanes of due examination of thinges, and for that cause to haue yor eare open to the hearing of either parte and so iudge and followe as reason illuminated by godes grace shall instruct you. ffirst of all therefore it is most certayne, and them selves will not, neither can they deny it, but that even then and from the first letter of ye Cardinall Protector, duringe wch tyme vntill the cominge of the Popes Breve the Archepriest was indeed theire lawfull superior, for so the pope him self did declare in the said Breve, affirminge wth all that whosoeuer did otherwise iudge or say his iudgment was of no effecte comaunding that in like manner every one should iudge accordinglie for the tyme to come. Therefore it must nedes followe that the iudgement of these men that tooke him to be no superior and therevppon resisted his authoritie, was even then when they so stood out of no value or effecte and consequently could not excuse them for reiectinge his autboritie wch indeede had ben a matter of greate effecte. Secondly they can not deny, but that whosoeuer did stand out wth the Archepriest before the Breve came vppon an opinion that he was no lawfull superior they were verily deceyved, becaus[e] in truthe he was theire superior, and consequently that theire acte of theire so standinge out, o^r not submittinge them selves, was an acte of disobedience because it was in deed a resistinge of a lawfull authoritie.

47, f. 186b

Thirdlie that it was no simple dissobedience but a playne rebellion, it is also evident because they did not only contemne to obey his comaundm^t but they reiected the authoritie it selfe, and would not acknowlecge or take him for a superio^r att all or submitt them selves vnto him as his subjects, wch is to Rebell against theire head.

ffourthly, that it was a culpable disobedience it is also most clere, first by the wordes of our savio^r him self when he sayth of the respect to be had to his apostles, and in them vnto all superio^{rs}: He that heareth yo^u heareth me, and he that contemneth you contemneth me. And in an other place, he that will not heare the Churche (that is to say theire pastors or prelates in whom the authoritie of

Christe his churche is represented) lett him be vnto thee as a heathen or publican. And St. Paule obey yor prelates and subiecte yor selues vnto them, for they watche over you, readie as it were to give accompte for yor soules. And in an other place. Let euery soule be subiecte vnto higher powers, for there is no power but from god, and the thinges that are are ordeyned of god, therefore he that resisteth power, resisteth the ordynance of god, and they who resiste doe gett damnation to them selues. Therefore by the verie testimony of god himself theire disobedience or rebellion against lawfull authoritie is not only sinfull but a most greevous and damnable synne.

ffiftly, that it was a most enormous, notorious and publick synne, it can not be denied, ffirst because it drew a greate number into a publick faction and dissention wch was an exceedinge iniury vnto the Churche and Clergie. Secondly, because it bred an open scandall and that in the heads of priests themselues, to the hurt of many soules and stayne of theire profession. Thirdly, because if made the authors thereof infamous for rebellion and disobedience vnto the whole nation. ffinally theire defence of the same made it most haynous, notorious and publick, and declared that it came not either of ignorance or infirmitie but of playne malice and an obstinate will not to obey: for wch cause they would take no notice of any superioritie appointed, and reiected all admonition both of theire knowne superiors the Protector and governor of Colledges and also of all others were they never so grave and credible reporters even of theire owne associates and punished for the same disobedience also.

Sixtly, that it came of a prowde presumptuous minde and a seditious spirite is to to clere. ffirst because vppon the verie hearinge of a new supior, and wthout any necessary examinacion or consideracion of the assignment and meanes of procuringe or appointinge the same, they began presently to resist as if theire owne designement of a superior of theire owne device and appointment had been crossed thereby of purpose against theire willes as if none

47. f, 187.

had righte or witt or power to appoint them superio^{rs} except them selves. Agayne, that hearinge it came from his holynes they durst notwthstandinge take in hand to resiste yea to overthrow his order even before himself, as if he had not done well or taken the best course: and therefore they would better advise him (seely men) then his owne counsell and consistory of Cardinalls, men experienced in suche affaires, could doe. Also that hearinge theire proceedinges were misliked at Rome and that theire solicitors were imprisoned condemned and punished for the same fact yet would not yelde but proceede [in] theire obstinacie. Moreover that they beinge so fewe in nomber that is to say 12 or 13 persons (as vppon the oath of theire sollicitors it was made manifest) and not all those either of the wisest, most learned, of greatest experience, of best fame and æstimation of vertue either at home or abrode (howsoeuer yor frend in his printed libell extoll both him selfe and them all vnto the skyes) yet would disgrace and expose them selves vnto the whole Clergie of England besides who did voluntarily, and wth many gratulations sent vnto the Pope and protector, accept of the Superior appointed. Yea, yor ffrend proceeded so farre in his insolencye, that he woulde notwthstandinge all this, compare him self wth holy Job for his innocency and wth St. Thomas of Canterbury, who in the defence of ecclesiastical libertie would not yelde vnto the kings ambition though the whole clergie had consented thereto, comparinge therein the Pope vnto an ambitious kinge, his obstinate disobedience vnto the see apostolick vnto the zeale of a saincte for obedience to the same, his licentious libertie from havinge a lawfull superior and subordination to keepe him in due subjeccion vnto ecclesiasticall immunities from temporall obligations for the more strict order and subieccion vnto the Cannons and Rules of the Churche and her pastors, condemninge all theire brethren either of rashnes, feare or flattery in that they woulde accept so soone or at all of his holynes order, and condemninge also the see apostolick (wch by Christes prayer was to haue the assurance of his spiritt to directe it, and against the wch hels gate should not prevayle) and the wholl Senate

47, f 118b.

of Cardinalls bothe for want of witt or honesty in affirminge that they doe all by favoure w^{th}out discretion, whereof my self wth many others are witnesses of yor frendes wordes in that behalf.

ffinally his laboringe still nowe after the Popes Breve, after his submission and promise made not to styr any more after so many scandalls and other inconveniences perceyved to sollicite verdits, gotton by misinformacion abrode, to sollicite new voices and suffrages at home for the revivinge of the old sedition, to sowe false rumors of theire owne proceedings, to invent false reportes and sinister caluminations of others actions and intentions approved vnto superir^{rs} and liked of all and agaynst all that are opposite vnto theire temeritie or irreligious pollicies to publishe and divulge in printed libells vnto the whole world theire owne follies indeede for the disgrace of themselves and iniury of others and so spreade abrode to the same purpose certayne exclamations of outragious iniuries and persecution sustayned for theire innocency, that theire innocent cause can get no audience, that all meanes to defend theire innocencye is stopped, that they can not be suffred to make a iust and lawfull Appeale vnto the see apostolick but are persecuted for the same, that superio^{rs} will admitt no triall, not so muche as iudge the cause them selves, it beinge put to theire owne consciences that it is the ambition and vayne glory of certen religious men that is to say Mr. Persons and his brethren that are the causers of all, that theire violent and iniurious courses discredite oure people and Clergie, they make vs to be accompted the worst Nation vnder heaven, they respect theire owne extraordinary creditt aboue oure Clergie, Churche and priestes, vniustly, they seeke to ouerrule in every place bothe Bishops Cardinalls and all and infinite suche false idle and seditious rumors in lamentable sorte doth yor frend and his associates cast into the peoples eares and others wth whom they may haue audience, never intending to acknowledge any fault in them selves or shewe any token of any due submission vnto theire superio^{rs} sentence or censures to chasten theire enormities but rather seeke to iniurye, and bringe all into a confusion that

47, f. 188.

them selves may seme innocent : all wch doe manifestly convince that they haue a seditious and most prowd presumptuous spiritt, the fountayn of theire disobedience.

Seaventhly, that theire disobedience even then tended to a seperation, division, schisme and fall of theire partie into further inconveniences it is in my conceyte verie palpable if you liste to examine theire owne wordes and the circumstances and sequele of theire proceedinges.

ffirst the intent of theere sodalitie (whereof yor frend was the principall deviser in the North cuntries) was to make a head and to oppose them selves against the societie of Jesus and this by the open profession of some of them selves and witnes of others, ergo they intended a division before there came any worde of a superior from the Popes authoritie.

Secondly they haue (at the least yor frend hath) a long tyme and that also before any notice of a superior bothe in his word[es] and writinges, made himself and those of his side an other bodie and company or congregation from oure societie, and those that he thought were adioyned vnto vs as if wee had no parte wth them either in charge spirituall functions and all endevours, but were a contrary or an other seperated body and congregation of an other comunitye, ergo in mynde they had even a separation from other members of the same Churche.

Thirdly, ymediatly after worde came of a superior by his holines appointment, yor frend declared that he was readie rather to want faculties, to forsake the cuntrie and give ouer all, then to live vnder the superior not appointed by them selves, the ground whereof he shewed to be this; because this superioritie appointed was the Jesuites deede and w^thout theire privitie to the end wee might over-rule in every place where wee came. ffor thus they vse to turn every thinge that cometh from his holyness, that is not after theire likinge that it is the Jesuits deede to over-rule   And not longe after hearinge that theire two sollicitors were like to be evill taken 47, f. 188b. w^thall by his holines, or that they were in prison for their temerarious attempt, he declared himself and his fellowes to be so farre from agrement or submission even vnto his holynes comaund that he affirmed desperatly that if those two were comitted, they would send other two, and after them other two, and after them others so longe as they had any left to take theire parte. And wthin a litle before the Breve came he affirmed resolutely that M^r. Parsons should never haue his head vnder his girdle so long as he lived, intendinge by meanes of this his holynes order appointed, to blynde the peoples eyes, they vse to prevent whatsoeuer commeth from the See apostolick that liketh them not, that it is M^r. Parsons dede to overrule all, erg^o before ever the Breve came they meant never to submitt them selves vnto the Archpriest or the Pope either, but they intended to stand out wth the Jesuites alone, but wth the Pope and superio^{rs} also, wch implyeth a division.

ffourthlie after theire submission (in colo^r only as the sequele declareth) albeit the Pope himself declared in his Breve that it was his owne dede and his will also that they should obey, yet did they it never vntill this day, at the least the heades of this faction either wth shew of likinge or contentment, but they were repyninge detractinge and quarrellinge att every thinge wth theire superio^{rs} proceedinges, as if all thinges were for theire punishm^t, and to beate and beare them downe wth mighte and tyranny and nothinge to comfort or doe them any good. To wch purpose yor frend in his late printed booke dothe compare his superio^r the Archepr: vnto a wilde Boare cominge out of the wood to destroy the viniarde of Christe, and vnto a singular cruell beast croppinge and devouringe all,[a] wch argueth playnelie how far theire mynde is separated from perfect vnion and accorde wth him and his that take him for no better then a verie Antechriste.

ffiftlye, yor frend in a late letter vnto one of his olde acquaintance

---

[a] Mush in his *Declaratio Motuum* addressed to Clement VIII. (1601), had besought the Pope to cast his eyes upon the English vineyard " ut videas et intelligas quomodo Archipresbyter, tua abutens authoritate, tanquam Aper de silva exterminavit eam, et quasi singularis ferus depastus est eam " (p. 80).

dothe not obscurely shew that him self and his fellowes are of some
seperated company. These are his wordes: I will blesse my self
from yor brother (meaninge me) and the rest of them that vniustly
haue and doe seeke the discredite of me and oure Clergie, respectinge theire owne extraordinary creditt aboue our priests more than
our Churches good or the glory of oure priests, but I hope god will
confound them. Marke well his phrase. What Church is this of
theires wch is not o{rs} also? Who be these priests of theires that
can not bothe clayme to vs and wee to them? Where is this
clergie of theires whereof wee also may not be accompted a parte
and haue as much interest in the same as any of them, if they be
of the same Churche Clergie and nomber or order of priests that
wee are of? how is not o{r} good theires, our creditt and glory
redound vnto them, but that they make them selves of an other
Clergie, priesthood and congregacion? And to what purpose dothe
he distinguishe himself from the rest of theire Clergie, saying they
seeke the discredite of me and o{r} Clergie if he did not insynuate
thereby that him self is some single or singuler personage over
and besides the Clergie of common priests or as one that would
seeme to be an odd man or the head of his congregation? doe not
these wordes savour a schismaticall spirite?

ffinally whether doe not these wordes in the end of the same
letter intend a fall yea or no when he sayth thus: Either must
wee suffer o{r}selves to be vniustly defamed of schisme and rebellion
to the see apostolick (to wch wee haue ben and are as obedient as
any Jesuite in the worlde) or be violently thrust from our place of
harbour and releef and consequently Starve wth famine, vnles wee
seeke for succour att the handes of our mortal adversaries heretickes. Of three inconveniences wch of them are they most like to
admitt? to be slaundered for Rebells, that you see they will no
way endure as theire whole proceedinge declareth: to starve wth
famine, it is intollerable especiallie to men of so litle mortificacion
as these wilfull men seeme to be, ergo they must of necessity (for
that will be theire pretence) seeke for succour vnto their mortall
adversaries, who, because they are mortall adversaries, they will not

47, f. 189.

yeld them any succour but wth some conditions deadly to theire soules if they will avoyde theire temporall deathes, decreed by theire lawes for wth them ordinarily no lawfull succour w^thout vnlawfull submission. How muche better counsell were it for them by a lawfull submission vnto theire lawful superiors and by an humble acknowledginge of theire manifest oversighte, as in duty they are bound, bothe to put away theire infamy iustly deserved, to keepe the places of theire harbour where they may still be maynteyned, and to avoyde all perill of their further fall by condescendinge vnto theire mortall adversaries? These things well considered may give a sufficient scantelinge vnto any of indifferent iudgement that theire disobedience even from the begynninge tended vnto a schisme and seperation and how farr indeede they did fall into it lett the cheife superior of vs bothe give iudgement when it shall come vnto his decision. neither intend I here to determine that belongeth vnto others censure, or to stand peremptorily vppon the terme schisme whether in most proper sense it may be applied vnto this disobedience of theires: it sufficeth me that vppon probable and sufficient groundes in myne opinion, and in the opinion of others more learned than I, it is so to be called, neither haue they been able as yet to purge them selves of the same neither will be howsoeuer they do exclame that they are vniustly slaundered.

47, f. 189b.

8. ffinally it is a thinge so evident in it self that theire first disobedience was a most notorious and greevous offence (whatsoeuer hereafter of the word schisme determined) that there can be alledged no probable or sufficient excuse either to defend them to haue done lawfully in standing out or to haue remayned innocent or w^thout blame in so doing. If I shew this I doe ouerthrowe the whole ground they stand vppon and then may it evidently appeare how vniustly they exclame that they are persecuted for innocencie or that they are slaundered w^thout cause. The former pointes do shewe sufficiently that the facte they comitted was a thinge in it[s] owne nature evill and a greevous offence. Wee must nowe declare whether in them it were excusable for any cause by them

alledged. Theire defence therefore consisteth in this that they affirme they had no sufficient notice that he was appointed a superior by his holynes. And of this they infer two thinges. The one is that he was not yet a superior as if his authoritie did wholly or principally depend vppon the promulgation and theire acceptance wthall: the other, that they were excused from synne by reason of ignorance that he was a superior: Admitt that he was one even then indeed. I will therefore first shew that they had no such ignorance that could excuse them admittinge that he was a superior. Then will I declare that his authoritie did not depend principally or yet materially in this case vppon the promulgation to every one or any of them in particular, as if that made him a superior and otherwise he were not. Lastly I will conclude that the notice they had was a sufficient warninge or promulgation and therefore that they were bound also to acknowledge him for theire superior & to accept of him.

To the first therefore that they had no suche ignorance as would excuse them. admitt he were a superior, as indeed he was by the testimony of the Popes Breve, it seemeth evident. ffirst they will not deny but that they heard by reporte and also by the sight of the Protectors letters (at the least some of them) that suche a man was appointed a superior over them all (I speake not of suche as had heard nothinge at all, for it is evident that those might be excused if there were any suche amonge them) els would they not haue gone about to ouerthrowe a thing they know not. This beinge supposed, I would aske of them what ground they had or notice to the contrary that he was not appointed for a lawfull superio^r? ffor if they had none it is manifest that they ought not to haue resisted him. Admitt they were not bound to beleeve the reporte that he was a superio^r. But the only ground they had that he was not appointed by his holynes authoritie, was, that them selves either did not, or could not, or would not beleeve that it was so, it was a thinge by them so vnexpected from his holynes, though them selves indeed were about suche a matter at the same instant,

47, f. 190.

erg⁰ the ground they had to resiste was theire owne conceyte and no proofe or reporte besides theire owne to the contrary. If this be true as I never heard vntill this day that they alledged any other proofe but that they supposed it was not his holynes deed : I would then demaund of them vppon what proofe or ground of reason they were induced to suppose, whereof if they can alledge none or at the least none that is sufficient to make a good man suppose suche a thinge, it must nedes followe that theire supposall or suspition was rashe and sinfull and consequently that theire ignorance came not of any probability or meere simplicity but vppon theire owne malice and temerity, and therefore could not excuse them to accept of the same notice wch sufficed others to acknowledge and knowe him to be theire superio^r muche lesse to be a warrant for them that they might lawfully reiecte and resiste him. But what groundes did they alledge for themselves where they should suppose that matter not to come from his holynes, because (say they) the Cardinall protector mighte forge suche a matter w^thout the Popes privitie. Admitt that to be true that he might so doe because it is not impossible absolutely but that suche malice might raigne in the hart of a Cardinall to attempt suche a matter : but what reason or probabilitie was there to induce them that either there was so greate a resident in Cardinall Caietanes harte, or that if there were he did or durst attempt suche a matter? ffor if they thought so badly of so greate a personage so well reputed and reported of amongest all w^thout cause or probability it was a most sinfull and vniust conceyte they had of him and therefore could avayle them nothinge toward theire probable ignorance, that they could wth no probability suppose suche a matter of the Cardinall but rather that they ought to have supposed the contrary : it argueth first because all men tooke him for a verie good man. Secondly because he had ben imployed in embassage of greate credite and moment, and had shewed him selfe a verie notable man as in the matters of ffraunce, and duringe the seige at Paris, and therefore would never stayne his credit nowe in a matter of suche perill and lesse honor. Thirdly because he was in a greate office as beinge head Camerarius in the Popes palace and he through whose authoritie all thinges were to passe duringe the absence of a Pope, and therefore would he not hazard so great a dignitye for suche a treacherous interprise of no profitt. ffourthlie bicause he was the protector of oure Nation and he whom the Pope did imploy in all matters concerninge our affaires and to whom for the benefite of oure Cuntrie the Pope had committed the charge of our seminaries and missions wth all suche faculties and authorities as before him Cardinall Allen had and practised : and therefore it is most like that he would doe nothinge but for o^r Cuntries good, and that by the knowledge councell warrant and authoritie of his holynes. ffiftly bicause the letters sent by the said Card: and all his manner of proceedinge was no secrett plott not able to abide the lighte, but a thinge subiecte unto the viewe and controllment of all, and a matter of execution: for all his letters concerninge the institution and progresse of the office and subordination were letters patente vnder his owne hand and seale and in his holynes name, and by his holynes comaund and appointment and not only the office so appointed but also large faculties and authoritie graunted and renewed and encreased by the same wth amplifications of newe directions & comandm^{tes} of retorninge answeres and informations about the practise execucion and effectes of the same. And what man of witt could suppose that this was don wthout the Popes privitie good likinge and appointment, or who can ymagine that a man of suche vertue, wisedom and accompte would attempt any matter of suche moment wthout sufficient warrant, his whole state and creditt lyinge in hazard if his bad attempt should once come to light, as it was no otherwise like to doe his dealinges beinge so open? And all these thinges were done before any notice came of the Popes Breve wch was not sent nor to be sent but only to stay the mindes of those malcontents from a further ᵃ and not then or

47, f. 191.

ᵃ Left blank in MS.

thereby to institute a newe the office before appointed by his owne authoritie as the wordes of the Breve it self doe declare, erg⁰ these men had a sufficient notice to knowe that this order was sett downe by the Popes privitie and authoritie vppon the sighte of the Cardinalls letters wch decreed the same.

Therefore theire excuse of ignorance is taken away. But say they it might haue ben otherwise and that the matter might haue ben forged. Wee doe not enquire what might haue ben done or what was in the possibility of the malice of man to doe (as I said before) but [what] was probable and most likely to be done, and what was by sufficient notice knowne to be done, and a Cardinalls letters patents is no flyinge tale or vncertayne reporte of a thinge but an evident proofe and weightie relation that the thinge was done and by them it was done and therefore ought to suffice for the takinge away of every mans ignorance who should haue sight of them or probable testimony of grave and trustye men that had seen them. But (said yor frend) there was once a Cardinall or Bishop (I did not well remember whether) that deceived all the Bp^s in Spayne by a false Comission forged in his holynes name: lett it be so, albeit my selfe doe not knowe of any suche matter save only by his owne relation wch many tymes I have found vntruthfull: must one swallowe make a somer? Or may one particular example infer a generall conclusion? Or is one malitious mans treacherie a sufficient ground wth any colo^r to bringe all others, or any one good mans creditt into any question or sinister suspition? Wherefore seinge the good Cardinalls letters did give them suche notice they were bound to give creditt vnto them, or at the least not to discredite them, muche lesse to attempt any resistance, an order so declared to come from his holynes w^thout sufficient proof or reason to the contrary. O but, say they, it was thought and so bruted that it was only the Jesuites deed to overrule and tryannise ou^er vs Then say also who thought or so bruted and vppon what groundes or occasion did they either thinke it or report it. Sifte this vnto the bottom, and you shall finde no better ground thereof then was found in the former obieccion that is to say a sinister conceyte of seditious mindes and a reporte of their owne fiction. Who are the Jesuites, or what haue they done to give men any iust occasion or grounde to thinke of them so perversely? Are they not honest and catholick men? Are they not cathol: priestes and religious priestes and of an appointed order of religion, and knowne to be most strict and diligent observers of the approved rules of theire order, and such diligent observers that if any of theire order be either noted of the worlde or amonge them selves to be of naughtie conversacion treacherous or scandalous, but that forthwth they detest him themselves and expell him out of theire order. But wee are suspected and reported (say they) to be seditious men & to persecute and tyrannise over our brethren. Then lett our actions be examined and sounded vnto the bottome: lett o^r accusers come forthe and lett vs be called vnto o^r triall, and if wee be found to be such men as they reporte vs to be wee aske no favour in iudgement: if wee be not able to purge o^{r}selves, lett vs be condemned hated and defamed. But we are so mightie none dare accuse vs, wee haue the Popes eare and countenance, wee haue the Cardinalls att comandment, wee rule and overrule all and euery one is affraid to speake against vs. What? is there never a good man that hath zeale of god and his afflicted clergie, not yor frend himself who was wont to spare nobody that dare shewe his face in open Consistorie to oppose him self against oure tyranny for the deliverie of his brethren? Will they whisper sinister suspitions of vs privatly in every mans eares and wthout names of the authors spreade infamous libells against vs bothe in printe and writinge and when they are either challendged by vs or have leave by superiors (as they alwaies have indeed) to come forth and accuse vs wth assurance given to haue audience and iustice against vs and yet still to put theire heades vnder a bushell and content themselves wth theire owne cry sayinge among theire people at home wee are persecuted, wee can not be heard, all wayes are stopped, the tyranny of the Jesuites perverteth all? Who seeth not theire fraud? who

47, f. 192.

will accompt them innocentes? who can not conveyve that not ignorance but malice is the ground of all their suspitions and reportes against vs? Them selves will confesse that the Jesuites haue ben the principall founders and meanes to erecte and maynteyne the most of theire Colledges beyond the seas. The Cardinall Allen of blessed memory would ever vnto his dyinge daie acknowledge that by theire helpe and meanes he was from the begynninge furnished wth mayntenance, assisted in his affaires, advaunced to creditt and honor: them selves will acknowledge that both for their advauncement in learninge, education, vertue and Religion they haue ben and are beholden to o^r societie: the world knoweth and will beare witnes wth vs wth what care & travell wee have endevored to profitt them, wth what good will and alacritye we have employed o^r talentes o^r frendes o^r persons to ayde them in all thinges for the glory of god and good of theires and oure Cuntrie. wth what patience wee haue endured theire infirmities, vngratefulness, detractions, mutinies, and rebellious proceedinges against vs: o^r actions haue ben examined and sifted into by men in authoritie: o^r bookes of accompts haue been perused and cast: o^r goverment hathe ben weighed and deliberated vppon, and in all wee have ben found faithfull, o^r actions vncontrolled, and oure goverment approved and confirmed and the proceedings of o^r adversaries against vs have still ben condemned. Wherefore that these men doe nowe so much exclame against vs for tyranny and ambition, and theire iniurious and violent courses it will retorne into theire owne bosome, and declare it self to be nothing ells but a sinister suspition wthout foundation and consequently they can derive no sufficient proofe or presumption thereof against the playne testimony of the Cardinall protectors letters, but that they were of sufficient creditt and authoritie to putt away all ignorance of the popes determinacion in appointinge them a superior; ergo they synned in resistinge him havinge no probable ignorance to excuse them.

An other argument to convince they had no probable ignorance was the generall acceptance and submission of the whole

Clergie in England besides them selves. ffor what perticuler reasons had those twelve disobedient persons to think those letters of the Card[ll] no sufficient warrant to acknowledge him a superior seeinge they did satisfie all theire brethren? Must we of necessity thinke y[t] these 12 persons in learninge iudgement experience and vertue farre exceede all the Clergie besides that that of right theire suspition alone must be preferred before the probable opinion or knowledge of so many wise, grave and vertuous men? They are never so arrogant in the conceyte of them selves that they dare thinke so well of them selves. And for those 12 them selves it is well ynough knowne that not any one of them was of any suche extraordinary knowledge iudgement or experience but that many of the other side did far exceede them in all settinge theire presumptuous mindes and busie heades aside.

ffurthermore it is well ynough knowne that a greate part of those 12 did excell in no talent at all and some of them, men altogether vnlearned and of no ripe iudgement, but rather were ledd and builded themselves whollie vppon the opinion and will of others. Also it is manifest that some of the best of them were ever noted for busye and seditious spiritts, yea no one of theire cheifes almost but he was noted w[th] some particular fault or excepcion whereby theire iudgement and authoritie was the lesse to be regarded in comparison of all theire brethren amonge whom there were many that lived w[th]out touche of discreditt and euery way better qualified then any of them, and for theire nomber exceeded 20 for one person of theires. And who then will excuse the ignorance of those 12 persons (if it may be called an ignorance) that still would presume to stand out yea endevour to ouerthrowe the order appointed when they did see all others w[th]out difficultie to haue submitted themselves. But say they, it was the Jesuites importunity and threates that did make them to submitt and to subscribe theire names against theire willes. Lett them then bringe forth one man amongest suche a number, that will say that any Jesuite or any for them, did threate or importune him to subscribe against his will. In this they might only say truly of vs and so it was indeed that if there had ben any amongest them that had been slack to submitt himself to his holynes order, wee would haue done our endevour to haue made him willinge not by threates or violence but by good persuasion for that had ben bothe his dutie and o^rs if we wished him any good, and to that effecte were wee charged by the protectors letters and o^r owne superio^rs bothe to sett forwarde his holynes order and to assist him whom he had assigned for the superio^r as nede should require and perhaps it was thought more convenient that wee should be somethinge employed in the begynninge in the establishinge of the subordination who were to be as frendes and not subiectes altogether vnto him: then y^t he shoulde whollie install himself there beinge no other superio^r w^{th}in the land or other direccion given to performe the same excepte the protectors letters in his holynes name: for if he had done it only by himself what exclamations it is like that these Rebellious would haue uttered against the Archepriest himself wth more colo^r then they doe now against bothe him and vs that he had intruded him self, that he was ambitious, that he did tyrannise on the Clergie, and more pretence would this haue had of pleadinge ignorance and suspectinge false measures, and that he was partiall and not to be trusted in his owne cause the wch now by havinge vs so many witnesses, and fortified also by o^r small assistance he is better able to confute and to put them to silence. And this it may be is a parte of their greefe and stomack against vs in that assistinge theire lawfull superio^r wee semed to crosse theire factious designem^{ts} but yet no ground sufficient to excuse them of ignorance in theire not obeying.

A third reason why they pleade ignorance in vayne was the manifolde notice sent them from beyonde the seas by men of accompte that the subordination came from his holynes expresse will and appointment and in particular from Cardinall Bellarmine the Popes Nuncio in ffflaunders, the Rectors of Doway and Rome who would not graunt faculties vnto theire priests sent into

England but wth condition and promise to be subiect vnto the Archepriest in England; and from divers others. But especially notice being given them that their two sollicitors were evill taken w^thall by his holynes, a Commission directed against them, as against malefactors disobedient to his holynes comaundment; they were apprehended imprisoned and in force of lawe examined vppon theire oathes, had lawyers allowed to pleade or advise them in theire cause: they were heard vnto the vttermost and by two Cardinalls deputed by his holynes, and by his holynes privity and assent were iudged guiltie, condemned and punished, and what ells was the fault of these two sollicitors but that they did sollicite the causes and intentions of these seditions at home them selves beinge of the same confederacie, albeit they did it wth muche more moderacie and shewe of peace and submission then these did at home. Might not this notice have sufficed them to haue yelded? Yes. But they would also haue heard worde from theire two sollicitors that it was his holynes will and then they sayd they woulde yelde. They had theire desire: both theire sollicitors did write vnto them, they signified that it was his holynes expresse will that they labored in vayne, that they repented them they had taken the matter in hand and in good sorte persuaded them to submitt themselves. Was not this bothe notice and warninge ynough to take away theire pretended ignorance? yes verily: yet would they not yelde accordinge to theire promise but they expected a greater notice and nothinge would suffice them but either the Popes owne Breve or an oath of the Jesuites in England, that it was the Popes owne deed. In the meantyme they exasperated their superior wth outcryes, tumultes, and other iniurious and scandalous proceedinges so farre, that after a whole yeares patience in forbearinge them wth hope and expectacion of theire pacificacion and submission they forced him to exercise his authoritie and function in correctinge some of them, of wch yor frend was one from whom he did withdrawe his faculties the first tyme. And all this passed before the Breve came in theire firste disobedience, the wch was a notice so

47. f. 193b.

evident, that he may be thought a madd man and voyde of all sense and reason that would seeke to excuse them from a most greevous synne by the only allegation of ignorance or want of true notice that he was a superior by his holynes deed.

A fourth reason may be added vnto these against many of them though not against all of them that stood out in that they affected theire ignorance and were cause thereof vnto them selves by avoydinge of sett purpose all such thinges and meanes as might give them notice of the same whereby they mighte seme iustly to plead ignorance and not to be bound to obey. To this effecte some of them sequestred them selves from the company of all such persons that were like to informe them excepte of theire owne faction and such as it semed unto them not sufficient to take notice at their handes: others refused to reade or heare redd the protectors letters or copies of the same testifyinge the truthe muche vnto them. Others put dowbtes that all was but forged thinges and the reportes of theire adversaries only: even the very letters of theire sollicitors they sought to extenuate by affected excuses that they were in prison and therefore durst not write theire myndes or that they were white livered men and therefore durst not proceede coragiously or that indeed the Jesuites had perverted them wth subtiltie. All wch doe argue that they were so farre from beinge excused through probable ignorance that theire synne was muche more increased by an vnlawfull affectacion of the same, seekinge in euery thinge wch way they might invent any colo^r of tergiversation least theire shame should appeare vnto all, wch in it self was evident ynough vnto euery one that had any iudgement or discretion.

Now will I come to the second ground they stand vppon, that is to say, that he was no superior before the promulgation of the authoritie vnto euery one and theire acceptance and voluntary submission made vnto him. ffor this cause they affirmed first that he was no superior before those letters Olim dicebamur wherein all the names of those that submitted were subscribed [and] were sent to Rome, as if that voluntary submission and acceptance of his authoritye signified vnto the Pope did make him a superior, and so they not acceptinge nor subscribinge (as it seemeth) they did inferre that he was no superior vnto them. W^{ch} if it were true it would followe that no superior could appointe any inferior officer of his owne eleccion wthout the consent and approbacion of the people, seeinge the Pope him self who hath plenitudinem potestatis over all the Churche can not in their opinion doe the same. And of this erro^r did it proceede that yor frend and others did so much exclame that a superior was thrust vppon them by the Jesuites (for they would never seme to nominate the Pope as an author of this subordination) wheras them selves would have chosen one by the consent of all, as if theire consent and election must needes have gone before, and then the Popes approbacion should have succeded to confirme the same. W^{ch} kinde of choosinge superiors in the Clergie dothe not take place but in particular cases accustomed and approved by the see apostolick, for in that sorte prelates are chosen by most voyces of their convent or congregation. Bishops by the Deane and Chapter, and the Popes themselves by a iust nomber of Cardinalls: but in case when suche courses faile or greate abuses are committed by the same it lyeth in the Pope's power to supply suche defectes or to alter the manner of suche eleccions. And when was it seen that the parishe priestes did ever choose them selves a superior? And yet are these men not so muche as parishe priestes but only extraordinary teachers sent wthout particular charge or comaund over any other then the voluntary acceptance of the people they deale wthall and whollie dependinge in all iurisdicion and forme of goverment vppon the Popes will. And may he not then appoint them a superior wthout regard vnto theire consent and approbation havinge no right or lawe sett downe by the cannons to make any choice of one by way of suffrages. The defecte of wch canons the pope hathe all authoritie ever to supply and alter also as necessitie and occasion shall require. Wherefore in this case _nether the defect of giving theire suffrages them selves nor yet

47, f. 194b.

the approbation of the other who did subscribe did make him a superior but the popes authoritie alone, and by the meanes of the Card: protector appointing the Archepr: whose letters patents did declare and divulge the same sufficiently and tooke effecte from the first sendinge as the wordes of the Breve did afterwarde declare and would have stoode good if no voyces at all had ben sollicited. And in this sorte wthout eleccion of any deane and Chapter dothe the pope nowe send lawful Bishops into Ireland and other cuntries newly converted and all other extraordinary superio^{rs} doth he appointe when he listeth not expectinge the consent of the subiectes. And suche was the office of the Archepriest in England. Wherefore this is but a false and frivolous ground to say he was no lawfull superior before theire acceptation or approbacion or suffrages from them selves when as the Popes authoritie alone did suffice and neither custome nor cannon gave them any righte or privilege to clayme a consent of theire voices.

Agayne they did affirme that he was no superior in that neither the Cardinall by theire knowledge was or had authoritie to appointe them a superior nor that his letters were of sufficient creditt to promulgate the same, ffor herein they thoughte nothinge to be sufficient except the sighte of the Popes Breve or that the Jesuites in England would swear that it was his holynes deed. But that the Cardinall was theire superior they could not be ignorant of it. ffirst because they knowe right well that the authoritie wch before was given vnto Cardinall Allen who was appointed theire superior, after his decease when the students of the college did laboure that they might be graunted vnto the Bishop of Cassana, contrary to their expectacion were given vnto Card. Caietane whereby he was made theire superior. So likewise they could not be ignorant that by the vertue of the same authoritie this Cardinall did directe for other Colledges of o^r Nation and appointed missions & gave faculties vnto those that came into England, all wch he did as a superior. Besides they knewe well that he was the Protector of the englishe Nation and employed by his holynes in all suche affaires or sutes as did concerne o{}^{r} Cuntry and therefore of sufficient creditt at the least to lett vs knowe his holynes favour or pleasure towardes vs in this as he had don in other weightie causes. Yea he was a fitt man for the Pope to depute as his substitute or Comissioner at the least to appoint vs a superior as his letters did importe and therefore they had iust cause to knowe that in this he was of sufficient authoritie. Neither was the office of an Archepriest a dignitie of such moment (though it be a greate one in deed) but that it might be appointed by an inferior officer vnder the Pope howe muche more by his speciall deputation and authoritie as the letters did declare. yea it semeth that in theire owne conscience they did thinke the Archepriest to be theire superior appointed by sufficient authoritie of the Cardinall in his holynes name. ffor some of them beinge demaunded by mr. Wrighte whether they would not vse any newe faculties if the Archepriest by vertue of the same authoritie would give them any. They answered that they would. Wherevppon he inferred that they then did knowe that he was their superior and thereuppon him self was satisfied. If then they did knowe the Cardinall to be theire superior and acknowledged in theire conscience that he was sufficient especiallie as his holynes deputie to appoynt them a superior why were not then the letters patentes of the same Cardinall protector of sufficient valewe to declare and promulgate the same? ffor whosoeuer hathe authoritie to appointe determyne or establishe anythinge: the same mans letters are an authenticall testimony to confirme and declare that he hathe don the same. As for theire demaund that Jesuites in England wolde sweare the subordination to be his holynes deed, it was but a frivolous exaction to no purpose and w{}^{th}out reason. ffor seeing they had the Cardinalls owne letters shewed them, w{}^{ch} were sufficient, why should they demaund any mans oathe, w{}^{ch} was more then nedefull? Agayne if they did not allowe of the Card: owne letters declaringe what was done by his meanes: when would they have ben satisfied w{}^{th} our oathe whom in all other thinges they did

47, f. 195b.

distrust as their adversaries: ffinally it was an absurd thinge to demaund an oathe of them that were not privie to the doinge of a thinge and could not . . . .[a] that it was done but by the same notice wch was deliuered vnto them selves. Yet if they would haue required an oathe of vs to declare that we thought in our consciences that the notice was sufficient to bynde them to obey as thereby havinge sufficient warrant that the subordination was by his holynes will and assignem^{t} wee would never have refused to haue pleasured them wth suche an oathe: but they only sought to wrangle, not to be satisfied by o^{r} meanes. And what reason had they to require a Breve in a matter evident almost vnto all and by so many other meanes confirmed as hathe ben declared before when as them selves in matters of no lesse moment will be credited either by theire owne worde or the relation of some private ffrend or acquaintance? They are priestes and by authoritie sent into England and here they bothe minister sacram^{ts} and some of them vse the graunt of extraordinary faculties suche as neither many of theire fellowes haue and were not graunted vnto Bp^{s} by theire ordinary faculties in tymes past: and what warrant shewe they? or what authenticall testimony doe men require at theire handes? dothe not theire owne testimony satisfie men because they haue the reputacion of honest men? yea in matters wch vse to be divulged by the Popes bulles and breves at Rome only yet apperteyning vnto the benefitt or government of the whole churche. How many bulls or breves are there shewed in other places except in Campo floræ or suche like places in Rome? Dothe not the reporte of honest men cominge from Rome give notice vnto others abrode in far Cuntries, and after such notice given or taken every man thinketh him self bound to obey w^{th}out further expectation of a Breve? And here in o^{r} case the letters patents of the Cardinall were sent into England and were shewed vnto divers and by them related vnto others abroade and they stoode in stede of a Breve no lesse than the Cardinall himself

[a] Omission in MS.

represented the Popes person in beinge his deputie in determininge the said authoritie? And why should not every man havinge suche notice thereof thinke it a sufficient promulgation and iudge him selfe bound to obey? Wherefore it is toe frivolous and absurd an excuse to thinke that they were not bound at the first to submitt them selves, muche lesse that they might lawfully oppose them selves vnto the authoritie of theire superior for want of canonicall notice (as they tearmed it) seinge they had as muche knowledge thereof as was reasonable and accustomed to be had in suche cases.

I will then come vnto the third pointe proposed wch necessarily is inferred vppon the former, wch is; that they had sufficient notice that theire superio^r was appointed by his holynes expresse direccon and therefore were bound to obey, ffor that they had notice it is evident by the first pointe and that the notice they had was sufficient is declared by that hathe ben said in the seconde and that it followeth of necessitie that they were therefore bound to obey. I will nowe declare it after this manner. Everie subiect is bound to obey his lawfull superio^r havinge sufficient notice that he is so appointed by authoritie. These malecontentes were subjectes and had sufficient notice that the Archepr: was so appointed; therefore they were bound to obey him as their lawfull superio^r. The first proposition is proved good by the wordes of the Apostle, Rom: 12 Where he affirmeth that the disobedient vnto the superiors doe purchase damnation. Wherefore if they will avoyde damnation they must obey of necessitie as a condicion they are bound vnto. The second proposition is proved by that hathe ben said before especially by the verie wordes of the Popes Breve, declaringe that even from the beginninge the letter of the Cardinall protector had theire effecte in appointinge him a superior, and therefore sufficient to give them notice thereof beinge shewed vnto them as they were. Therefore the conclusion followeth that they were bound even at the begynninge to obey him as theire superio^r before the Breve came and that vnder payne of damnation by the

47, f. 196b.

Apostles testimony; Ergo no man did them wronge or uniustly slaundered them in sayinge they synned greevously through disobedience when they did openly in the begynning refuse to obey and by all theire power resisted his authoritie yea rebelled against him by not acknowledginge him as theire head. And by this meanes every one may see what cause they haue to make these exclamacions as they doe of theire persecuted innocency, and what iustice or right they haue to make any Appeale from his censures when he would chastise them for such a notorious cryme.

Wherefore, good madam, ponder wth indifferent iudgement this wch I haue written for yor better instruction and suffer not yo^rself to be led away wth the sleightes and shiftes of contentieus persons into error and synne. Muche and longe haue you labored in the way of vertue and Catholick path of true religion, but all is well that endeth well, and a large losse may it be thought to forgoe in one instant either thorough want of discretion or perseverance the labour of yor whole life imployed wth comfort in the service of god. No more, but Christ Jesus blesse yo^u and inspire yor harte to see and followe that is most for yor eternall good. This last of June.

Yo^r La^{ps} to comaund in all that he may.

A. DUCKETT.

12. *Mr. Collington.*[a]

Accordinge to your request I send the bearer, and have willed him to shewe yo^u the coppie of two letters wch the importunitie of others made me writ. The cause I deliuered in my last to yo^u, and is laide downe againe in the letter of bothe. I praie giue yor opinion there in, wheather the sendinge weare to purpose or no. If they make no answeere, as I thincke nethier will, yet it will not be idle to tell thos who nowe so broadlie talke of our conceaved schisme, that neither of the two principals will saye so much, nor

---

[a] Written thus at the top of the letter by another hand.

wrotton too acknowledge so much, a chooke bone to thos of a feeling conscience. In the after noone I leave the citie, writ I beseeche you all the newse at large, or at least by word of moth send it. I heare, and a prieste was the reporter, that theire should be twelue artickles exhibited to the Consaile for removinge the Jesuits out of England. The said prist deliuered the newse in that order as the hearer vnderstood that theire was a feare, or a suspition, or more conccaved least they artickles shuld be drawen by the consent and helpe of some pristes. If you heare ought hereof I praie impart it. I take it a newe fabolous conceat but wtall slanderous. I have sent yor frend Ro : Laud(?) sixe shillings recommending to his prayers a living woman of my acquentance. Fare you well.

3 of March.

Copy, endorsed :

Of a report that a priest should draw xij Articles for the expelling of the Jesuites out of England.

[This endorsement is written twice, the first being struck out.]

13. *Letter from Blackwell concerning Robert Benson, Appellant.* 47, f. 114.

Charissime. Quod valde dolendum est, Intelligo iam, D. Bensonum, nimis obfirmatum in malevolentia, non solum contempsisse mea monita; sed etiam ad Superiorum voces se obduravisse, et obedientiam reliquisse. Certe, cor durum male habebit in nouissimo : Et, qui malignantur, exterminabuntur : sustinentes autem Dominum, ipsi hæreditabunt terram. Non expectabo de spinis vuas, neque de tribulis ficus. Qui sordidus est, sordescet adhuc : Virtus autem Patrum splendebit per sese semper, nec alienis unquam sordibus obsolescet. Tantum abest, vt Patrum luminibus obstruxerit hæc posterior illius quasi exaggerata altius oratio, vt inde nihil aliud, nisi intimam et reconditam ille animi sui ægritudinem aperuerit; et ita calumniam omnem adversus venerabilem

Societatem ipse suspiciosus, et malevolus obtriverit. O vtinam seipsum cognosceret et antecedentia vitia multis succedentibus virtutibus obtegeret. Sed, quoniam desinit esse remedij locus, vbi, quæ fuerunt vitia, mores sunt; restat, vt nos iam similitudinem apum moremque imitemur: qui quidem a natura hoc habent, vt ex herbis agrestibus spinisque asperrimis lenissimum mel optimumque eliciant, et ad hominum vsum atque vitam traducant. Perspicimus illud D. Chrysostomi verissimum esse: quòd quemadmodum incurabilia vulnera neque austeris medicamentis cedunt: ita anima semel captiua, si se peccato cuipiam fecerit obnoxiam, considerare non uult, quæ sibi vtilia: etiamsi innumera quis eius inculcet auribus, nihil proficiet; sed quasi mortuæ aures sunt; non quia non potest, sed quia non vult. Precemur Dominum vt auferat ab eo cor lapideum, et spiritum rectum innouet in visceribus eius. Et quamvis (vt loquitur Tertullianus) duritia vincenda sit, non suadenda; peto tamen a vobis vt in dando consilio divtius elaboretis, alijsque remedijs adhibendis; quibus ex oblectationum et pertinaciæ vadis faciatis hominem emergere; et se ad frugem bonam (vt dicitur) accipere; et pro inivrijs venerabili Societati tandem satisfacere.

     Valeat Reuerentia vestra, et oret pro me.
     Vester seruus in Domino
         G. B. Archep^t.

At foot of letter:

 Si quis Episcopum, aut presbyterum aut Diaconum falsis criminibus impetierit, uel accusauerit, et probare non poterit, nec in fine dandam ei communionem censemus.
    Damasus 2, q. 3. si quis.

14. *Letter from R. C. to m^r B.*[a]

Good m^r b. m^r J. C. & I myselfe had seen you before christmas but that I was loth to wander in the winter in the vnknowe waye for m^r C. had not according as he wyshed (when we appoynted the iornye) sent to him who shold hae bene our judges the cause of our not comming at this tyme, your brother can enforme you, when tyme shall serue, we will come unto you. I wold now haue come, but I think I cold not come to any great purpose, m^r C. not being in towne, wth whome it is necessary I shold reckon before I can determine any certayntye concerninge our principall iornye, yet haue I bespoke a good lodging for the first nyght or two, and I am promyssed that I shal speed wthout any fayle, wheresoever I shal take horse. I had written unto you, when your brother was laste in towne and because I could not meet wth him, I detayned also my letter, for that I had not written so fully as I wold, & ment to haue imparted my mynd vnto him; now haue I had talke ynogh wth him, he can tell you at lardge what soeuer may concerne us. It is so long since I heard thos matters of . . . [b], that the series of them is cle[an] out of my head, wch is a litle troble vnto me, especially hauing a determination to go so nowe to worke, as I wold not be found faltye in the least poynt. Yor brother can tell you wherfore I instimat(?) this, I am ready to hazard all wch I may, to doe any good, and I shall think it no hazard when I shall haue my head full, & my perse full, & a suffycyent warrant that, that wch I goe about is not the fancye of a few, but a generall consent ether of all, or the most part, for effecting of wch some are in trauaile, & vppon their retorne I will doe what lyeth in me;

---

[a] The writer and the occasion of this letter are uncertain. It was written apparently between Christmas and March, and cannot therefore relate to the journey to Rome undertaken by Bishop and Charnock towards the end of 1599. The several references to the "brother" of Mr. B. suggest that the letter, notwithstanding the endorsement, may have been addressed not to Bagshaw but to one of the brothers Bennet.

[b] Words illegible.

they doe not retorne untill about the middle of March, vntill wch tyme, not knowing any better course, I rest, wth as much desyer that thinges were to come to their perfection as may be, & commend me most earnestly to yor good devotions. I pray you talk wth yor brother, least hast make me leaue any thing imperfeet. I would willingly be ordered in this buysyness by you.

Yors most assuredlye
R. C.

I haue sent you a copy of the letter to be dd to his holiness to wch I think it fit as to such effect many doe sett their handes also to these articles or to lyke effect. yf any come vnto you, as be so ware as you can send conueniently vnto them who will ioyne in this action I pray you take their handes lest they who are gone an other way hitt not vppon them. deale wth none but such as you thinke wilbe secret in the matter.

> *Endorsed*: R. C. to Bagshaw for procuring handes secretly wth a copie of a letter to be sent to the Pope.

V.
DEALINGS WITH THE GOVERNMENT.

1. *A Memorandum by Bagshaw.*   38, f. 379.
Oct. 19, 1598.

Some yeare or more paste one fysher [a] came into Englande to vnderstande howe the estate of priestes stoode there, after he had bene cunningly shifted owt of the Romane college. Diverse priestes wth whome he talked, perceyvinge the privitye of Cardinall Toledo to his comminge, & readynesse to assiste the redresse of some wrongs wch by dealinge in the affayres of the Seminary he had some coniecture of, thoughte not to omitt suche an opportunitye, for compassinge whereof they intended by subscribinge theyre names to assure them selfes of mutuall helpe of prayers, advises, travayles & purses. Notwthstandinge by the deathe of the Cardinall, many differences in particular opinions, wante of monye, & specially for feare of sinister interpretations or suspicions at leaste to wch all suche thinges ar subiecte, leaste the endevoure of stoppinge practises mighte seeme some dawngerouse practise, & for y^t the wisest laye Catholiques ar most desyrouse yt the actions of priestes should not extende beyonde theyre spirituall function, the devise of associatinge priestes was vtterly disliked & lefte of.

The Jesuites saye & write y^t a memoriall was sent to the Pope by two Englyshe in the lowe cowntryes vppon the comminge of one fisher owt of Englande contayninge agaynst them diverse accusationes, whereof these occurre nowe to memorie.

The seekinge of superiority over other Catholiques.

---

[a] Fisher entered the college at Rome in July, 1593, when twenty-two years of age, and left for England in May, 1596. He had received minor orders at Rheims.

The infaminge of all sortes of men wch crosse theyre practises.
The not bestowinge of mony vppon the poore & such good vses wch for y^t purpose is given them.
The Vsinge of Equivocations as they terme them, to the greate offence of manye.
The medlinge in matters of state contrary to theyre profession.
The writinge of diverse seditious bookes & infamous pamphlets.

Assistants of the Achip^rsbiter
{ Henshawe.
Bavan.
Burkett.
Hans.
Standyshe.
Turwhitt.
Michell.
Shingleton.
Clennocke. }

Endorsement:

19 Octob., 1598.
Bagshaw of Fishers comming from Rome.
Of Cardinall Tol : his inclination.
Of the association.
The name of the assistantes.

38, f. 381.

2. *Fisher's Instructions.*

No greater faculties are to be granted to the Jesuits than to the secular preistes.

The College of Rome is not to be continued in the regiment of the Jesuits.

A visitation is to be granted for Englande, specially for Wisbiche, y^t without equivocation the true cause of the dissentions & scandals in Englande may appeare.

The Pope is to prohibite all practizes bookes and rumors against the temporall state.

The authority of Archpreistes is to be revoked as no ways beneficiall, but contrarye.

An Ecclesiasticall Hiearchye (if any) is to bee instituted in Englande.

Instructions are to be guine to Cardinall Toledo for continuance for his purpose for remouinge of the Jesuites out of the Englishe College in Rome & Englande, the prosecution wherof for directe Reasons he had fully determined.

[*The following notes are written across the page here in the hand in which many of the endorsements are made*]

The purpose of sending fisher was to deale wth Cardinall Toledo for ye removing ye Jesuites from ye College & to call them out of England. And they wrote to Mr. Paget & Dr. Gifford to further y^t point by theire letter to ye Cardinall. The institution y^t such as are there shalbe sworn to be priestes & to come for Eng[land] when they shalbe sent. And y^t ye Jesuites sought to drawe them to be of theire society wch Toledo disliketh. Beside, ye students there told hym y^t ye Jesuites deeling there further he vtterly disliked, ye book of persons & the dealing for the Spaniard against England.

Mr. Bluett [*this apparently again in another hand*].

Then follows in same hand as " Fisher's Instructions "

The effect of the Association.

One shall yearly bee chosen by the greater parte of the priestes to gouerne.

The Authoritye of the greater parte shalbe to displace him wch is chosen, if he doe not gouerne well.

The Superior shall procure continuance of charitie amonge the associated.

He shall reforme thinges amisse accordinge to speciall rules for y^t purpose allowede of by the greater parte.

Hee shall provide for the pore and distressed Catholiques.

Hee shall not suffer any practizes or pamphlettes wch may irritate the temporall state.

He shall procure (as he may) by the authoritie of the Pope, if other meanes cannot suffice, y^t cleargymen shall not intermedle in temporall negotiations.

He shall renounce by othe or protestation all other Societies or companyes which be not parcelle of the common wealthe.

In the same hand as the notes given on the previous page:

from D. B. to Mr. Wade in presence of the B. of L. [Bishop of London] & Mr. Liegt [or Leift].[a]

3. *Statement in the handwriting of Bagshaw.*

IHS.

[Winter of 1598-9?]

Althowghe in the space of these 23 yeares wherin the Jesuites have imployed them selfes in oure Englyshe affayres,[b] we of the Clergye of Englande have had greate cause to mislyke many thinges in theyre proceedinges, and to feare oure ruine by them, wch Cardinall Allen of happy memorie foresawe & foretolde at the beginninge of theyre combininge wth vs, yett hythertoe we have vsed patience & silence, so longe as hope of redresse was, ether amonge our selfes, or by true & syncere information of our superior.

Nowe the measure of the iniuryes done vnto vs beinge in our opinion growen to the full & litle expectance of perfectly instructinge our superior by the Jesuites beinge lefte, & much experience of false insinuatinge thinges by them vnto him almost dayly

[a] Mr. Macray conjectures "Mr. Lieutenant of the Tower."

[b] If this document was written, as it appears, during the absence of the two messengers sent to Rome and before the confirmation of the Archpriest's appointment by the Pope, the "23 years" must be reckoned from the origin of the college at Rome in 1576, when the first students sent from Douai were assigned Jesuit masters.

occurringe, we ar driven for the necessary defence of our credittes to divulge the cawse of our sendinge to him some wch may not be impeached & withstandinge of all plottes grownded vppon iniuste surreption, vntill we knowe his pleasure by credible relation of faithfull & indifferent messangers proceeding from his full & intire informacion.

The seeking of preeminence by the Jesuites afore the Englishe priests in Rome & elsewhere hathe manye wayes appeared. In Wisbych it was attempted wth a most scandalous & disorderly schisme. for the hatefullnes & better colouringe thereof, it is nowe proposed in the forme of an Archip^sbyterye, a practize begunne, folowed, vrged, & sollicited by & wholy dependinge vppon the Jesuites.

Some of vs have conferred wth them & in peaceble & priestly manner requested them to desiste from this seekinge vniuste & vnfitt superioritye, wch the Pope him selfe hath warned them of, & hathe made them odiouse wth Bishopps, Pastors, Universytes, & all ordinarie Ecclesiasticall estate in many places of Christendome.

We for shame of our religion, & pytiinge theyre imperfection, yett almost make dowbte to propalate what answeares they have returned to some very grave, learned & worthy persons, wth what indignitye, contumelye, lightnes, & vnlearnednesse theyre letters ar farced.

W^ch is so much the more intoleerable, for y^t we expected at theyre hands vppon priestly & brotherly warninge not evill & disdainfull speeches, but good & Catholique behaviour.

1. Helpinge, or not impugninge, our seminarie wch is vppon dissolution by theyr meanes, as we heare. 2. Satisfaction for detraction wch as an arte hath bene by them professed, & y^t against very many & those w^thout exception. 3. Realevinge the poore Catholiques & specially prisoners wch ar like to be starved, all collections beinge in theyre handes or disposition, very fewe & small ons excepted. A desistinge from all practizes in temporall

state, wherby the have indaungered vs & infamed our order & ar likely to bringe the temporality to destruction.

Yett from these & many the like proceedinges so farre they ar to dislike, as they have mightely labored so have the cown·tenanced by a supposed authority of an Archip^r bit^r derived from on Cardinall Caietane whom the name the Protector of Englande.

From wch Authoritye, as preiudiciall to the dignity of the sea Apostolique, & promise & piety of his holines, & obtained only by intervention, shufflinge, glosinge, & false intimation, reputed by our Prince & countrye as trayterwise & disloyal, preiudiciall & nowayes profitable to our religion & callinge, for many iust causes at large to be declared, we have appealed & doe appeale to the Popes holinesse him selfe, etc. W^ch appeale god willinge we will —all good sorte prosecute, not wayinge or respectinge any sentence, iudgemente, or action to the contrarie, etc.

Endorsement:

D^r. Bagshaw: how the Jesuits have had to deale in England 23 yeares and of theyr proceedings in seeking of superioritye till at the last by false suggestion, they had procured theyr Archpresbytership by the meanes of one Caietane, from the wch he and his company have apealed and doe meane to prosecute the same.

4. William Watson to the Attorney General.

47, f. 97.

April, 1599.

Righte wor^ll.

Syr, althoughe the report w^the proofe now made of yor innated clemency, noble disposicion, & highe prudence hathe yeelded me noe lesse comforte then hope of redresse in the midst of these my miseries: inocency, integritie & a cleare conscience, comby nd w^the loyalty, love & duety, to god, my prince, countrey & yo^rselfe in autority, affording me as ready, simple & plaine an answer (voide of all equvocacion, sophisme or doubling, & confirmed by that oathe wch I esteeme dearer then my life) as yor demaunde was politique, wise & round unexpected of me. Yet feare, affection, & former felte smart making me iealous (pardon good syr my boldnes) least some vnfriend of mine by sinister suggestion, or misconstruing some clavse in my writings (wch are of many & those intricate collecions) mighte avert that good conceite of me wch of yor owne inclining hearte to pitty, it semed to me you have : & soe I to loose an vmpire of my cause : & such a frinde (though w^thout my defects) as the place & person you reprysent in censuring of me, may worke my well or woe, & yet noe doubte secundum allegata & probata w^thout preiudice of that vprighte minde you cary. I therefore have presumed (necessitie constrayning me for mine owne discharge and desire of satisfying all parties into whose handes my writings may have fallen, but yo^rselfe aboue the rest, as it semeth apointed for this matter) to declare at large in this breife, what my studies have bene; what the intencions of all those collections, bookes & writings were : & what have bene the causes moving, of all the doubts that eyth^r have or may rise vpon those manuscripts or otherwise. And becaus I must herein open as it were my whole life to explaine the meaning of those writings you have, therefore my onely hope, desire, & humble suite is that of civill courtesie you will conceale that wch can do no man good to be revealed, I meane as well suche fovle defects as in those writings may appeare in the contention betwixte vs & the Jesuites; as also what I shall here deliuer pertayning to the same or like obiectes.

ffor my selfe in few since I was able to conceive anything I have bene brought vp in learning, sent to Oxforde at 10 years of age w^the my tuto^r (a perfect linguist wch my fath^r kept to teache) at 14 I came to the Inns of covrte : at 16 I passed the seas to Rheims : at 26 I returned home;[a] was broughte of the sea in

---

[a] According to the *Douay Diaries* he received confirmation at Rheims in March, 1581, minor orders in 1583, and priesthood in April, 1586, and was sent back to England on June 16 of that year.

mariners apparell, presented before her ma^ty (vnknowen vnto me) committed to the Marshalsea; deliuered thence to have bene banished by syr francis Walsinghams meanes, affirming that her ma^ty of her owne princely, wonted benignitie, had promised I shold not die nor suffer any extremitie, before my date of departure was runn; being taken againe, & by Mr Topcliffs cruelty comitted to Bridewell wth this comission to have all the plagues & torments of that place inflicted upon me (whereof fewe I think were lefte oute, & some I dare say vnknowen to her ma^ty or councell that ever I suffered, as whipping, grinding in the milne, w^the the like, by no lawe to be lade vpon such, etc.). Breaking oute thence throughe this his cruelty, I passed over the sea againe, lived at Liege some 2 yeares; returned backe,[a] remained most parte in the West, vntill there betraide, taken, & committed againe w^the more favo^r by Mr. Waades meanes yet not put in execution as he comanded & in the end that litle I had being abridged by Mr. Topcliffe as my kep[er] saide) who seing me one day taking the ayre vpon the leades, or some one (for none but one) frend came vnto me, he threatened the porter, swore I wold run away: & by that meanes restrayned, & hearinge of a fovle slander was like to happen vnto me aboute 200^li w^che one had taken vp in my name (I not knowing the dryfte) I made an escape the second time, taking an occasion of the dores set wyde open vnto me; and nowe being comitted againe, this is the 41th yeare of my wretched life, vpon St. George day nexte, the 15th since I first came into Ingl.[b] & the 31 since I first went to Oxforde.

My studies vntill I was 18 yeares of age were in the 7 liberall sciences intermixte, w^the the tongues, phisicke, common lawe (& especially histories all my life time for recreacon) from 18 vntil 21.

[a] It was reported at Rheims, Oct., 1590, that Watson, "qui et antea duras carceris molestias pertulit," had returned to England (*Diaries*, p. 236).

[b] If the endorsement gives the date of this document correctly, "April, 1599," Watson had not yet completed the thirteenth year since his first coming into England.

I studied the lawes canon & civil w^the positive divinitie & perfecting of my metaphisicke and philosophie. after that vntill my returne home I plyed schoole divinity (the whole covrse being then read orderly in 4 yeares). Since my first comming over vntill w^thin these 2 or 3 yeares : my studie hathe bene how to draw all handmaides to their mystres, I meane all families & knowledge to serve for some vse in a schoole divine finding Mr Fernes words true in his Glorie of Generositie, that as a perfect Heralte at Armes oughte to be exquisite in all sciences: soe (seing that labia sacerdotis custodiunt sapientiam et legem requirimus ex ore illius quia angelus domini exercituum est, Mal. 2°) an herhalt in gods churche oughte to have a sighte in all lawes, professions, & faculties to be able in conscience & before god to iudge secundum tempus, locum et personam what is mete in such a case, & how to draw it to the fountaine of all knowledge, etc. These latter yeares I spent most in such collections & studies as there, yor wor[ship], may finde : wch that they may neith^r be scandalous nor offensive whereby eyth^r those of the Spanish faction maye thinke them done of malice towardes them (wch I thanke god I never bare to any, noe not to Mr Topcliffe that most deserved it) nor others of simplicitie (ignorance comonly being subiect to take scandall) thinke me eyth^r to have spent my time unfruitefully, or els voide of all religion, as (god forgive them) some have saide, I temporized wth time & studied onely Machiavel) finding there at mie chamber onely lawe bookes Machiavels werkes, tragedies, cronicles, colleccions of Doleman, Philopat^r, Leycesters commonwealthe (all 3 one man as is said) the bishop of Londons Genevian platforme, the discovery of the originall cause & begining of our dislike of the Jesuites & their procedings : & many other notes colleccions & breifes of prophecies, genealogies, discents of hunting, hawking & the like : this then I answere as wth an apologie of my doings.

Whither it were of a hard conceite the Jes[uits] have had of me from the begining, being euer (by good fortune) brought vp vnder suche tutors since I was 19 or 20 yeares of age in companie w^the suche as were wholy opposite to their designements as at Rheims, I heard the case canvased ad vnguem about Leycesters common wealthe & adjudged of as an vnmete obiect for a priest much more for any religious person to handle. In the Marshalsea I was one of the 24 priestes then prisoners that vtterly disliked & condemned Babingtons attempt with his fellowes all executed, & in this contradiccon of Sem[inarists] togither against the ruine of o^r poore country w^che we greately feared by that Spanified league; I was thoughte to have had a depe share & in good will to prevent any inconvenience I was (sure) as forward as any: or els that this dislike came vpon some speaches I have often let passe againste their busie medling in state matters: & taking vpon them autority aboue all oth^r, being by their ord^r (indede) inferio^r to all other as in my writings I have proved; or that it grew first of some letters I writte to Rome & other places in dissuading diuerse of my frendes to enter into that societie: or what els may be the cau[se] (as some oth^r there are) I had rather conceale then utter, wishing there were not soe much in my papers to be sene as there is; but my hope is of yor greate humanity. Yet this I must confesse (for that my papers will affirme it) that my persecution hath bene more heavy & burdensome vnto me by their tongues & such as are their folowers then that wch I felte (though it hath bene greate) by civill magistrates: & this moved me to these kind of colleccions & studies, at the last.

I humbly giue god thankes I never wanted friendes styrd vp (oftentimes) unexpected (as now I hope to fynde your wor. one) to defend my inocencie in all externall actions: neith^r did any want or necesitie of requisites to my vocation ever force me eyth^r to come in or passe oute of the lande: yea yf eyth^r desire of doctorship or oth^r degrees in schooles or dignities in churches, or oth^r preferments aboue my desarts, offered vnto me, wold have moved, I neded nev^r to have bene molested here: But as love to my native contrey did drive me to affect here to liue in the greatest affliction that my swete sauio^r shold suff^r to be laide vpon me (vtpote suauiter dis-

ponens omnia) rather then in any other land wth all the delightes
were offered: soe have I dearely boughte my love that way & as I
thinke none more, that is of my profession & calling now on live.
ffor soe vehement hathe my persecution bene by their meanes as in
truth it hath sometimes made me almost weary of my life & in
minde to leave of that course w^{che} I had taken against them, in
suppressing their plots & devises. for what shold I doe, I was
soe hardly thoughte of (eyth^r by Mr. Topcliffe or others meanes) that
my happe was ever to suffer extraordinary cruelty & hard vsage in
prison: I cold goe noe where abroade: but there were warrants
oute for me yea .16. at one time in the west (as I was informed) &
that by an Hyspanized politicians meanes: It was generally blazed
abroade that I was let oute of prison by the late L. Treasorere, that
I was in & oute of prison when I lyst & onely of policie gave out
that I was hardly vsed, that I had money at will allowed vnto me
to play the Spie: that I defended ffixer & Cicill [a] wch had warrants
as all the world knew from the saids L. Treasorer to goe & liue
where they lyste & none to be troubled for them (and in dede ffixer
I did defend finding him wholy opposite to the Spanish faction) &
commended the L. Treasorer & Mr Secretarie, his son, togith^r
wth Mr. Wade that they were noe persecutors; but well affected
(wch I also did, marry not that ever I had any such dealings as they
infered was the cause of these commendes, to witte, as set on & maintained by them) that I had continually when I wold secrete accesse
to Syr Robert Cicil, that I never went nor came to any place, but I
gave Mr. Waad presently to vnderstand thereof: soe as he knew all
whatsoever I knewe: These w^{the} the like did they soe vniustly
slander and wthall as I knew not what to doe, for euery one affected
unto that Spanish faction believed verily that these reports were
true: those whoe of themselves or other of my brethren the Sem.

47, f. 97b.

[a] John Fixer was sent upon the mission from the seminary at Valladolid. For
an account of the career and character of Dr. John Cecil see "Documents illus-
trating Catholic Policy in the Reign of James VI." in the *Miscellany* of the Scottish
History Society.

persuasions or by my owne meanes were quite opposite w^{the} dislike of that faction although they never beleived otherwise then charitably & well of me, & that yf I had any such accesse or dealings it was for some good end to o^r countrey & them all : yet hearing me deny it (as otherwise I had lyed) they were put in that feare (least some or oth^r of that faction wold betray me as I pray god, it were not nowe soe in dede) that they durst not kepe me for yf they heard I had bene in any place or countrey they nev^r seased vntill they learned oute where I was : & then eyth^r some was set on worke to make them believe I was a spie & soe disgrace, discredite, & supplante me as noe beinge there ; or els that I was soe dangerous a man as whosoev^r were taken wth me shold be sure to die bringing ni twoe wch procured my first escape oute of Bridewell for an example (executed by Topcliffes cruelty)^a to terrify them for receiving of me : or otherwise a feyned surmise of a searche or greate troubles were alledged to be towards these parties w^{the} whom I was & onely as was thoughte & reported bycaus it was knowen of my being & lying close there : & soe vpon the sodeine, & comonly when most troubles dangers & searches were, must I nedes flie & expose my selfe to all dangers that mighte happen vnto me. To yeald my selfe voluntarily to prison I mighte not doe it knowing what extremities I had there bene put vnto : & expecting the like againe, yf ever I came in the civill magistrats handes thoughe I thoughte ever there was least cause to afflicte & most cause to favo^r me or as much as any of my profession yf that had bene then wch nowe is knowen. To vtter my greife & hard case to any civill magistrats or oth^r Protestant my profession, religion & function did all forbydde me, it being not my parte to accuse any man (especially of my owne religion) in particular except in matters of fact lesæ maiestatis diuinæ vel humanæ, as in heresie against god or treason against my prince, neith^r in trueth wold I ever to deathe have written or saide thus much but that my writings (wch I am sory for) declare this & muche more wch they have done bothe against me & others whom they have abused & therefore am

Margaret Ward and John Roche, executed Aug. 30, 1588.

I bounde herein to open the trueth so far forth & noe farther then pertains to my discharge. To avoide the lande I founde noe comfort nor hope of ease that way now these latter yeares, for that having vpon these occasions bene driven to defend my selfe & offend them, in gathering these collections you now have & casting oute & sending abroade diuerse letters in confutacion of their Spanishe title faction & devises & now the matt^r being hotely prosecuted on bothe sides; the passage I shold have had must have bene by stealthe and therefore doubtfull of escaping & yf taken then sure to be as now I am, committed to prison & perhaps greater suspension had of me on all sides. yf I had escaped cleare over, then had they laide a traine for me (as themselves confessed hearing I intended (as I did) such a matter) to have laide me fast & eyther to have bene put to death there or cast in prison to my dying day. To continue in the case I was in here it semed to all my frends a thing impossible but that eyther they wold force me, as they did Mr. ffixer, at length to departe, or els I was sure to be taken, & having not that good warrant w^{che} he had, I knew best my selfe what I was to looke for, even as nowe I fynde. At last I resolved to giue place to fury for a time & gette me into Scotlande, intending to have gotten over into france that way & soe to have liued at Paris, where I knew I shold be saife from them or els to have byllited in Scotland for a time. But there also finding as greate a division as here touching that Spanishe faction & not that comforte nor harbor for priests eyth^r English or Scots as had bene heretofore, I returned thence into the Northe, where newes being come from London by those that lysten and inquire still after me wch way so ever I goe: then began a new conflicte & there in dede being moved to see their folly I was bothe rovnde & plaine w^{the} them that they of all others towards the borders shewed smalle eyth^r witte, religion, or affeccion towards their country that wold any way lysten to that Spanish faction or title, it being certain that the lordes of Northe were all opposite against it, especially Westmerland & Dacree, & that the Dacree being then in Scotland soe well beloved of all the

borderers of both nacions as he was: the Scots lying upon them as
they did to enter in a trice: yf they shold leane vnto the Spaniard,
of whom could they or were they to expect ayde or succor but to
be made a pray for Scot. Span. & the South of England w^the all
other. In fine I was forced to fly thence & come Southward
againe to London. But ere ever I came here they had rung me
such a peale as I knew not where to put my heade. They had given
oute euery where to take hede of me that I was (nowe) set on by
my L. of Essex, & met w^the the L. Dacree in the northe in Cum-
berlande, wch my L. of Essex privie vnto, that I went into Scotland by Mr. Secretaries apointment, that I slandered Dolemans
booke, that I w^the other Sem[inarists] soughte to bring in the Scot.
that an army was presently there to be levied for that purpose.
That I was become an apostata, an excomunicate person, & suspended from the altar, & neither mighte heare masse, heare confessions nor vse any oth^r priestly functions (& in dede by this
meanes a greate many did shun my company, yea even of my
friends thinking that it mighte welbe (as true it is) by their procurement of malice against me), that I cared for noe religion, was
an atheist, sought to set vp heresie, and prefered rath^r the Scot an
herite then the Span. soe sounde a cathol., that I was a deadly
enimy to all the Jesuites, & soughte by all meanes possible to gitte
them banished oute of the lande, etc. These heavy calamities
vrged me far being every word as falsly & uniustly laide to my
charge as to the childe new borne as god is mie witness. But
carying a cleare conscience I cared not for them, & soe I
remayned.

Now whither it came by their speaches given oute of purpose
against me, that I had written a booke for the Scots title & was set
on by the king to doe it: they thinking hereby eyth^r to stoppe my
writings & obieccions against them & their Span. title, w^che they
feared I was in hand wth all, & therefore charged me depely vnder
paine of deadely sin to take away all writings that he could fynde
of mine : or els that they hoped by this false alarme to bringe me

& all the Sem. my brethren, into the like tearmes for Scotland as they were in for Spaine: & thereby to have confirmed their reporte & slander raised of a sodality that we shold have entred into (forsothe) opposite to their hispanized title & dealings: or els for that I had told some (to daunte them wthall) that their Spanish succession was answeared: or for that hearing oure such revyling speaches against the king of Scots as in trueth are not to be vsed against the greate Turke nor any y^t sitteth on the throne of ma^{ty}. I saide be the Scots king as he is yet I will ever prefer him before the Span. bothe in word & wrytinge; or that my speaches against them in the north gave this suspition: or howe it came to passe I know not. But ere ever I set pen to paper, or in good faith intended it, one came to me & told me how her ma^{ty} & honorable counsell had intelligence of such at worke set oute by a Sem: against Dolemans succession: & were not onely well contented wth it but yf it were not yet published were very willing & desirous it shold, soe as they mighte have first a sighte of it: and persuaded me in any case to publishe it before any broyles by Span. Scots or Irishe were begune, it being thought by many, bothe cathol. & protestants, to be the nedefullest werke that ever was set in hand wthall. All their vaine hopes by this means being dashed: a greate good worke, for settling of wauering mynds, moving all to ioyne wth one consent in defence of o^r contrey as many examples be alledged for the like notwthstanding difference in religion, a speciall cooling carde against the Dolemanists slanders raysed against all Sem. & others that are not of their faction; especially in clearing my selfe for my speeches vsed in comparing or preferring Scotl. before Spaine: as also for discharge of Doctor Bagshawe aboute Squires treasons: & acquitting Mr Doleman the priest of the suspition had of him to be the autho^r of the booke of titles: & in generall to stoppe all their mouthes that wold shuffle of these bookes & other medlings of & in state affaires from the Jes. & their folowers to the Sem. & other cathol[ics] & lastly wold shew plaine that plot to be theirs by that ye Scot. should wonder why noe Sem. wold answere Doleman for him.

47, f. 98.

To this I answered that in dede I was about a pece of worke wch I meant onely shold goe amongst cathol. to shew what men the Jes. were & wherevnto their ambitious Span. pretence did incline & that I had made sundry colleccions for mie owne private knowledge & to be able to defend my selfe against them in all things. y^t may pertayne eyther to England Scotland or Spaine intending to make Calvins platforme, Machiavels prince, & Dolemans succession but all 3. words of one significacion, viz. turkized atheism: but for setting oute any booke or other worke y^t mighte touche the title in particular eyther for one or oth^r I neither had nor did intend. And as for the Scots title or the Kings setting me on worke, none of any witte, but will see it is a ridiculous toy proceding of their wonted malice against me, 1°. for there is (as I heare) a very learned answer oute against Doleman on the Scots behalfe, 2° my going into Scotland being onely to voide the danger I was in of being taken here by them, I had bene madde to have come theare wth any such meaning, espicially to have published such a worke or once set in hand wth it in England. 3°. yf it had eyther bene motioned or by me intended, it had bene the onely colo^r most saifety & preferment I could have had to have stayed there; going of purpose (as I did) to have stay^d yf I had founde any saifety & maintenance convenient. 4°. I founde noe comforte nor cause at my being in Scotl. & lesse sinne to further the Scots title yf I mighte meddle in such matters, they being all (except those affected to the Dacree who hate a Span[iard] for his sake) eyther puritanes or Spanified against their owne king (noe doubt for gaine) and bearing generally a revenging minde against all English vsing such opprobrious words as none that hath an English heart can brooke. 5°. considering how the Dane is linked neare in blood wth Spaine & the first in the holy league, I euer was of that minde that it proceded of singular highe prudence to fede the Scotte a farre of w^the hope, thereby to kepe him from admitting Span. ayde rather then ever to further his admittance here to the English crowne for many reasons wch I could alledge by that I heard & sawe whiles I was there. 6°. soe long as Doleman was Scots, & Leycesters commonwealthe in request, there were diuerse Sem[inary] Dolemanists thoughte to be affected that way, in soe much as I heard my selfe a Scots puritaine at a noble mans table in Scot. say that it was the papists of England that must helpe King James to the crowne as Leycesters book had given it him or els he wold never gitte it. But after Dolemans dryfte was once descried I thinke there was not, neither is there, any one Sem. this day on live y^t wisheth a Scots gouernment except respectively rather then a Span[iard] shold have it and the reason is for that all who favoured the Scots title before time, were then Dolemanists, & therefore now bend eyther to Spaine wth him : or els finding at length what his dryfte was, first for Scotl. & then for Spaine, they vtterly have abandoned, abhored & detested all his practises & bookes of state, seking to suppresse them to the vttermost as tending to noe end but raising of slanders against prince & peers, exasperating of authority to persecute all for his faulte exciting foraine invasions unnaturally against our countrey ; setting all nacions togith^r by the eares, inviting to open rebellion & making all iealous of one an othe^r & seo to cut each one an others throate. W^{ch} course being contrary to all sound & apostolicall examples noe Sem. nor oth^r cathol. or protestant (as I thinke) but will avoide, & and I know it y^t daily both the cleargy & laity decline more & more from that good opinion they had of him & his society. and therefore it is but eyth^r a false alarme of theirs of my intituling the Scot thereby to hinder all replies that mighte be made to cleare o^{r}selves & leave them to their Span. title: or els (quoth I to the motioner) you are set on by some Dolemanist to intrappe me. But he insisted in his suite wth depe protestacion of all sincerenes.

Continuing in his earnest suite vnto me w^{the} 3 sundry supplies from the courte at last I, looking vpon him smiling, saide well this is but a trappe for a syllie mouse, but doing or not doing it I shalbe suspected & some enimye of mine wil in the end set out such a worke on the Scots behalfe in dede & lay it vpon me as

Parsons doeth on Doleman, wch to prevent I will goe gitte me oute of hande into Scotl. where I am sure I shall be most welcome, have security w^the princely reward & many thankes & publish it withe autority & credite for ev^r aft^r at the kings hand, but then (quoth I wth all) I must nedes make the title cleare on the Scots parte w^che I am neith^r willing to, neith^r thinke I that her ma^ty or councell wold have it soe on any side. The conclusion was that yf he dealt bona fide wth me, w^the humble thankes vpon my knees to her ma^ty & honorable councell for so mercyfull an acceptance of such a worke thereby to cleare our selves her highnes faithfull subiects wth our loyalty in discarding the Span. clayme & favorable proteccion to secure me from daunger. I would lay all my notes & colleccions togither & make one of Dolemans workes confute an oth^r. And hereupon a draughte I drew of the whole worke, made 2 epistles, one as a preface ioyning England & Scotl. togith^r (least the Scot. shoid say I wer set on to confute his late booke against Doleman) an other as dedicatory to her ma^ty alone, declaring my whole intent w^the the rest of my brethren minde herein (for y^t ere I wold begin it I talked wth diuerse & sent to m^r Doctor Bagshaw aboute it, for his opinion) this done I began the worke dialogue wise & had written 15 shetes thereof ere I was taken, all wch were perused w^the greate good liking (as I was tolde) of her ma^ty, my L. of Essex, my L. Chamberlaine, m^r Secretary, m^r Comptrol^r & others but especially syr John Stanop, whoe I thinke by the bishop of Lymericke or m^r Udalls meanes was first made privie vnto it & acquainted her ma^ty therew^th all, to my most comforte of her soe gracious acceptance of my poore myte, her highnes keping one copy & my L. of Essex an oth^r of the sum or contents of the whole worke. The epistle to her ma^ty syr Robert Cicil saw in my L. of Essex hand and disliked only or rather doubted (as was told me) of this word *tolleration* y^t her ma^ty wold not grant it. It was sent backe to alter it, I did soe & returned it againe (the very day that I was taken on), my L. of Essex vsing these honorable speaches that he coulde wishe wth all his hearte y^t we mighte have liberty of conscience. The methode I observed was all well liked of soe as I wold put oute such names of the nobility and others as I had broughte in obiectively oute of Philopat. & others in the person of the opponent protestant against the defendant Romanist where I had named my lord Treasorer, syr ffrancis Walsingham, & others & wthall not to touch Calvin in matters of religion. In bothe w^{ch} & all oth^r doubts on my parte I resolved then that their will in this case shold be to me a lawe, wth promise to put oute all names or what els as mighte offend eyth^r prince, pere, or state. This answeare was marvailous pleasing & well liked of, as also the answeares to the twoe first obieccons of Dolemans succession (for I was taken ere I heard what became of that of bastardy of the house of Scotland, the lady Arbella Hertford & Derby house) and especially it was noted wth well pleasing conceitethat I quite shutte out all foraigne titles and drew the clayme rather to Yourke than to Lancaster, wherein, to speake gods truth, I meant covertly to have defeated Scotland in the end by y^t & other groundes as occasion shold have bene offered me obiter wthout suspition to ye Scot. to writte ex proposito against him & wthall to have intituled the house of Yorke or England to the kingdomes of Castile, Aragon & Portigall (to teach Doleman to be soe busie against his native contrey) by a surer pretence than any Spanishe Lancastrian can make to our Englishe crowne. 47, f. 98b.

Thus (Wor^{ll}. syr) I have presumed to lay open vnto you my whole course of life, how unwilling I was to have entered into the worke, yea althoughe all my brethrene (opposite to these foraine titles, factions, state matters and persons that seke the ruine of our whole countrey & vs all) did assuredly thinke this discovery of Dolemans sucession to be most necessary aswell to cleare the inocent as also to abate the peoples fond affection to that Span. title & those persons & by none soe fitte to be handled as by my self who had still bene trayned vp in opposition against them. And althoughe I had all firme promises that might be & thos from time to time to set me forward, shewing as from her ma^{ty} &

cheife aboute her regall person, what greate good I mighte doe to o^r whole countrey hereby; what singular liking & good speaches there were had of it on all sides: her ma^{ty} glad to heare y^t all Sem[inarists] were not of Dolemans minde, that she thoughte ere this, all priests to have bene consenting to that Span. faction: that her highnes was of opinion that we Sem. wold ever take in hand to answeare that booke: that now she hoped both Sem. & Jes. wold in the end become more loyall subiects: she of her owne mercifull benignitie not willing to afflict, but to conive at their religion & ceremonies therevnto pertaining. These w^{the} many oth^r comforts came vnto me as are yet for the most parte to be sene in the letters that there are amongst my writings as also the condicons concluded vpon on bothe sides to be observed aboute this worke viz. 1º to leave the title indiffrent w^{the} confutacon of Doleman onely. 2º. to touche noe matt^r of religion in particular against Calvine. 3º. a wishe (but no commande) was, not to touche any of her ma^{ties} nobility or of her honorable concell (wch I never ment but soe as in the end to cleare them w^{the} blaming of Dolemans Philopat^r for accusing them). 4º. that euery page mighte be pervsed before it came in printe; all wch I promised & performed on my parte soe far as I had gone. But now what promise was kept w^{the} me? 1º. it was promised me that a warrant sholde be granted to printe it privately alwais provided that noe Jes. nor fautor of theirs mighte know thereof nor that her ma^{t}y or any of the councell were privie vnto it (before it were done) in autorizing the printing of it. 2º. that it was a thing expected & wished for bona fide & wold most favourably be accepted of. 3º. that I shold be secured from all dangers that might happen hereby vnto me. 4º. yea, hope & promise was given & made vnto me to be protected, defended and freed from all imprisonments yf hereafter I fell into civill magistrates hands for this good service done herein, yet was I still in feare (all this notwthstanding) that some Spanified Machiavell had a hand herein to gitte me (at least) laide fast, soe as I shold never hinder their vncivall & disloyall procedings & attempts any more hereaft^r. And now they have their will of me, and whiles I ment in all feare of god, loyalty to my prince, love to my countrey to shew anie desire of drawing all home w^{the} deare affeccon pugnare pro patria, as all lawes divine & humane do bonde vs abstracting from the least thoughte of Scotlands favour intencion or motion for him or from him, as god & his angels are my witnesses in the testimonies of all my actions wth these I have dealte the worke it selfe beganne here as you see: the diuersitie of letters yet extant amongst my writings & all my brethren, especially M^r. Doctor Bagshaw, will make it manifest. yet I am drawen, as I suspected, & even like a shepe in the shambles boughte & solde; quite cut of from all humane helpe or succor & made a pray for euery one to fede vpon. The Spanish faccion persecuting me wth their tongues to the vttermost; and here by the autority of the state (thoughe not for me to say why doe you soe) laide close in prison for my greate good will, deare love & duetifull affeccion to my contrey, stripte quite of all my money writings, bookes & other smalle necessaries: and not allowed (now almost this moneths space) y^t common benefite called liberty of prison (wch I was promised never to have nede of) that others both priests Jesuites, ministers & and other lay persons of all sorts enioye.

And herein (the promisses considered) how heavy & lamentable my case is I leave it to yor wisdome w^{the} all tender compassion to consider vpon: & of yor owne pitifull nature in christian charitie to helpe me w^{the} redresse of these calamities I sustaine: assuring myselfe her ma^{ty} nor honorable councell of her royall & their noble hearts wold never afflicte but spedily release me to my comfortable constrainte to sounde forthe their mercy extended towards the afflicted, most for his loyall & dutifull love towards them: and onely my hard hap that my cause was never laide open as yet to the eye of pitie, nor view of honor. wch charitable worke yor selfe (noble syr) preferring you shall not onely affect an act worthy yo^{r}selfe yor place & calling to yor lasting credite acceptable to god & man; but wthall bynde me, and all my friends opposites to all disloyalty to remaine yo[rs] in whatsoever we may be able to shew a thankefull minde. And thus craving pardon for my long & tedious letter w[the] humble suite for a comfortable answeare I leave farther to trouble your worship at this time comitting you to the tuition of the Almightie, & my selfe to yo[r] effectuall remembrance.

yo[r] worships poore afflicted
Willm Watson.

Endorsed on the copy on a blank leaf marked ' 105 ':

Aprill 1599. A letter from William Watson, a Prist unto M[r]. Attorney-Generall, and in his absence to William Waad.

5 *Forty-five Articles of Enquiry.* [a]

47, f. 107

D. B.

[Winter of 1600-1601.]

1. It semeth that the Jesuits about 27 or 28 yeres since beganne to resorte into England, and imploy them selves in Englishe affaires. Inquire the circumstances hereof : viz who came first hither : who sent them : what faculties had they : and how did they behave them selves.

D B.

2. It semeth that when the Jesuits did first combyne them selves wth the Englishe priests, Cardinall Allen foretold that he feared they woulde be the ruyne of the priests.[b] Inquire howe this may appeare.

---

[a] These articles of enquiry, which have no title or heading in the MS., were probably prepared by the Bishop of London. They were written after Nov. 1600 (as is shown by the references to the correspondence between Charnock and Cardinal Borghese), but before the publication of any of the appellants' books which first appeared in print early in the following year. The marginal notes are in various hands. On folio 106 there is noted in Bagshaw's hand : " Parsons collections afore his flyghte, the Spaniards letters for the Jesuits to Rome. Parsons labouring for a redde cap." But this can have no reference to the present document.

[b] This seems to refer to the opening paragraph of the preceding statement by Bagshaw (p. 208).

3. It appeareth that Campion wth others about one time, and Heywood and Holte wth some also at an other tyme were sent over hither. Inquire the particuler occasions of theire sendinge: what faculties they had, and howe they imployed them. It appeareth that Heywoods dealings were not approved amongest many of the popishe Catholicks—the specialties hereof are muche desired. D. ffarb.^a
To D. B.

4. It semeth that the priests at Wisbiche wth theire company there have ben reputed amongst the popishe Catholicks for the visible Churche of England. Add herevnto what may be thought convenient for the better openinge of it. Sondry l̃res to D. B. and others.

5. It semeth that Edmonds the Jesuite for 6 or 7 yeres affected to be the cheife of the said visible churche, and that for that purpose he hathe practised diverslye, viz., by Insynuatinge himself into the favoure of the younger sort at Wisbiche: by labouringe to haue place and sitt before a D^r. of Divinitye: by thrustinge himself forwarde to make collations when straungers came to see them, and by insistinge commonly in his said collations vppon the necessi^{tie} of order and discipline. Many things towchinge his carriage and packinge for this purpose may herevnto be ioyned. D. ffarb.^a conference wth Curye.
D. B. to D. W.
D. ffarb.

6. It appeareth that about christmas 1595 Edmonds havinge made his faction sure vnto him entered into a separation & schisme devidinge himself wth 19 of his companions from the rest of the priests at Wisbiche as from disorderly and wicked persons, suche as they could no longer holde company wth: Insomuche as he wth his faction refused to eate or drinke wth the other priests: and therefore desired a severall kitchine, severall offices, and so to eate and drinke by them selves. 47, f. 107b.
D. W. to d^r W.
Conference betwixt Medley, Southworth, and d. B.

7. It semeth that after the said separation Edmonds and his faction contrived certeyne accusations against d. B and his syde conteyned in two or three sheets of paper, charginge them to be Mr Dolman.
D. B.

---

^a Perhaps Dr. Farbeck, a doctor of medicine, who lived in Holborn but made frequent visits to Bagshaw at Wisbech, where he died November, 1598.

straglers, susurrones, livers ex raptu, extortioners, impugners of order, men of confusion, violent deteyners of other mens goods etc. Inquire for his writinge and the circumstances thereof, and particulerly of theire defence of detraction: so as the parties be not named.

ffarb.

8. It semeth that this separation was not made w'thout the consent of Wallye, the provinciall for the Jesuits: and that the faction of Edmonds made choice of him the said Edmonds to be theire governo^r or Agent wth an absolute authoritie: desiringe the approbation of theire said choice from Wallye, and that he yealded therevnto so as all might be compassed sine invidia sui. Peradventure here is some mistakinge. ffor example: It may be that theire said choise of Edmonds: Contulimus inter nos etc. Was some fortnight or moneth after the said separation. Inquire the certeyne course that was helde in this matter: as for Wallyes letter to Edmonds in approbation of his agencie, wch was shewed (as I take it) to m^r. dolman; or for any other letters or particlers apperteyninge to this purpose: As namely againe: Whether Walley havinge pervsed the letter: Contulimus inter nos, with theire xxij articles, did not sett downe some particler directions or forme of Edmonds Agencie.

Dolman against Southworth.

47, f. 108.

9. There are certeyne orders tearmed Regulæ sodalitatis nostræ in latine wth a preface beginninge: Cum nobis non sit colluctatio. Inquire to what company those apperteyned: who drewe them, and what was the devise for the practise of them.

10. There are other orders in Englishe intituled thus: orders to be observed of Catholick prisoners begynninge viz: that none live of charitie, etc. and endinge wth this subscription: sine ordine necesse est vt omnia corruant G. J. Inquire when these orders were made, by whom, and vppon what occasion.

11. There are other orders also in Englishe wth theire titles in latine: as first de Rectoribus, and begynninge: There shalbe chosen everie yere one father etc. and endinge thus: Diminution or separation in these orders. Inquire the purpose of the said

DEALINGS WITH THE GOVERNMENT. 229

orders: who devised them, and the occasion thereof, wth suche other circumstances therevnto belonginge.

12. It semeth that vppon the occasion offred by Edmonds his Agencie, that the priests who were opposite vnto him and against the Jesuiticall faction devised an association or vnion wherevnto hands were procured. Inquire the whole course thereof: what the said association was, and wherevnto it tended: who devised it: were the rules of it wth suche other circumstance as may make the same apparant to be of a farre different nature from the Jesuiticall complotts and vnions. D. B. Mr Char. & other l̃res.

13. It semeth by a letter of mr. Charnocks to D^r. B. that there was about this tyme a iarre betwixt the priests in the North and in the South of England about a generall association and vnion: and that they affected to haue one cheife for the North and an other for the south but bothe to governe accordinge to certeyne rules. Wth this letter m^r Charnock sent a booke of rules, not differinge muche from an other booke: Savinge that the one is in Englishe and the other in latine. Inquire of this iarre, and of that devised goverment, and procure the said booke wth any other thinge herevnto apperteyninge.

14. It semeth that after the said separation, before mentioned, when many popishe Catholicks abroade beganne to dislike it, Edmonds concealinge his Agencie approved by Walley was contented in shewe to haue the quarrells betwixte him and the rest comprimitted: supposinge that D^r. Bavyn one of them whom he named as an Arbitrator woulde approve theire separation, and plott out for him some forme of goverment not muche differinge in effect from his said Agencie: wch if he could haue effected by the consent of the other Arbitrator m^r. Dolman, it would have bene more gratefull vnto him, the said Edmonds, as proceedinge from secular priests: and then he should not have been driven to have detected his secrete intercourse wth Walley the Jesuite: wch he knewe would be hardlie borne by the other priests. Some things may herevnto be added for the more apparent vnfoldinge of Edmonds hipocrisie in this action. 47, f. 108b

Collected out of Dolman's discourse against Southworth.

15. Mr. Dolmans large confutation of Southworthes letter is sufficiently perused concerninge Dr. Bavyn and his proceedings as also Dr. Bavyns Geneva platforme and his paltringe and packinge for Edmonds : as it appeareth by sondry letters wch passed betwixt him and D. Bag : Likewise the quarrell betwixt Dr. Wyndham and the two Arbitrators that Edmonds and his faction sinned by theire said separation. But the narration thereof might be made more cleare by suche as knowe those affaires more particulerlye.

16. Vpon notice what Walley had done as towchinge Edmondes agencie, it appeareth that D. B. did write to Walley challenginge him of partialitie & iniustice in proceedinge so farre as he had done before the other side was heard, etc. Inquire for the particuler letters that passed betwixte them.

47, f. 109.   17. It appeareth by a letter of Thomas Awdleys to Dr B. 1595 [a] wherein he perswadeth wth him to yealde to Edmonds agencie that the yeare before in lent suche a matter was allowed of, and commended to all by the absolute superior. In the said yeare 1594 there was a mission to Rome, wch receyved the popes benediction. The further explanation of these particulers is desired : what formes or matter was so commended : what the mission meaneth, the cause, and successe of it, etc.

18. It semeth that many dealt wth D. B. this yeare 1595 for his yealdinge to Edmonds and so to the Jesuits : and namely Tho. Awdley assuringe him that the Jesuits were then in suche credite, that whosoeuer opposed themselves against them would loose theire creditts. Likewise he telleth a longe tale of Cardinall Allen his commendation of the Jesuits, advisinge the priests in England to be advised and ordered by them, etc. Inquire more hereof and what was the cause of the Mission then to Rome at that time.

To D. B., Idibus Jan., 1596.   19. It appeareth that certeyne priests remayninge in London did deale ernestly with D. B. that one might rule the rest, if not

---

[a] This letter, dated 26 June, is in the archives of the Archbishop of Westminster and was printed by Dr. Knox in *Letters and Memorials of Card. Allen*, p. 378.

Edmonds yet some other: and that they sent to D. B. librum regularum. It is desired to knowe the names of these priests and to obteyne the said booke wth some further instruction of the author of it, and to what end and for what company it was compiled.

20. It semeth that vppon D. Bavyn and m^r Dolmans givinge over the cause as not beinge able to compound it, notwthstandinge they had dealt in it for two or three monethes or more D. B. did contynue his writinge somewhat sharpely to m^r Walley: and that he the said Walley therevppon did write two or three letters in answere vnto him: wherein he promiseth that so the priests in Wisbiche would yeald to any good order of goverment amongest themselves, he would recall m^r Edmonds againe. W^{ch} it semeth he performed in some sorte as havinge a further matter in his head to plott at Rome thinkinge that the fittest way to wynne time for his purpose. Walley to D. B., Oct. 22, 1595.
47, f. 109b.

Some particulars may here be added for the makinge of this more manifest.

21. It semeth that vppon the said offer of m^r Walley to recall the said Edmonds agencie D. B. and his side subscribed to certeyne articles for the better goverment of that house: wch Edmonds and his partie dislikinge, theire quarrells were referred to one m^r Mushey and m^r Dudley: who the sixt of November 1595 compounded them, and gave vnto them 19 rules for theire said goverment wherevnto all sides subscribed: Mr Edmonds for modesty sake subscribed the lowest of all his faction. Hereof Walley beinge certified writt to D. B. a glorious letter dated the 17 of November resemblinge the said agreement to the place of the heavenly Jerusalem; whereby a man would have thought he and his faction would have contented themselves and sought no further. Add herevnto what may be convenient.

22. It seemeth that the priests at Wisbiche conforminge them selves to the said orders lived in a kinde of scamblinge and choppinge manner of frendshipp almost for a yere. In wch time a *The treatises.*

greate contention fell out betwixte Edmonds and D. Bag: about the Stewes, and shortly after, exceptions beinge taken to the said orders made by Mushey and Dudley, and to Walley in that he kept not promise in lookinge to his subiects, there was a newe breache, D. B. and his side refusinge to be governed any longer by them.

D. B.
47, f. 110.

23. It semeth that the Jesuits were growne to be very odious about this tyme to the sæcular priests by reason of theire pride and ambition and of theire collection of money and misimployinge the same, etc. Insomuch as there was written A° 1597 a treatise in latine against them tearmed memoriale and dedicated to the Pope. This treatise I desire greatly wth all the circumstances that doe concerne it as also if any thinge may be added vnto it towchinge the Jesuits proceedings.

24. It appeareth that m^r ffisher and an other were sent to Rome about these matters. Inquire the cause, theire interteynement and successe.

G. G. to D. B.

25. It semeth that whilest the priests at Wisbiche were quarrellinge together about theire goverment and about the Stewes,[a] that Walley was practisinge wth Parsons for an other manner of goverment and association, and that D. B. was advertised of Walley's intent viz: to have all the priests in England either governed by a Jesuite, or by one so addicted to the Jesuits as that they might be sure to have them at theire commaundment. The circumstances are desired to be sett downe more particularly.

26. It semeth that Walley so wrought wth Parsons as that he obteyned a newe kinde of goverment directed from Rome by Cardinall Caietane, 7° Martij 1598. I haue a copie of the letter and of his iustructions, and desire to vnderstand who were sent by

---

[a] See Bagshaw's *True Relation* (reprint, p. 66-7). The propositions of Giles Archer, reported to the Pope, are set down in a paper signed by Cecil, Bluet, Mush, and Champney (Petyt MSS. xlvii., f. 276), and were printed in the *Declaratio Motuum*.

Walley to Rome, and howe that matter was contrived, wth other circumstances.

27. It semeth that vppon the arrivall in England of the said Cardinalls letter and directions for Blackwells Archpriestdome etc. he the said Blackwell did publishe his owne praise and authoritie by an insolent letter written to all the preists in England, etc. requiringe them to be obedient to him and his assistants, etc. : the copie of wch letter I doe desire as also to knowe the Nuncio or messingers that brought the said Cardinalls letters wth suche other circumstances as doe therevnto apperteyne. By diverse lettres.
D. B.

28. It appeareth that D. B. and many other priests in England tooke sondry exceptions against this newe subordination, shewinge the absurdities of it as D. B. had done of Edmonds agencie : exceptions are taken against Blackwell and against his proceedinges, wch it appeareth are verie papall and rigorous, suche as were disliked by verie many priests: and that therevppon, as also in many other respects an appeale was made from this newe authoritie vnto the Pope. Here also many things may be added perteyninge to this narration. I haue D. B. letter begynninge pro instituendo in ecclesia Anglicana Archipresbiteratu, etc. 47, f. 110b.

29. It appeareth that the priests who disliked of the newe goverment vppon theire Apeale made, or purposinge the same, sought handes to some other crosse course, and devised to send to the pope theire opynions and desires aswell concerninge Blackwells hierarchy, as what they thought most fitt for the good of the priests in England and for the erecting of popery. Many thinges here also may be added by suche as were acquainted wth these matters, besides the particulers to be sett downe wch here are mentioned : as what the said crossinge course was : and howe the said appellation was caryed and fortefied.

30. It appeareth that vppon the said appellation Blackwell and his adherents tooke greate offence, and many threatnings were vsed : he writt sondry prowde & threatninge letters : and together wth his assistants tooke away from suche as they disliked and gave Charnock.
Bishop.

vnto others faculties at theire pleasures: sondry raylinge letters were written by his faction against the other priests as against D. B. that he taunted the Cardinalls orders: did teare the copye of the Nuncio his letter etc. The copies of as many of these letters of Blackwells as may be had are greatlie desired as also a more particler and cleare declaration of this pointe.

47, f. 111.   31. It semeth also that some of Blackwells faction dislikinge the said Appellation, did write a treatise against all that opposed them selves against it, or rather deferred the yealdinge vnto it, vntill they knewe the popes pleasure. In wch treatise the author taketh vppon him to prove that all suche priests as so opposed them selves were schismaticks. The copie of this treatise is desired together wth suche circumstances as doe concerne the same.

32. It appeareth that whilest D. B. and the other priests were about the contrivinge of theire message to Rome condemninge theire Appeale, Blackwell and Walley procured almost 200 priests to subscribe a letter to Cardinall Caietane of thanksgivinge for appointinge the Archep^{rs}bitershipp on them: wch letter beinge shewed by the Cardinall to Parsons, he writt back to Blackwell of his ioye in respecte of that newes, etc.

33. It appeareth that after deliberation D. B. and other priests sent m^r Bishop and m^r Charnock to Rome wth divers instructions. I haue seen m^r Mushey his letter wch was then sent to Rome concerninge the desire of the sæcular priests to have a goverment by Bisshoppe, together wth the conditions, wch beinge graunted, they might haue yealded vnto the Archep^{rs}bitershipp.[a] When these

[a] This was probably the important letter, already referred to, written by Mush to Mgr. Morro, and printed in the *Declaratio Motuum* (pp. 122-142). Mush wrote to Bagshaw, May, 1599 : " Desire Mr. Cauerley to copye out my letter to Mr. Morus y^t is sent back by Fa. Parsons & come into the Bishop of London's hand." Petyt MSS. xlvii. f 204, printed in *Jesuits and Seculars* (p. 147). In the endorsement of this letter it is noted : "The B. of London hath his lre. to ye Cardinall." Morro or Mora, an Italian prelate who assisted Cardinal Sega in the visitation of the English college, in 1596, was not a cardinal. The letter in question, addressed to him by Mush, lays down no conditions of yielding to the archpriest. The conditions referred to may be those laid down in the paper printed below (p. 98).

parties were sent to Rome they had some further instructions wch I would gladly knowe, as also suche other circumstances as are herein materiall, as the letter subscribed by the priests against the Archepresbiter : the letter to the pope mentioned by Charnock, and any other letter then sent to Rome either by D. B. or any other.

34. It semeth that Blackwell vnderstandinge of D. B. and the other priests intent (m^r Bishop himself acquainting him wth his goinge to Rome) did send some of his cursitours before to advertise Parsons and his faction there what was intended Insomuche as the Pope was purposed if they had come to fferara, where he then was, to haue cast them in prison and haue chastned them. Ex literis episc. Tricaricensis pridie Idus Jan. 1599.
47, f. 111b.

Inquire who they were that were sent thither and desire to be informed in all suche materiall circumstances as doe belonge herevnto.

35. I haue pervsed m^r Bishops longe letter to Parsons: whereby it appeareth howe he and m^r Charnock were handled at Rome. It semeth that m^r Bishop at his cominge from Rome writt some shorte letter to Parsons: wch Parsons answered at large: in the Reply to wch answere m^r Bishop writt the said letter. I would gladlie haue a copie of the said shorte letter to Parsons and of Parsons said answere therevnto: wch gave m^r Bishop the occasion to write this second letter.[a]

36. It appeareth that when m^r Bisshop and m^r Charnock were to appeare before the two Cardinalls in Rome m^r Parsons had appointed to procters (beinge some cheife priests there) to informe by Parsons directions fr Blackwell against them, and suche as sent them; as to prove them schismaticks and what not, etc. I 2 lettres from Rome.

---

[a] "The copie of a letter written by F. Rob. Parsons, the jesuite, 2 Octob. 1599 to M. D. Bish[op] and M. Ch[arnock], two banished and consigned priests," etc., and " Doctor Byshops Answere to Fa. Parsons Letter of the 9 of Octob." 1599, were afterwards printed, with other correspondence on the same subject, in *The Copies of certain Discourses*, published by the Appellant priests in 1601 (pp. 49-67 and 178-186).

desire to knowe theire names or any thinge more concerninge theire dealinges in Rome then is expressed in m^r Bishops letter to Parsons.

37. I haue the copy of two letters written from Rome into England bearinge date the 19 and 20th of November 1599.[a]

In wch letters reporte is made of m^r. Bisshop and m^r. Charnocks interteynement farre otherwise then m^r. Bisshop writeth of it, viz: that they were interteyned verie kyndlie : that they showed themselves verie simple men : that they were so handled by Parsons and one of the said proctors as that they had nothinge to say for themselves : that it was made apparant by the said proctors that both they and the priests that sent them were schismaticks and hereticks : that they were imprisoned for theire apparant schisme : that certeyne of D. B. letters beinge there read he was greatlie blamed and charged to haue left Oxford because he missed a mastership : to haue ben expelled the Colledge at Rome 1584 for his factious behavio^r : that he is a man of litle learninge but malitiouse, and that his end will prove sutable to his begynninge or to that effecte. Suche thinges as are convenient for the truthe herein may be added.

38. It appeareth that Parsons so handled the matter as that whilst he caused m^r. Bishop and Charnock to be kept in prison he procured the Popes ratification of the Archep^{r}sbitership and of all that Cardinall Caietane had before prescribed. Inquire what course the priests doe nowe holde that were opposite consideringe that they have not yet been heard by the Pope who hathe suffred him self to be led by Parsons and the said Cardinall and is not yet thoroughly informed, etc.

39. It semeth that m^r. Charnock is come into England notwth-standinge the Cardinalls commaundment to the contrary. Inquire

---

[a] The letters of Martin Array, printed below (pp. 109, 123), were dated respectively Jan. 18 and Feb. 20. The earlier letter of Dr. Haddock (p. 101) is shewn to be erroneously dated "Nov. 19," really Dec. 19, 1598.

howe his so doinge is taken by the Archep : and Walley : whether he hathe not since ben blamed from Rome : by whom, and what he hath answered.

40. It semeth that as many as submitt them selves to the Archep: doe subscribe to certeyne Articles touchinge the disposinge of the Crowne of this kingdome, etc. intermedlinge wth state matters in the highest degree.

Inquire hereof what is expedient to be knowne, and namely whether Parsons be not the author of the Englishe book touchinge succession and published vnder the name of Dolman.

41. I haue seen the censure of Paris that the priests against Blackwell were in no schisme nor sinne in that respecte : and likewise m^r. Blackwells controllment thereof emboldened thervnto by Walley and the Jesuits who are in no greate charitie wth that Universitie. Adde herevnto some other pertinent circumstances : many there must nedes bee in a matter of suche importance.   47, f. 112b.

42. There haue been at sundry tymes greate stirres in the Englishe Colledge at Rome (as appeareth by a large discourse penned by ffissher concerninge one quarrell) sondry persons haue ben expelled 12 or 14 at once : many crimes haue ben published wch m^r. Sicklemore would haue to be concealed.[a] I would gladly haue an historicall narration of all those ambitious practises and cruell designements of the Jesuits. M^r. Siclemore told D. B. one discourse 1598, and is angry that he gave it no better credite. Desire the effecte thereof.   Siclemore to D. B.

43. It appeareth that Parsons hathe ben the cheif author of the quarrells betwixt the priests and Jesuits condemninge the newe subordination : and that he is a meere polititian, and a man voyde of all conscience and honestye. One threateneth to laye him out in his colors :[b] and it is reported that Charles Pagett hathe displayed bothe him and his practices.   A lettre to D. B.

[a] *Infra*, p. 48.
[b] Note to letter of T. P. to Bagshaw, June 4, 1599, printed from the Petyt MSS. xlvii. f. 155, in *Jesuits and Seculars* (p. 146) : "Parsons must be layd out in his coolers."

238   THE ARCHPRIEST CONTROVERSY.

A paper of D. B.   44. It semeth that the treatise to prove the priests wch hold against Blackwell to be no Schismaticks is answered: and that the said answere is confuted. Inquire who answered it, and who hathe confuted it etc.

G. G. to D. B. and J. M. to D. B.   45. It semeth that the Jesuits wth theire Archep^{r} doe so behave them selves as that the priests who haue stood against them, doe greatly feare theire tyrannye. Inquire of some particulers.

47, f. 113.   6. *Answers in Bagshaw's handwriting to the foregoing Articles of Enquiry.*

[Draft,[a] without title or endorsement: on one leaf.]

1. The first were F. Parsons & F. Campion, sent by theyre generall abowte xxij years agoe.[b]

2. Cardinall Allens speachees were knowen to diverse than conversinge wth him.

3. F. Heywoode misliked F. Parsons his superiority, chalendginge & wante of myldnesse in proceedinge.

4. Wisbyche was accowmpted the most conspicuouse place of Catholiques in Englande.

5. M^{r}. Edmunds his cariadge was as muche as mighte be concealed all wch were not his consorts (*but y^{t} wch is heere is true*).[c]

6. It is true y^{t} some were so accowmpted *& the rest is certayne as Mr. Medley*[d] *can tell.*

7. These accusations were especially against three or foure. . .[e]

---

[a] Certain interlineations and additions, here printed in italics, appear to be in the same hand as the body of the documents, but to have been written subsequently. The writing in many places is very faint.

[b] The Jesuits arrived in England in the summer of 1580. This was probably written in 1601.

[c] Interlined: refers apparently to preceding paragraph.

[d] The keeper of Wisbech prison.

[e] The words "I think" have been struck out.

DEALINGS WITH THE GOVERNMENT.

Scarce any papers be extante of those things, many beinge loste & torne by tracte of time & searches &c.

8. Contulimus inter nos was afore the separation & so was F. Walleyes answeare. whose letter was showed to diverse but (as theyre manner vsually is) y^t it should not be copied. Theyre dealings ar wth secrecye vntill time & as they thincke advantage bringeth them to lighte.

9. Regulæ sodalitatis (as far as memory serveth) was some device for the better vnitinge of the sæcular priests wch the Jesuits conceyved to be done against them.

10. Orders are thowghte to have bene for Hulle.

11. 12. 13. 19. De Rectoribus was made by some sæcular priests *for some better vnited order.* But all associations or combinations intended amonge them were stopped & hindered by some of the prisoners in Wisbyche *amonge other things dowbte gave them jealosy of the temporall state.* It shoulde have been voluntary to have entred into it, & likewise to have lefte it agayne. . .^{a} The rules should have beene from time to time arbitrary as mutuall likinge & experience should have directed, wthout irritation of the temporall state. Wth many other differences from the Jesuits from the northe & sowthe diverse priests proposed diverse opinions, but wthout any iarre or resolution. *It so differed from the Jesuits plotts as they thowghte it to be done against them directly.*

14. It is thowghte exactly true.

15. D. W. & M^r. Dol. vppon true information dislike the separation.

16. Suche letters than passed.

17. 18. Thomas Audeley *conteyned diverse untruthes wherof he was convinced.*^{b} A mission is nothinge but a company of students goinge to, or cominge from the Englyshe College in Rome.

---

^{a} " governed only by " struck out.
^{b} This interlineation substituted for the words " was not true."

20. 21. 22. They ar true savinge y^t F. Edmonds and his consorts first disclaymed the rules.

23. 24. 25. They ar true. It is thowght Fisher was putt into the galleyes at Naples or otherwise made awaye.

26. 27. One James Standyche was sent to Rome, who vntruly in the name of the sæcular priests informed the Pope. He was assisted by D. Haddocke & one Martine Araye & Parsons him selfe. He is thowght to have brought the Cardinalls letters. M^r. Blackwells letter was sent to Wisbyche, but not to be copyed, yett some coppyes ar elsewhere extant. *Whither also it was directed.*

28. 29. 30. M^r. B. (?)[a] was disliked *bothe for generall & particular reasons.* The sæcular priests would ether have bene lefte to governe them selfs or required an ecclesiasticall Hierarchye, if any should be instituted. The[y] sent D. Byshoppe & M^r. Charnocke to Rome. *Those raylinge letters (as others of the same stampe) are stuffed wth litle else than absurde vntruths.*

31. Suche a treatise of schisme is extante. *It was made by Lister*[b] *who ranne out of ye Marshals[ea].*

32. 33. 34. 35. It is thowght y^t Cardinall Bellarmine by letters was a meanes to informe the Pope against D. Bys. & M^r. Ch. The rest is true, *& the letters at opportunity may be hadd.*

36. Theyre names were D. Haddocke & Araye.

37. Those letters (as many the like) be devised to gayne time by false reports.

38. The sæcular priests havinge no favowre in Englande, are driven to try theyre friends in other cowntryes, specially in Fraunce.

39. M^r. Charnocke is disliked by M^r. Blackwell & Walley. A letter is sent him or fayned to be sent from Cardinall Burghesius,

---

[a] The letter is obscure. It might be read as P or H, but it is evidently Blackwell who is referred to.

[b] A copy of Father Lister's treatise *Adversus Factiosos* is among the Petyt MSS. It was first printed by Bagshaw in his *Relatio Compendiosa,* pp. 37-49.

to mislike his comminge into Englande wch he is sayde to have answeared, & yett to have harde nothinge agayne.^a

40. The dealings of M^r. Blackwell are as much as may be concealed those wch dislike them yett time will discover them. F. Parsons made the booke of titles.

41. There is a letter sent from D. Dorrell dwellinge in Agen in Fraunce abowte that matter.^b

42. The Romane stirres ar best knowen to the Romanists lately there. It may be som[e] of them may be willinge exactly to publishe them.

43. Parsons feareth some will discover him wch some iustly therto provoked to defende truthe innocency & loialty may perhapps effecte.

44. There is no iuste answeare to the libell of schisme, but some fewe notes passed from [one] to another, vntill further opportunity.^c

45. Excepte state matters & detractions, & suche stuffe be lefte by those wch professe virtue it is not to be dowbted but the authors will be at the leaste fully discovered.

7. *The Declaracõn of James Clercke of the Middle Temple London, geñ. made septimo Junij towchinge Parsons the now Jesuite.* 47, f. 44.

M^r. Parsons the now or late Jesuite and my sellffe havinge first

---

^a Cardinall Borghese's letter of remonstrance to Charnock, dated 15 Sept., 1680, and Charnock's lengthy reply written from London, 4 Nov., 1600, stilo veteri, are printed in the *Relatio Compendiosa*, pp. 84-95. Blackwell suspended Charnock and warned the faithful to avoid him in a letter printed in Cal. S. P., Dom. Eliz. cclxxv. 115.

^b This letter of Darrel or Dorel, dean of Agen, is printed in Bagshaw's *True Relation*. The original or a copy is among the Petyt MSS., 47 f. 86.

^c An ill written draft of a reply by Bagshaw himself is in the Petyt collection.

lived diuers yeeres together in good likinge, as boies and scoolefellowes in the free scoole of Taunton in the Countie of Somersett; we both departed thence neere about his age of nineteene yeeres, and about the ende of the seaventhe yeere of the Queenes Maties raigne that now is, he to the Vniuersitie of Oxforde, and my sellff to the s^rvice of the right honorable the now Lord Cheeff Justice of Englande then of the Middle Temple of London: And about eighte or nine yeeres after this the saide Parsons came to the Middle Temple to me from the Vniuersitie of Oxon withe resolucion as he saide to travell beyonde the seas: and then was verie often with me at the Middle Temple for the space of seaven or eighte weekes. The first place wherevnto he meante to travell was Padua, where one Lane a M^r of Artes and of his olde acquaintance in Oxford then was as he saide. He also affirmed that he meante to make Phisicke his proffession: and his travell was with purpose to be better seene & instructed therein: and neere about his departure he amongest other thinges tolde me that he muche desired to be broughte acquainted with certeine gentes of the Middle Temple as namelie with M^r. Alexander Popham, M^r. Tristram Mitchell and others: And then we grewe into further speeches in this maner. M^r. Parsons saide I, their are now divers yeeres paste since we were scoole boies together. But in this time that is required which in those our childishe yeeres was not to be looked for at our handes; I must deale plainelie with yo^u: I haue often hearde that yo^u since that time are become a great papiste. I woulde be gladde to be satisfied to the contrarie before I procure yo^u any acquaintance with those gentes yo^u name, or wordes to the like effect. And he aunsweringe therevnto assured me there was noe such matter. It was as he saide a slaunder bruited forth against him by some enemies of his, amongest wch he named M^r. Doctor Squier as I now remember: and protested to me, that he neither then was, nor never meant to be any papiste; and that he woulde soe satisfie me not onelie vpon any conference, but alsoe vpon his oateh: And afterwardes we fell into some discourses in matter of

Relligion, wherein I colde not finde that he did holde or mayneteine any pointe of papistrie to my vnderstanding : And shortelie after he departed towardes Padua as he had before determined.

JAMES CLARK.

Endorsed :
  James Clarke of M^r. Parsons purpose to study phisike when [he left England ?] ^a

54, f. 400.

8. *News from Rome respecting Parsons' Book and the Spanish Faction.*

Mr. Blackwell required all priests and Catholicks to celebrate and pray according to his intention: Vpon or a little before the last cominge of the Spanyards into Ireland. Whereas the nuntio in fflanders [had authority] his nuntiatura^b extended over England Scotland and Ireland. Parsons procured Archer the Jesuite ^c to be nuntius for Ireland wch the nuntius in fflanders took in evil parte.

The booke was first drawen in fflanders by the Jesuits, and delivered by one Dennis to the Nuntio, who sent the same to Cardinall Aldobrandino, the pope's nephew. It afterwards came to Parsons handes, and hath therevpon receyved an alteration. The popes finger is in it, and the second draught is wth Blackwell or Garnet, or where they have apointed.

In the sayd book where the designements there mentioned doe seeme to ayme after her ma^{ts} death, it is more then coniectured that the first opportunity offered shall be taken to hasten her death.

---

^a The last three words are cut off, except the tops of the letters.
^b The words in brackets are erased, and "his nuntiatura" substituted.
^c Giles Archer, sometime prisoner at Wisbech and afterwards resident at Rome, was not a Jesuit.

Cardinall Aldobrandino the popes nephew is altogether Spanish and doth leade the pope very much. There are three nephewes of the popes that sway much. Petro Aldobrandino a Cardinall, the Cardinall S^{ti} Georgij, and Petti the popes nephew by the mothers syde. Wherevpon Pasquill moved the Romans to pray hard, because there was a g[reat] schisme in the Church, viz. fowere popes, Pope Peter, pope ffrancis now dead being the popes brother, Pope S^{ti} Georgii and old pope Clement.

Pope Peter is in such æstimation, as every Ambassado^r having had Audyence wth the pope; doth presently addresse himself to Pope Peter Aldobrandino.

The Courte of Rome is very greatly swayed by the Spanish faction. The most of the Cardinalls being eyther his Pensioners, or having theyr livings or estates in regno. Besydes all that are of any account abowt the popes person are eyther Spanyards or receyve pensions frome the king of Spayne.

47, f. 255.

9. *Swift's Declaration.*

List of the Members of the English College at Douay, with an Account of the Jesuit's Seminaries.

[About March, 1600.]^a

There are in the Colledg of Doway about fourscore schollers & Doctors & seruants: The President of the Colledg is D^{tor} Worthing-

---

^a This document represents the membership of the College as it stood early in 1600. Dr. Thomas Worthington had assumed the government of the College in succession to Dr. Barrett in August of the preceding year. Rayne, Neville, Butler, and others mentioned as "divines not priests," were ordained priests April 1, 1600. Curtes, however, described as "priest" and Clarkson "divine, not priest" were according to to the *Douay Diaries* (p. 17) ordained priests together Feb. 26, 1600. Dr. Kellison, lecturer on scholastic theology, here entitled "Vice President," had previously acted in that capacity for Dr. Barrett, at Rheims, in 1589.

DEALINGS WITH THE GOVERNMENT. 245

ton: the Vice-president is D^tor Kellison. The rest of the Colledg is deuided Into

Seniors & Preists.	D^tor Weston D^tor Bretton D^tor Harrison D^tor Webb Mr Redman Mr Jackson Mr Peale	Penkeuel Stapleton Egerton Priests not Seniors. Jones or Evans Curteys	Batman Rayne Rudal alias Diuines not Preists. Neuel Butler Clarkson Foynes alias Sims

Those y^t studie Logick, Philosophy,[a] Rheto: Poetry, Syntax.	Nathaniel Egerton
	Barthol: Smith
	Thomas Foscue
	  alias Greene
	John Jarueys
	John Burrel
	Thomas Briggs
	Harry Deuonish
	Thomas Deuonish
	Francis Low
	William Webb
	Thomas [b] Thyrsby
	Steuen Dowgle
	Clement Dowgle
		Robert Mallet
		Philipp Linn
		Robert Parkinson
		Edward Greene
		Will: Collier
		Jhon Trim
		Jhon Sweete
		
		wth 12 seruants
			Greenal
			Pett
			Moorton alias
			  Fitz-James
			Moorton
			Cocks
			Clark
			Morris
			Harris
			Owin

The Jesuits gouernment being in the forme of a Monarchy, hauing for their head one whom they call their Generall, whose seat is at Rome, wch Generall hath under him substitutes in all parts of the world whome they call Prouincialls, for that they gouerne all the Jesuits that are in that Prouince, as the Pro-

---

[a] The words in italics are inserted by another hand.
[b] Substituted for "Charles."

uinciall of the lowe cuntryes gouerneth all the Jesuites that are in that Province. Theise Prouincialls haue vnder them the Rectors of all the Colledges in their Prouinces, every colledg hauing in it three kinds of Jesuits, Statesmen or Politicians, who doe not only study but also practice matters of estate ; Readers, for bycause by their profession they are bound to teach children where they liue. Writers, who sett forth bookes of all kinde of learning, hauing amongst them some or others who are excellent in all sort of knowledg. By the first they enlarge their gouernment, working them selues into all actions both priuat & publique. By the second (wch is reading) they chuse out the finest witts & entice the noblest youths into their order. By the thyrd they make them selues famous through the world & thus all their actions & all their proceedings tend wholy to the creditt & commodity of their order. For the wch cause, they haue euer sought to gett possession of all the English Catholiques or Papists beyond the seas, that by them they mought the better come to be placed in the Realme of England, as they are in other cuntryes. For the better effecting whereof they had gotten into their hands all the English seminaries beyond the seas as that in Ciuil & Vale-de-leyds, & Rome. And to that end built and erected the semenary of St. Omers by the help of the King of Spayne for the receipt of English youth, whereof the greatest part are Gentlemens sonns, wch four Colledges liuing under their gouernment, & being violently gouerned by most seuere orders wch they instituted, at the last in the Colledg in Rome did break into a violent faction (whereof I doubt not but that your Honor hath heard, or else at better opportunity I would set downe) beinge an action of great note, wherein was discouered much knauery. Howsoeuer, yett hauing gott those four Colledges into their hands, only remained that they gett the Colledg of Doway into their hands that so noe man should come to liue beyond the seas that should not be of their humor; hauing also, for the other sort of men, wch are not schollers, a Jesuite belonging to the Arch-Duke, named Father Baldwin, to hinder those wch are against them, & preferr those wch are of their faction & not Schollers. So they haue in Spaine Fath. Creswell belonging to the King, so in Rome Father Parsons in high fauour wth the Poape, that so noe man may be preferd by either the Poap, K of Spaine or Archduke but through their meanes. Wherefore it remayned only that they gett into their hands the Colledg of Doway, for the effecting whereof they caused Cardinal Caietane Ld Protectour of the English seminaries to chuse, or rather in his name they chose D^{tor} Woorthington to be president of the Colledg after the decease of D^{tor} Barrat who held it out of their hands. W^{ch} D^{tor} Woorthington being a man wholy of their seruice and altogether of their faction although not of their order, & whose actions altogether depend vppon [their]^a wills, they haue made him their instrument to bring into the Colledg their government, wch now they haue affected, although it [is] not altogether established. First they haue instituted that noe man shall be sent out of England vnto that Colledg that not . . . . commended thither by the Archpreist Mr. Blackwell or some especiall Jesuit in England. Also that euery one shall take oath to be preists at their pleasures when the superiors shall call vppon them, & in all controuersies & dissensions that are & may happen between the Jesuites & other Preists, they should take the Jesuits part. Also that euery preist that commeth ouer shall submitt him self vnto the pleasure & order of the Archpreist M^r. Blackwell & his Assistants. Likewise that noe man liuing in the Colledg shall vppon an oath; haue or keepe any mony to his priuate vse, but shall surrender it into the hands of the Colledg wth diuerse other orders both priuat & publique as are in other Colledges beyond seas, wch as yett are not & will not be confirmed vntill Christmas next. For the wch cause, they haue procured of the Poape that two English Jesuits shall come into the Colledg & be Confessors vnto the Schollers of the Colledg, exhort, prescribe meditations, & catechize. The cause why they seeke all

^a Edge of the MS. mutilated.

this, is the hope wch they haue to be brought & settled in England by the Spanish forces, that now having euery man depending vppon them, they may, if they be brought in, haue the whole gouernment of ecclesiasticall affaires in their hands, as they haue in India, Japonia & such like places. Thus much briefly & [abruptly] by reason of the breuity of times.

[*Original?*] *Endorsed:*

Swifts declaration of the state of the College in Doway.

Printed in the USA
CPSIA information can be obtained
at www.ICGtesting.com
LVHW022134041023
760082LV00002B/59